The Concept of America

ISBN 978-0-578-17831-8

Printed in USA by Ingram Content Group (www.ingramspark.com)

About the Authors

We are a forgotten nation. We have *forgotten* our past. Our schools no longer teach the founding principles and the civics which made this country unique among nations. There are 196 countries on this planet earth, and when people choose to leave their homeland for a new beginning, the most sought-after destination country has been the United States of America.

The authors of the *Concept of America* decided it was time to re-educate our children as to the exceptionalism of the United States and tell America's story through the great discoveries and inventions we have gladly shared with the rest of the world to improve civilization. This book is the first in a series highlighting our greatness for all to see.

Ed Mattson: Contract writer, author, columnist, medical research specialist. Mr. Mattson has been a long-time Rotarian who participated in close to one hundred humanitarian projects. He served in the Marine Corps from 1965 to 1972, and served as the spokesperson for the National Cord Blood Registry from 2000 to 2004. His book, *Say NO to the Undertaker*, about the future of biological response modifiers, cancer vaccines, and targeted gene therapy, sold  thousands of copies to cancer patients fighting for survival and to the medical community.

He has spoken to more than 3000 service club audiences on state-of-art cancer treatment protocols in 43 states and five different countries, and provided cancer research services to numerous physicians. Having spent two years studying the effects of the Chernobyl disaster with the Medico-Ecological Center and Dr. Nadia Panchenko, he went on to spend eight years developing medical facilities in Eastern Europe, including the Echo of Chernobyl Foundation and the Cancer Screening Center of Romania. He worked with numerous U.S. Embassies supporting the National Guard Bureau of International Affairs State Partnership Program serving former Soviet Bloc countries transitioning to democracy.

C. Robert Brawley: Born and raised in Iredell County, Robert Brawley went to Raleigh in 1962 to pursue a bachelor's degree in Engineering at NC State University. As a student athlete, Robert was the ACC Wrestling Champion in his division in 1964 and 1966, as well as being voted the ACC Tournament's Most Outstanding Wrestler in 1964 and 1966. May 15, 2016 Robert will be inducted into the North Carolina Chapter of the National Wrestling Hall of Fame.

In 1967, while attending college, Robert began his service to the people of North Carolina when he joined the N.C. Army National Guard where he served for more than twenty-four years as a helicopter pilot and retiring as a Lt. Colonel. He was later inducted into the NC National Guard Academy Hall of Fame.

He earned his degree in Engineering Operations from NC State University in 1968 and by 1980, his public service expanded into the political arena when he launched his bid for the North Carolina General Assembly, successfully campaigning to represent the 43rd house district, which included parts of Alexander, Catawba, and Iredell counties. He used his education to build insurance agencies, a construction business, and a ladies dress shop. This was necessary to give five children an opportunity for college.

Robert served the citizens of the 43rd District for eighteen years, from 1981 until his retirement in 1998, and received the "National Legislator of the Year" award in 1995 by the National Republican Legislators Association and serving as President of the National Republican Legislators Association in 1996. During his service he served as chair and/or vice chair of various committees and received numerous awards for meritorious service. Robert served as Sunday School teacher and church lay speaker for over thirty years.

About our cover

Edward Moran was born on August 19, 1829, in Bolton, Lancashire, England. His family first emigrated to Maryland in 1844, and then settled in Philadelphia a year later. Moran is most famous for his series of 13 famous historical paintings of United States marine history; representing a painting for each of the original thirteen colonies.

Unveiling The Statue of Liberty, **1886 by Edward Moran**

In Philadelphia Moran apprenticed under James Hamilton, who also had emigrated to the United States from his birthplace of Entrien, Ireland. Hamilton, who was a great admirer of the renown landscapes of English painter J.M.W. Turner, tutored Moran on how to capture the realism of marine life.

Not satisfied with learning the single but brilliant style of Hamilton, Moran also studied under Paul Weber from Frankfort, Germany who emigrated to the United States, in 1848. Weber was a known artist and a frequent exhibitor at the prestigious Pennsylvania Academy.

Moran began to make a name for himself in the Philadelphia artistic scene while working in the same studio as his younger brother, Thomas Moran, who was a famous artist in his own right. Edward Moran, though lesser known than his brother Thomas, received numerous commissions, completed some lithographic work, then traveled to London and became a pupil at the Royal Academy of Arts in London for two years before returning to America and settling in New York.

Shortly after completing his 13 painting series representing the Marine History of the United States, considered his most important work, the series was displayed at the 1893 World's Fair in Chicago to great acclaim. Moran lived in New York City until his death in 1901.

Dedication

The Concept of America is dedicated to all those great Americans who have come before us and led the way to the present. There are no "native" Americans; we all came to this continent from somewhere else looking for something . . . For some it was better hunting grounds, for others it might have been for freedom, and for still others, the opportunity for success, unencumbered by repressive governments.

God blessed this land with beauty and natural resources and entrusted us to keep it free for all, that no matter what race, color, creed, or national origin, you would be welcome to come participate in what has become the American Dream so long as we all honor the traditions that have made America unlike any other country on earth.

Our forefathers gave us a government formed by men of great wisdom and the deliberations carried on in the Constitutional Convention of 1787 that were held in strict secrecy.

When their duties were completed in forming a government, anxious citizens gathered outside Independence Hall when the proceedings ended in order to learn what had been produced behind closed doors. A Mrs. Powel of Philadelphia asked Benjamin Franklin, "Well, Doctor, what have we got, a republic or a monarchy?" With no hesitation whatsoever, Franklin responded, "A republic, if you can keep it."

He went on to say, "We have been assured, in the sacred writings, that 'except the Lord build the house they labor in vain that build it.' I firmly believe this; and I also believe that without His concurring aid we shall succeed in this political building no better than the builders of Babel; we shall be divided by our little partial, local interests, our projects will be confounded and we ourselves shall become a reproach and a byword down to future ages. And, what is worse, mankind may hereafter, from this unfortunate instance, despair of establishing government by human wisdom and leave it to chance, war, or conquest."

Our hopes lie in the future and we can only pray the current generation will forgive the shortcomings of our generation and boldly lead America in the tradition of our forefathers.

Table of Contents

Preface with Colin Powell

In 2002 General Colin Powell said to critics of US policy…

"Far from being the Great Satan, I would say that we are the Great Protector. We have sent men and women from the armed forces of the United States to other parts of the world throughout the past century to put down oppression. We defeated Fascism. We defeated Communism. We saved Europe in World War I and World War II. We were willing to do it, glad to do it. We went to Korea. We went to Vietnam; all in the interest of preserving the rights of people. And when all those conflicts were over, what did we do? Did we stay and conquer? Did we say, "Okay, we defeated Germany; now Germany belongs to us? We defeated Japan, so Japan belongs to us"? No. What did we do? We built them up. We gave them democratic systems which they have embraced totally to their soul. And did we ask for any land? No, the only land we ever asked for was enough land to bury our dead. And that is the kind of nation we are." [1]

Introduction

"The greatest advances of civilization, whether in architecture or painting, in science and literature, in industry or agriculture, have never come from centralized government."

Milton Friedman

Laying claim as to who first arrived on the North American Continent has been the subject of debate for many years and will probably be so for well into the next century and beyond, provided the country we proudly call the *United States of America* continues in existence. With the current political climate, the failure of America's school systems to teach the history of the country, and the attempt by liberals to diminish the relevance of the greatest nation ever conceived, it is quite possible that just who settled this vast continent first may become a moot point.

History is replete with the success and failures of civilizations dating back to the narratives recorded on the walls of caves, and has proven to be cyclical and predictable . . . in short, it continues to repeat itself, because man has refused to learn from the mistakes of civilizations past. All great nations, dynasties, and empires, are seldom defeated from without, but inevitably collapse from within.

If one were to listen to the voices of liberal America, the United States is but a mere blip on the radar screen of civilized countries, no more exceptional than any other country since man began to walking upright. As students of history we find this lack of appreciation about our great country to be a great disservice to our ancestors and to all those who have been charged with the task of insuring the continuation of America's unique position as the greatest nation in the history of civilization.

The United States was an experiment in governance by the Founding Fathers who truly believed there are certain natural laws, handed down by an Almighty God, that people are to be free to pursue their dreams, unencumbered by government; that all men (and women) are created equal, with certain inalienable rights that include life, liberty, the pursuit of happiness, and that they should never be prohibited from the ability to defend themselves and their families from tyrannical efforts of government, or any being who might attempt to harm them or take their property without just compensation.

Unfortunately, these facts are being rewritten by a cadre of misinformed and arrogant *pseudo* historians, who haven't the slightest clue as to the important and noble principles on which this country was founded. They do not understand the basic concepts of our democratically elected representative republic or the magnificence of a capitalistic market-based system which has proven to be the only type of economy that allows one to flourish and reap the fruits of his/her labor; the only one that enables a person to rise from poverty and achieve vast wealth.

They instead choose to view the *free enterprise system* as one in which only those who cheat the system will succeed, and that fortunes can only be made at the expense of others. They preach there is a zero sum^2 rule in play in any system of capitalism where someone's gain always results in someone else's loss. Nothing could be further from the truth. In fact, it is the *collectivist systems* that redistributionists see as ideal, much in line with Karl Marx and his doctrine of Marxism, that always results in a zero-sum transaction and insures equal misery for all.

For one to be successful in a free enterprise capitalistic system, the key is *self-responsibility* . . . self responsibility to maximize your education; develop a sound work ethic; live within your means; and invest wisely. Perseverance is one of the most important traits to making it in the free market. There is no assurance one will be successful on the first try, so having the desire and willingness to stay vigilant in reaching your goal will inevitably lead to success for most.

This is not possible in a Marxist society where the fruits of one's labor are confiscated to support the *classless society*, where

11

everyone shares equally, but it never works out that way. In fact there is no record of such a collectivistic system being successful in any society throughout the history. To hold such societies together in most cases requires the use of force often including at the point of a gun.

It is ironic that even in today's modern world, people simply cannot see that taking away the freedom to keep the fruit of your labor stifle's ingenuity, productivity, quality of workmanship, and results in people settling for the lowest common denominator.

The Soviet Union was the most startling example as demonstrated by a comparison of The Gross Domestic Product of the Unites States and the USSR/Russia for the period of 1946 through 1992, based on 1990 dollars:

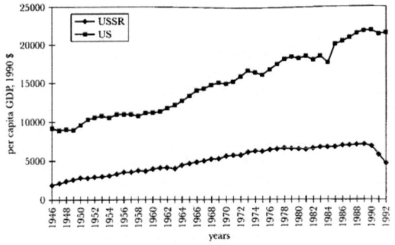

To provide a clear insight into just how wrong-headed and misguided the rewrite of American history is becoming, we can learn a great deal by studying the report by what would be an unbiased observer, Philip Hanson[3], who is Emeritus Professor of the Political Economy of Russia and Eastern Europe at The University of Birmingham, located in Edgbaston, Birmingham, United Kingdom. Professor Hanson relied on personal experience and literary sources, including memoirs, as well as available economic data and analyses, to illustrate the reality of everyday life and of economic policy-making in the post-war Soviet Union. The European History Quarterly called Professor Hanson's study, "a lucid and compelling study."

The author argues, *"the Soviet economic system was capable of producing economic growth, and did for most of its existence exhibit growth. But it revealed over a time a key weakness compared with capitalism: a systemic inability to cope well with technological change, which doomed the Soviet economy in the long-run. Moreover, 'success' in partially liberalising (sic) Soviet society, so that terror receded into the background, reduced the effectiveness of a top-down economic system that relied on authority and obedience."*

Hanson further reinforces his position which points out the flaws of collectivism using Hayek and von Mises' [4]1920 arguments that were amply supported by historical evidence. The argument noted that everyone . . . socialists and non-socialists alike . . . had long realized that socialism suffered from an *incentive problem.*

If for example, *"everyone under socialism were to receive an equal income, or, in another variant, everyone was supposed to produce 'according to his ability', but receive 'according to his needs', then . . . who will take out the garbage?"* In other words . . . *"what will be the incentive to do the grubby jobs, and furthermore, to do them well?"* Under the socialism/collectivism scenario a question begs to be asked . . . "What would be the incentive to work hard and be productive *at any job?*"

Von Mises[2-1] summed it up perfectly as follows:

> *"Naively, the traditional socialist answer held that the socialist society would transform human nature, would purge it of selfishness and remold it to create a New Socialist Man. That new man would be devoid of any selfish, or indeed any self-determined goals; his only wish would be to work as hard and as eagerly as possible to*

achieve the goals and obey the orders of the
socialist State.

"Throughout the history of socialism, socialist
ultras, such as the early Lenin and Bukharin and
later Mao Tse-tung and Ché Guevara, have sought
to replace material by so-called moral incentives.

"This notion was properly and wittily
ridiculed by Alexander Gray (1882–1968) *as 'the*
idea that the world may find its driving force in a
Birthday Honours (sic) List giving to the King,
365 birthdays a year."

In drawing a conclusion to all the myths about the glories of socialism/collectivism, socialists soon found that voluntary methods could hardly yield them their *New Socialist Man*, and that even the most determined and bloodthirsty methods could not avail to create this mythical creature.

It is a testament to the spirit of freedom that cannot be extinguished in the human breast that the socialists continued to fail dismally, despite decades of systemic terror.

Throughout the 20th and so far into the 21st centuries, these observations have become apparent and very easily verifiable because of our instant access to information thanks to the one of the greatest *American* inventions of all time . . . the computer.

It has been and will continue to be the goal of the liberal-progressive establishment to mislead those who will be entrusted to carry-on the traditions that have made America the greatest experiment in government ever envisioned. They are doing so through our public schools which have been commandeered by the Department of Education and the Federal Government.

They continue to chase the foolish vision of a strong monolithic central government destroying the very U.S. Constitution that ensures our freedom, liberty, and way of life.

Regardless of which political party is in power, the public's vigilance must not be deterred.

We felt compelled to set the record straight and tell the truth about American Exceptionalism so one could witness what the world would be like if there was no United States of America. The remarkable discoveries, inventions, and products that have been produced by unleashing the free market capitalism of America, should forever be held as a beacon of light to guide the rest of the world.

Chapter 1 - America is more than a country, it is a *concept.*

"A simple democracy is the Devil's own government."

Benjamin Rush

America. When the Founders of the United States were pondering the form of government under which the new nation would function, they approached the task with a strong affinity for a democracy, but were keenly aware that all democracies were very short lived. James Madison summarized "democracies" as follows:

> *"In a pure democracy, a common passion or interest will, in almost every case, be felt by a majority of the whole; a communication and concert results from the form of government itself; and there is nothing to check the inducements to sacrifice the weaker party or an obnoxious individual.*
>
> *"Hence it is that such democracies have ever been spectacles of turbulence and contention; have ever been found incompatible with personal security or the rights of property; and have in general been as short in their lives as they have been violent in their deaths."*

What the Founding fathers were seeking was a form of government that would be founded on the principle of a weak centralized power, and that power which was not specifically granted by the people to the federal government was to be reserved for the states or the people. Since they had had the experience of a weak centralized government under the Articles of Confederation, they well understood the federal government under the U.S. Constitution had to have more power to govern. We often use Thomas Jefferson's words that the people have *certain unalienable rights of life, liberty, and the pursuit of happiness*, however, these words were overlooked in the U.S. Constitution itself.

After the Revolutionary War was won, the new American Congress passed the Constitution of the United States. It would surprise most Americans that as originally adopted, the President of the United States and the American government did not have to abide by specifying these words: life, liberty and the pursuit of happiness for the people.

So the U.S. Constitution was an imperfect document and had to be amended to insure the rights of the people. The lack of this protection from the government as well as people's other individual rights was so bad that the Congress had to pass ten amendments to the original Constitution; collectively known as the *Bill of Rights*.

The *United States of America* as the country was titled in the Articles of Confederation differed in many ways from the America that began anew with the U.S. Constitution, still designed to limit the powers of the central government, but with enough power to govern effectively:

The term of legislative office under the Articles of Confederation was one year with no Executive Branch (no President), and specified term limits no more than three out of every six years. Congress was unicameral (one house of government). Each state was allowed between two and seven members, all appointed by state legislatures, selected in the manner each legislature so directed, and each state would receive one vote in legislative matters.

Under the U.S. Constitution, the federal government included an Executive Branch (President), a Legislative Brach or *Congress* made up of a Senate, with each state having two members appointed by the state legislatures and a House of Representatives, with members elected by the vote of the citizens with each state granted a number of representatives based on population.

Senators were to serve for six years and House members were to serve two year terms with no term limitations. Each member of Congress, Senator and Representative, were to be allowed one vote each.

The Seventeenth Amendment, enacted in 1913, changed the selection of the senate members to popular vote by the people of each state, instead of appointment by state legislatures. The long term ramifications of this *blunder* remain and are still being debated today.

In addition to the Executive and Legislative Branches, the U.S. Constitution established a Judiciary Branch called the Supreme Court, with its members appointed by the President and ratified by vote of the Senate. The Supreme Court Justices were to *serve for life* to prevent having them *stand for election* and to protect them from being biased by a vote of the electorate.

Each of the three branches were to share power equally with Congress writing the laws, the President ratifying them into law, and the Judicial branch standing in judgment as to the Constitutionality of each law. The House of Representatives, being subject to the will of the people, was to have the ultimate tool at their disposal to insure the rule of law by having *the power of the purse*, enacting bills to fund the government.

No document of governance ever written could anticipate a country's needs into the future. Therefore the signers of the U.S. Constitution developed a way to amend the laws under which we live, by specifically outlining the procedure which requires ratification of three-fourths of the states. Such amendment process can be undertaken by Congress or, under Article Five, by a Convention called for by the States. This *Convention of States* was seen as necessary should the federal government become out-of-touch and to be found to overstep the boundaries outlined in the Constitution.

While the new government was a democracy, it was technically a *democratically elected representative democracy*, in short, a *Republican form of government*, with the people electing representatives to represent them in the operation of the country's governance.

The basis of the new government of the United States dates back to the English charter of 1215, called the Magna Carta, aided by the experience gained under the Articles of Confederation. The U.S. Government can aptly be called a high-bred, experiment in governance, which has lasted nearly 2-1/2 centuries.

Although far from perfect most probably can agree that it is far superior to whatever system of government is in second place. The remarkable fact of our government is that we have the freedom to discuss political matters, criticize those who are elected to office, protest the government with our list of grievances, run for elected office, to vote or to not vote, and to live our lives with freedom of speech, freedom of religion, and the right to bear arms to protect ourselves and our families from those who would do us harm, including the government.

Such wisdom of the Founders is seldom discussed with school children, so they grow-up with very little knowledge of just how sacred and precious our freedoms and liberties really are.

What the people of the United States have enjoyed for 2-1/2 centuries is a country that has exceeded anything the Founders could have imagined. Our freedom, liberty and pursuit of happiness, coupled with our right to own property and free enterprise capitalistic economic system has led to the most advanced civilization the world has ever seen.

In short, people have come to America, not just because it was a country different from the one they left, but because **America isn't a country per se, it is a concept.** Since its inception people have risked life and limb just for the opportunity to seek a better life for themselves and their families, crossing oceans and seas, often in leaky boats, in search of their dreams.

America is a homogeneous mixture of ethnicities who have built a one-of-a-kind country where, "if you can visualize it in your mind, you can more than likely achieve it". They have succeeded because they have assimilated into our blended culture, learned the language, and succeeded because of the personal responsibility they took to become Americanized.

Ed Mattson, *Veterans Today*

As our children go through our educational system, they are no longer taught what America is all about. They are not taught our history, the achievements Americans have made to the growth of civilization, and the transformative effect that American agriculture, medicine, industry, science, technology, and commerce have had on the world stage. Our *free enterprise capitalism* has been responsible for more than 8 million patents[5], many which have changed to world and nearly all have been eagerly shared with people all over the world.

People who came to America learned that if they developed an idea and *patented* the concept, they would have an opportunity, unlike in countries where freedoms are curtailed to benefit the state, to succeed. In this great country they have had the freedom to exercise their creative talents, develop their concepts, and harvest the financial benefits of their ideas.

It is this freedom that is an American Concept. Such wisdom of our Founding Fathers is what has set America apart from all other countries, yet our school children do not hear this message from the government controlled, public schools.

Our technology has led the world in transportation, manufacturing concepts, electronics, and production methods. This is not to say that all the advances in civilization were made at the hands of and by the ingenuity of Americans. The world is far too old for that, however, of the 8 million patents on file in the U.S.

21

Patent Office, as of 2001, 82% are owned by Americans. Corporations account for the largest number of American owned patents, but 23% are owned by individual American citizens. Growth of American owned patents continues unabated, and has increased significantly since 2001.

This brings us back to what our children are learning in school these days. Our faltering education system, under the control of the federal government since October 17, 1979, has enabled the once *beacon of educational light*, American education, to sink sadly into the sunset, as international test results clearly show.

The Program for International Student Assessment [5](PISA) is an international assessment agency that measures 15-year-old students' literacy in reading, mathematics, and science every three years. Their assessment validates the fears of every American parent:

> *"The latest 2012 PISA test results, released Dec. 3, 2013, show that the U.S. lags among 65 countries (or sub country entities) even after adjusting for poverty. Top U.S. students are falling behind even average students in Asia. Asia is emphasized because Asian countries (or sub entities) now dominate the top 10 in all subjects: math, reading and science".*

Even worse according to U.S. News and World Report[6], today's school children absolutely fail at geography in a world that requires knowledge on a global scale. They also are taught nothing about civics and economics and know so little about the history of our country, it is downright embarrassing.

According to Slate.com, a left of center think-tank owned by the Washington Post Newspaper:

> *"In America, high school is for socializing. It's a convenient gathering place, where the really*

important activities are interrupted by all those
annoying classes. For all but the very best
American students—the ones in AP classes bound
for the nation's most selective colleges and
universities—high school is tedious and
unchallenging. Studies that have tracked American
adolescents' moods over the course of the day find
that levels of boredom are highest during their time
in school. "

Not a day goes by that we don't hear on the public airwaves, about the pure nonsensical gibberish that is permeating our schools in the form of **political correctness.** To say it is running amuck would be to minimize what it is doing to our school aged children. Forgotten is the real reason we send our children to school and why so many parents are opting out in favor of home schooling.

Kids need an education to compete in the world to get a job or career to support their families, and our public education system is failing, and failing miserably. Furthermore, student discipline is a major problem in nearly every inner-city school where teachers and children are held hostage by teenaged thugs with whom the school administrations simply won't deal.

Foreigners who come to American and assimilate into the American culture, who are willing to sacrifice for their families, insist on their children getting ahead with a good education. They fare far better than the children of Americans who have lived in the United States their whole lives, and who take for granted the government has their best interests in mind. For most, schools are nothing more than *daycare centers* while the parents are at work.

The awakening of *Conservative America* in the last ten years, is evidence the people have had enough of the politically correct crowd who go out of their way to diminish the greatness of our American way of life. They discount everything that has made America great, and try to instill in our children that there is nothing at all exceptional about this great country.

It is long past the time for us to tell our children and the people of the world, the truth about the greatness of the United States. Why amongst the freedoms we enjoy, is the *freedom to be ignorant acceptable?* It is everyone's right to be taught the truth about the freedom, liberty, and opportunity one has as a citizen of the United States.

There are 196 recognizable countries[6] in the world, but *there is only one America. America however, is far more than just another country as our children are being taught today* . . . **America is a concept.**

Chapter 2 - America has given the world liberty and freedom

"Let every nation know, whether it wishes us well or ill, that we shall pay any price, bear any burden, meet any hardship, support any friend, oppose any foe to assure the survival and the success of liberty."

John F. Kennedy

History is replete with tyrants, thugs, dictators, and two-bit rulers who have sought to enslave their own people as well as whole nations in a thirst to become a dominant force in the world. This has been a fact since cavemen began hitting each other over the head with clubs in order to get their way.

Such mentality has led, according to the Chris Hedges[7], author of *What Every Person Should Know About War*, to upward of one billion people killed in all wars since records have been kept. Counting military personnel and civilians this of course is an estimated number because many people simply disappeared.

War is the final answer to conflict and an action in which some always get rich. This is a fact and one which civilization will forever have to face. As former *Commander of the Marine Corps School*, "The Fighting Quaker", Gen. Smedley Butler, once said, *" War is a racket. It always has been . . . A few profit - and the many pay. But there is a way to stop it. You can't end it by disarmament conferences. You can't eliminate it by peace parleys at Geneva. Well-meaning but impractical groups can't wipe it out by resolutions. It can be smashed effectively only by taking the profit out of war."*

In Chapter One we said every school age child should be told the truth about the country in which they live. This would include America's participation in armed conflict, whether good or bad.

According to military records, sourced via militaryfactory.com[8], *"In its first 100 years of existence, over 683,000 Americans lost their lives, with the Civil War accounting for 623,026 of that total (91.2%). Comparatively, in the next 100 years, a further 626,000 Americans died through two World Wars and several more regional conflicts (World War II representing 65% of that total). Using this comparison, the Civil War might very well be the most costly war that America has ever fought"*.

Yes, since its inception, the United States has fought in many wars. First and foremost, was our own war for freedom from British rule in the Revolutionary War. Born out of this violent beginning when we established the fact that *freedom and liberty* were worth fighting and dying over, the entire world has benefited at the cost of American lives.

As in all matters, one can debate the issues, even on the issues regarding U.S. participation in wars. It is not our purpose here to debate right or wrong, but to educate about the fact that many Americans have been sacrificed on the altar of freedom and liberty.

Each war has its own set of circumstances as to the cause and the actions our politicians took in committing our country's resources. As hindsight is almost always 20-20, most historians will forever be debating our involvement in each of the wars, and as we review the various conflicts discussed in this book, it is best to just briefly present the facts and let the readers draw their own conclusion. Most grown-ups understand that *freedom* is never free (to repeat an old cliché), and that some things are . . . well . . . just worth fighting for.

Our involvement in armed conflict can be divided into wars over domestic issues and wars that involve global issues. Some were necessary to right injustices, such as the issue of slavery in our own country, while others have been deemed necessary to eliminate armed aggression of one country over another, or to put a halt to a conflict where genocide was the issue at hand.

In recent years we have been drawn into conflicts where terrorist acts are being perpetrated on innocent civilian populations, and in instances where those involved were fighting over geographical or economic concerns.

The very *Concept of America* needs to be understood from viewpoint of what makes America and Americans tick. The issues regarding the price we put on freedom and liberty as a country, are as equally important to the value we put on our independence to pursue the American Dream with our entrepreneurial, free market, capitalist economic system. These concepts are American, and need to be passed down, not glossed over or hidden from view, for every generation that follows.

Chapter 3 - Domestic wars and conflicts - wars fought on U.S. soil

"That we here highly resolve that these dead shall not have died in vain - that this nation, under God, shall have a new birth of freedom - and that government of the people, by the people, for the people, shall not perish from the earth."

Abraham Lincoln

American Revolution (1775–1783) The Revolutionary War waged by the American colonies against Britain was our War of Independence which influenced political ideas and revolutions around the world. The thirteen original colonies formed a largely disconnected country which won its freedom from the greatest empire and military force of its time.

At the heart of the revolution was that Great Britain was forcing its 13 American colonies to pay taxes but would not give them representation in the British Parliament. This and other injustices led the colonies to declare independence on July 4, 1776.

With much unrest across all the colonies that were situated along the eastern seaboard, many of those clamoring for a voice in government were deemed the radicals of their day. They were by no means in the majority, but were able to stir up sentiment around their perceived unjust treatment with the rallying cry of *"no taxation without representation"*.

The business owners, farmers, lawyers and common workers in the Colonies were thriving. The economy in general was strong, with some plantation owners and merchants becoming quite wealthy. America could have boasted the best quality of life in the world. Times were good for many others as well. It might have been envy or just the fact that the British were jealous, but they wanted a slice of the American life in the form of *cash* and were taxing it out of the Colonists. As resistance built up, a backlash was bound to occur.

Schools do still teach about the Boston Tea Party which was a result of the building resistance to British rule. On December 16, 1773, 50 or 60 *Sons of Liberty*, as they called themselves, disguised as Mohawk Indians, boarded merchant ships in Boston Harbor to protest the 3 cents per pound British tax on tea, seized the cargo, and began dumping chests of tea into Boston Harbor. Most schools never teach that this occurred on *two separate occasions*[9], the first in December 1773 followed by a repeat performance on March 7, 1774. The two tea parties cost the British around $3 million in today's dollars.

The resistance escalated against the British. The Colonists were convinced their prosperity and liberty were at stake without proper representation in the British Parliament. Virginia's Patrick Henry summed up the colonists' position when he announced for all to hear, "Give me liberty or give me death!"

As discontent began to peak, armed conflict was to follow. A major incident in Boston was the initial confrontation that involved the first death of the Revolutionary War.

Crispin Attucks[10], an escaped slave of African and mixed Native American descent, was part of an angry mob that surrounded eight British soldiers on March 5, 1770 outside the Boston customs house. The soldiers fired on the crowd and Attucks was killed, along with four others. The shootings were quickly dubbed the "Boston Massacre" and held up by angry colonists as a case of British brutality.

2

The Battles of Lexington and Concord[11], fought on April 19, 1775, kicked off the American Revolutionary War which lasted from

1775 until 1783.

According to History.com- A&E Television Network,
"Tensions had been building for many years between residents of the 13 American colonies and the British authorities, particularly in Massachusetts. On the night of April 18, 1775, hundreds of British troops marched from Boston to nearby Concord in order to seize an arms cache. Paul Revere and other riders sounded the alarm, and colonial militiamen began mobilizing to intercept the Redcoat column. A confrontation on the Lexington town green started off the fighting, and soon the British were hastily retreating under intense fire".

An accurate accounting of the Lexington and Concord Battles is posted at that website:

"At dawn on April 19, some 700 British troops arrived in Lexington and came upon 77 militiamen gathered on the town green. A British major yelled, "Throw down your arms! Ye villains, ye rebels."

"The heavily outnumbered militiamen had just been ordered by their commander to disperse when a shot rang out. To this day, no one knows which side fired first. Several British volleys were subsequently unleashed before order could be restored. When the smoke cleared, eight militiamen lay dead and nine were wounded, while only one Redcoat was injured.

"The British then continued into Concord to search for arms, not realizing that the vast majority had already been relocated. They decided to burn what little they found, and the fire got slightly out of control. Hundreds of militiamen occupying the high ground outside of Concord incorrectly thought the whole town would be torched.

"The militiamen hustled to Concord's North Bridge, which was being defended by a contingent of British soldiers. The British fired first but fell back when the colonists returned the volley. This

was the "shot heard 'round the world" later immortalized by poet Ralph Waldo Emerson."

By the end of the Revolution the death toll was estimated to be 6,800 Americans killed in action[12], 6,100 wounded, and upwards of 20,000 taken prisoner. Historians believe that at least an additional 17,000 deaths were the result of disease, including about 8,000–12,000 who died while prisoners of war.

Independence was achieved in 1783, when the Treaty of Paris was signed with Britain.

War of 1812 (1812–1815) This war which lasted three and a half years came about initially because the British were interfering with American trade, and conscripting American seamen from the ships they detained at sea, forcing them to serve in the Britain Navy. At the same time, the U.S. began expanding westward into then controlled British territory and into territory controlled by Canada to the north.

On June 18, 1812, U.S. President James Madison signed a congressionally approved declaration of war against Great Britain. The War of 1812 is not well remembered because it came between the Revolutionary and Civil Wars.

The legacy of the War of 1812 left its mark on the United States, Britain, and Canada as well. Americans rationalized their move into Canada by believing they were "liberating Canada from the

Andrew Jackson and the heroic battle of New Orleans with his makeshift army of soldiers, gamblers, cowboys, former slaves, pirates, and representatives from several Indian tribes, route the British.

32

Brits", but in reality they were credited with forging a national identity for the Canadians as they united to repel the series of American invasions.

Hostilities concluded in 1815 with the Treaty of Ghent (Belgium), following the resounding victory Andrew Jackson had in defeating the British with a rag-tag assortment of a make-shift militia in the Battle of New Orleans.

The war is remembered for two main reasons . . . The Star of Spangled Banner which became the national Anthem of the United States, and the launch of the political career of Andrew Jackson who went on to become the 7th President of the country.

In reality, the War of 1812 was a reenactment of the Revolutionary War. The trade issues between the United States and England went unsettled as the war had to be considered a "draw", but the biggest losers were the American Indian tribes who fought alongside the British and Canadians.

With the British and Canadians no longer the protectorate of the tribes, westward expansion of the United States went on unabated, and led to a long series of wars with the native Indians who had settled on the Continent long before the Europeans.

Mexican War (1846–1848) The stage was set for the Mexican War with the Texan's War of Independence from Mexico ten years earlier. The Texans declared their independence from Mexico, and as history has proven independence has been a trait of Texans ever since.

The Texan's war with Mexico will long be remembered because of the Battle at the Alamo. The Alamo was an old Spanish mission in San Antonio, where Col. William Travis, his co-commander Jim Bowie, and their troops, fought a battle to the death alongside such folk heroes as Davy Crockett, against a massive Mexican army commanded by Antonio Lopez de Santa Anna.

Col. Travis and the men of the Alamo fought to the death for Texas independence.

The significance of the Alamo was that the Mexican army was moving up through San Antonio on the way to San Jacinto on the southeast part of the Texas Territory to put down the Texas army being formed by General "Sam" Houston. At the time Houston's group would have been *easy pickins'* for the Mexican army to wipe out as they were still trying to organize their force and declare independence from Mexican rule.

The *battle cry*, "Remember the Alamo" became famous among Texans as they feverishly tried to recruit more soldiers to fight the Mexican army.

Col. Travis draws the famous "Line in the Sand", which became a lasting metaphor.

The notorious *Line in the Sand* metaphor - Col. Travis had known for several days that his situation inside the old Spanish mission was hopeless, far out-numbered, out gunned, and desperately short of ammunition. Travis was only 26 years old and was not a professional soldier but had read enough military history to understand that in a siege, the army on the outside usually prevails over the army on the inside.

As he gathered his troops around him he made the case to all . . . *"We must die in this fight as it is our business not to make a fruitless effort to save our lives, but to choose the manner of our death."*

He clearly stated the three possibilities before them: *"Surrender and summary execution; try to fight our way out only to be "butchered" by Mexican lancers; or remain in this fort...resist every assault, and to sell our lives as dearly as possible."* He then challenged his men to make the choice by drawing his sword and slowly marking a line in the dirt. *"I now want every man who is determined to stay here and die with me to come across this line."*

It is irrefutable that with Travis drawing that line with his sword - be it truth or legend – has given Texas, America, and eventually, the world, one of its most enduring metaphors. The *line in the sand* metaphor gets its power because it represents something that is absolutely true: Making a courageous decision often comes with a high price.

The Battle of the Alamo began on February 23 and lasted 13-days until March 6, 1836. It was the pivotal event in the Texas Revolution. The number of Texans who died in this battle has long been forgotten and often referred to as "a handful", but the manner in which they died and the valor they displayed will always be remembered by historians. The action caused a delay for the Mexican Army in their pursuit of General Houston, and enabled Houston's men to be prepared for the forthcoming Battle of San Jacinto.

The 11th president of the United States, the great James Polk.

When Santa Anna's troops finally arrived at San Jacinto, located southeast of Houston, the cries of *Remember the Alamo,* could be heard above the noise of battle, as revenge was inflicted on the Mexican Army enabling Texas to secure its independence in a very swift 18-minute battle.

In the aftermath of the Texas War for Independence, the 11th president of the United States, James Polk[13], a native of North Carolina, was serving as president. Though he elected to serve only one term in office, the Texas War of Independence with Mexico enabled him to achieve his desire to acquire California and the rest of the Mexican territory of the Southwest.

Upon being elected president Polk reiterated his goal to secure the westward expansion of the United States into the Oregon Territory to the north, and insure the acquisition of the southwest land that eventually became the states of California, Nevada, Arizona, New Mexico, Utah and Texas. Polk has been recognized as a *great* President among those who have served because he achieved his goals and forced Mexico to give up two-fifths of its territory.

Civil War (1861–1865) As we look back at history, slavery has been around since nations have gone to war with each other. Captured soldiers have helped facilitate the concept of slavery as punishment, and once the idea of getting free labor as the *spoils of war* became popular, slavery was institutionalized around the world. In many countries today, slavery is still an issue even if some countries no longer call it "slavery".

In the United States our liberal progressives have used the slavery-issue to drive a wedge between ethnicities, in an effort to enforce their so-called version of "justice" on the country as a whole. They condemn the very country that affords them the right to free speech to belabor the fact that the United States participated in the abominable slave trade seen in the South.

Never spoken in their diatribe about how evil that makes America, is the truth that the slave trade was mainly perpetrated by African tribes which had conquered other tribes, taking the enemy warriors as prisoners to be sold into slavery in the new world which included the United States, the Caribbean, Central and South America.

Unfortunately our American educational system has long forgotten the truth and/or has simply turned a blind eye to the facts about slavery. The blight of slavery is one the educators want to *blame on all Americans,* and that simply is not the case. In politics, it is was mainly the Democrat Party, which was the political party mostly responsible for fostering the *business of slavery.*

Additionally, it was the Democrat Party that, following the end of the Civil War, used every effort at their disposal to deny Black America their right to equal access to American life, even after hundreds of thousands of Union soldiers (the North) had perished in the fight to insure slavery would be abolished.

As nations go, the United States is the only country that literally fought a war to ensure the end of slavery. Yet today, our historians want to *shelve the story* of those who gave their lives to end the practice, and want to revert back to the 1860's whenever anyone wants to have a meaningful discussion about equal rights for all Americans, affirmative action, or race relations in general.

Slavery was not a universal problem for all Americans back when our country was founded. It was a problem with the plantation owners who wanted low cost farm labor and those who would financially benefit from the slave trade.

That brings us around to the fourth major war fought on the domestic front . . . the *Civil War*. The North (the Union) fought The South (the Confederacy) over the issue of ***state's rights***, meaning the Confederate States, which were far more

Sen. Charles Sumner. Nearly beaten to death in the well of the Senate for his anti-slavery views.

agriculturally oriented, wanted the right to have slavery, and the independence to determine their own destiny by breaking away from the northern, industrialized states.

Following often bitter debates in Congress over laws forbidding slavery, and after Massachusetts Senator, Charles Sumner[14], was nearly beaten to death in the well of the Senate during one such debate, the discussions were over, guns were drawn, and bullets began to fly.

The economic and political rivalry between an agricultural South and an industrial North grew into the civil war because the South feared that losing the free labor of slaves would take away their competitive edge in agricultural markets.

Were it just an issue of free labor perhaps going to guns could have been delayed if not avoided, however the issue became more unbearable because of the inhuman treatment of slaves by many slave owners, *including Black slave owners*. The brutality involved whippings (for insubordination or runaways), branding (to insure identity for the owners), and rape and sexual assault, so as not to diminish the value of the work a slave was able to produce.

From Black historian, J.A. Rogers[15], we learn that, *"perhaps the most insidious or desperate attempt to defend the right of black people to own slaves was the statement made on the eve of the Civil War by a group of free people of color in New Orleans, offering their services to the Confederacy, in part because they were fearful for their own enslavement: 'The free colored population [native] of Louisiana ... own slaves, and they are dearly attached to their native land ... and they are ready to shed their blood for her defense. They have no sympathy for abolitionism; no love for the North, but they have plenty for*

Louisiana ... They will fight for her in 1861 as they fought [to defend New Orleans from the British] in 1814-1815'."

Prior to the Civil War, slavery was a major issue in the formation of the country, but was put on the back burner by the Founding Fathers in order to form a government. Had the issue of slavery been debated thoroughly by those in attendance of the Constitutional Convention, it is doubtful we would have ever seen the formation of the United States.

It was decided slavery would be addressed later in amendments to the Constitution. In *The Collected Works of Abraham Lincoln* the U.S. president during the Civil War (edited by Roy P. Basler, Volume III, "Lincoln-Douglas Debate at Quincy" - October 13, 1858, p. 276) we read:

"In the first place, I insist that our fathers did not make this nation half slave and half free, or part slave and part free. I insist that they found the institution of slavery existing here. They did not make it so, but they left it so because they knew of no way to get rid of it at that time."

Abraham Lincoln. Arguably the greatest President the United States has ever elected.

... and from Roy P. Basler, Volume VIII, *The Collected Works of Abraham Lincoln,* "Speech to One Hundred Fortieth Indiana Regiment" - March 17, 1865, p. 361, we see the further thoughts of Black America's first champion of freedom, Abraham Lincoln, when he stated:

"Whenever I hear any one arguing for slavery I feel a strong impulse to see it tried on him personally."

While the United States (and the British colonies that preceded our independence) played no prominent role in creating the institution of slavery, or even in establishing a long-standing African slave trade developed by the Dutch, Arab, Portuguese, Spanish and other merchants long before the settlement of North America, Americans did contribute[16] mightily to the spectacularly successful battle to end slavery with the Civil War.

Indian Wars (Early settlements through the westward growth of America) Conflict between the Native American Indian and the settlers of the New World began in the seventeenth century with the Powhatan Confederacy[17], and specifically in that of the Paspahegh[17-1] tribe whose near annihilation of the settlers of the Jamestown settlement in Virginia with large-scale attacks in 1622 and 1644, brought strong reprisals by the English, and resulted in the near elimination of the tribe.

The Powhatans, also known as the Algonquians, was made up of about thirty different tribes and were also in constant conflict with the Iroquois Indians. It wasn't until the 1722 that the Algonquians and Iroquois settled on a peace treaty, but by then the Algonquian tribes were greatly diminished in size, much in part due to sickness and disease inherited from the white settlers.

Many of the early battles with America's Indians involved tribes where the Indians and white colonists lived in close proximity. Perhaps it was the early cohabitation problems that set the stage for the anti-Indian animosity that prejudiced the colonial expansion of the white population. Whatever it was throughout America's first two centuries, relations between the natives and settlers was tenuous at best and outright hostile up through the nineteenth century.

40

These Indian wars were not just between the Native Americans and the Western Europeans who were settling the east coast of America. The Spanish were busy in the west making inroads into creating their own settlements in the new world. The Spaniard's purpose in colonizing New Mexico[18] was to explore for gold and silver, but the missionaries who traveled with the soldiers were determined to Christianize the Native Americans.

In the decades that followed the initial contact the Pueblo Indians had with the Spaniards, they were subjected to severe oppression under Spanish rule and were forced into labor, required to pay demanding taxes in goods, and their religious activities were suppressed.

The Great Pueblo Revolt[19] threatened the entire Spanish-held territory in 1680, when the Natives forced the Spaniards to flee to the Santa Fe area of New Mexico. In fierce fighting the Pueblo Indian revolt took the lives of many of the Franciscan missionaries and as many as 380 Spaniards. The Spaniards eventually made their way to El Paso, Texas. From the files at The Library of Congress we learn:

"The Pueblo rebellion effectively under the leadership of Popé, Tewa medicine-man, and native of the pueblo of San Juan, ended Spanish rule in New Mexico for the next 12 years. However, Popé died and the de facto confederation of the Pueblos fell apart. Since there were no Spanish troops to offer protection, the traditional enemies of the Pueblos, the Apache and Navajo, launched their attacks. The succeeding Spanish governor of the territory, Diego de Vargas Zapata y Luján Ponce de León (ca. 1643-1704), began a successful military and political reconquest in 1692." The resurgence of Spanish control was inevitable[20] because the Indian tribes were decimated by disease.

Traditionally, the Indian tribes fought to avenge the deaths of kinsmen rather than to acquire territory. When a clan member was killed by Indians from another tribe, a war leader related to the deceased formed a war party composed of kinsmen and unrelated young men who sought the prestige that came through success in battle. As fate would have it however, the Indian revolts and subsequent battle between the Indian tribes were probably equally focused on ridding the Pueblo region of Spanish influence as it was to avenge the death of tribesmen by the Navajo and Apache tribes.

Although Popé died during this turbulent period, he and the other Pueblo leaders began a systematic eradication of all signs of Christianity and Spanish material culture while fending off assaults by Navajo and Apache war parties. Regardless of how adamant the Indian tribe was about killing-off Spanish influences, they found it was *easier to order the eradication* of all vestiges of Spanish presence than to *accomplish it*. Many items of material culture[21] which had been introduced by the Spanish such as iron tools, sheep, cattle, and fruit trees, had become an integral part of Pueblo life.

Moving into the nineteenth century there was constant conflict between the two sides as the vast hunting grounds of the Indians were being overrun by first the settlers, ranchers, farmers, and then prospectors searching for treasures of gold and silver. The expansion of the coast-to-coast, Union Pacific Railroad, sped up settlement of the West.

According to History.com[22] research regarding the American Indian Wars, the 1800's was a period when the federal government attempted to move the tribes onto protected reservations to make room for western settlements. Because the treaties tended to be far one-sided, with the Indians on the *short-end of the stick*, the battles between federal troops and the tribesmen were often fought-to-the-death by the Indians who were often out-gunned, and out-numbered.

> *"On the Pacific Coast, attacks against the native peoples accompanied the flood of immigrants to gold-laden California. Disease, malnutrition, and warfare combined with the poor lands set aside as reservations to reduce the Indian population of that state from 150,000 in 1845 to 35,000 in 1860. The army took the lead*

*role in Oregon and Washington, using the Rogue
River (1855-1856), Yakima (1855-1856), and
Spokane (1858) Wars to force several tribes onto
reservations.*

*"Sporadic conflicts also plagued Arizona
and New Mexico throughout the 1850s as the
army struggled to establish its presence. On the
southern plains, mounted warriors posed an even
more formidable challenge to white expansion.
Strikes against the Sioux, Cheyennes, Arapahos,
Comanches, and Kiowas during the decade only
hinted at the deadlier conflicts of years to come".*

9-Chief Sitting Bull   10-Chief Crazy Horse   11-General George Custer

The culmination of the Indian Wars ended in 1890 but not
before the key battle which signaled the beginning of the end in a
battle which became known as Custer's Last Stand[23]. Sioux
Chieftains Sitting Bull and Crazy Horse had been successfully
resisting the government's efforts to confine the Sioux people to
reservations for more than a decade.

With gold being discovered in the Black Hills, the Indians
were no longer able to hunt freely, and the federal government
refused to keep white prospectors out of the Sioux Reservation.
The two chiefs decided it was time to defend their way of life.

By the late spring of 1876, more than 10,000 Indians had gathered in a massive camp along a river in southern Montana called the Little Big Horn. *"We must stand together or they will kill us separately,"* Sitting Bull told them. *"These soldiers have come shooting; they want war. All right, we'll give it to them."*

According to reports as documented by America's Story from America's Library of the U.S. government:

> *"On the morning of June 25, 1876, Lieutenant Colonel George A. Custer and the 7th Cavalry charged into battle against Lakota Sioux and Northern Cheyenne Indians. Custer's orders were to wait for reinforcements at the mouth of the Little Big Horn River before attacking the Indians, but Chief Sitting Bull had been spotted nearby, and Custer was impatient to attack.*

> *"A treaty had given the Sioux exclusive rights to the Black Hills, but when gold was later discovered in the area, white miners flocked to the territory. Despite the treaty, the U.S. government ordered the Indians away from the invading settlers and back to their reservations.*

> *"Custer's job was to force the Indians back to their reservations. Some of the Indians refused to leave their sacred land, and other hunters were camped in remote places and never learned of the order. The U.S. Army prepared for battle anyway.*

> *"Custer planned to attack the Indian camp from three sides, but Chief Sitting Bull was ready for them. The first two groups, led by Captain Benteen and Major Reno, were immediately forced to retreat to one side of the river, where they continued to fight as best they could. Custer was not as lucky.*

"Custer's troops charged the Indians from the north. Quickly encircled by their enemy, Custer and 265 of his soldiers were killed in less than an hour. The Indians retreated two days later when the troops Custer had been ordered to wait for arrived.

"The Battle of Little Big Horn was a short-lived victory for the Native Americans. Federal troops soon poured into the Black Hills. While many Native Americans surrendered, Sitting Bull escaped to Canada".

Crazy Horse lived only one more year and was killed in 1877 after leaving the reservation without permission. The Sioux Indian Tribe did finally surrender to federal troops in 1888, and the armed resistance between the Indians and federal troops was over. The remaining Sioux were forced into reservation life at gunpoint.

With their traditions and way of life rapidly disappearing, many of the Sioux looked for spiritual guidance from their tribal leaders and medicine men, which came in the form of what became known as "The Ghost Dance"[24], which was used to ward-off evil spirits. This tradition spread rapidly from tribe to tribe, but the prayers of the Indians did more to spook the white population than deliver on the hope that *"an Indian messiah would come and the world would be free of the white man. The Indians could return to their lands and the buffalo would once again roam the Great Plains".*

The white population of South Dakota demanded that the Sioux end their ritual of the Ghost Dance, and when the Sioux ignored the request, the U.S. Army was called-in. A group of about 300 Sioux left the reservation to continue their spiritual prayers, but the federal troops believed their movement was to prepare for war against the white settlers. When the troops caught up with the Indian group and the two sides came into contact, the Sioux reluctantly agreed to be transported to Wounded Knee Creek on Pine Ridge Reservation.

45

When the army demanded the surrender of all Sioux weapons, a shot rang out, though nobody can say for sure who fired the shot, the army opened fire, cutting down the Indians as they fled. When the shooting ended, the Seventh Calvary had accounted for the death of almost all of the 300 men, women, and children. Some died instantly, others who were wounded, were left to freeze to death in the snow.

This massacre marked the last showdown between Native Americans and the United States Army. It was nearly 400 years after Christopher Columbus first contacted the *Indians*. The 1890 United States census declared the frontier officially closed, and Sitting Bull was shot and killed by a Lakota policeman, marking the end of 1890. The massacre at Wounded Knee[25], S.D., is generally considered the last of these conflicts.

Spanish American War (1898) If you ask the average American today about the Spanish-American War, most probably wouldn't have the foggiest idea what you were talking about. That's understandable, as American history classes don't teach much about the wars in which the United States has been involved. What you're likely to hear is that *"the U.S. is bad and every other country has simply been caught up in America's industrial-military's thirst for profit"* rhetoric.

Regardless of what you might know or what you might have been led to believe, the Spanish American War had tremendous implications for the United States, Spain, Cuba, Philippines, Guam, and Hawaii. History classes that do mention this important piece of American history usually gloss over why it was important simply waving it off as a three-month skirmish engineered by politicians with no real gain to be had for America.

Like most wars of any length, they leave a lasting legacy. Many have heard the refrain *Remember the Maine*[26], but haven't put two and two together to know what it means. On February 15, 1898, a massive explosion sank the battleship USS *Maine* in Cuba's Havana harbor, killing 260 out of the 400 crew members aboard. The battleship was resting peacefully in the harbor where it had been sent to protect American interests after a rebellion against Spanish rule broke out in Havana in January, 1898.

Though everyone thought the ship was blown up by a mine, an official U.S. Naval Court of Inquiry ruled that out, but the American public placed the blame on Spain and demanded that Congress declare war.

Slow to move forward with a war declaration; the people's indignation over Spain's brutal suppression of the Cuban rebellion, added to diplomatic failures to resolve the Maine issue, and continued losses to American investments, led to the outbreak of the Spanish-American War in April 1898

In reality, the U.S. supported Cuba's desire for independence from Spanish rule and wanted to seize the opportunity to expand U.S. influence in Cuba and extend its power in other parts of the region . . . war became inevitable. At the end of the brief conflict, Cuba gained its independence, and the U.S. gained several former Spanish territories including Puerto Rico, Guam, and the Philippines, and annexed the independent state of *Hawaii.*

The Spanish American War was relatively bloodless from the American perspective, the most memorable event of the short-lived war was the Battle of San Juan Hill, which made a legend out of Teddy Roosevelt and led to his eventual election as the 26th president of the United States.

In May 1898, one month after the outbreak of War, a Spanish fleet docked in the Santiago de Cuba harbor. A superior U.S. naval force arrived soon after and blockaded the harbor entrance. The U.S. Army Fifth Corps landed on Cuba to launch an attack on Santiago in a coordinated assault with an attack from the sea.

The ground troops included Theodore "Teddy" Roosevelt and his ensemble of "Rough Riders," which was a collection of

Western cowboys and Eastern elitists. Together they made up the First U.S. Voluntary Cavalry.

July 1st, after fighting its way to Santiago's outer defenses, the Fifth Corps was ordered by General William Shafter to attack the village of El Caney and San Juan Hill[27]. Shafter wanted to secure El Chaney before tackling the heavily fortified heights of San Juan. With 5000 U.S. infantry however, the small band of roughly 500 Spanish soldiers held them back. Even though El Caney was not secure, 8,000 Americans soldiers pressed forward to the base of San Juan Hill.

At that point the forces split up into two groups to take both San Juan Hill and Kettle Hill. The Rough Riders were among the troops in the right flank attacking Kettle Hill.

Teddy Roosevelt and The Rough Rider taking "San Juan Hill", however contrary to the popular myth of horse mounted troops charging up the hill guns a' blazing, Roosevelt led the charge up Kettle Hill on foot, without the aid of horses. They had been left behind because of transportation difficulties.

The order was given that *"the heights must be taken at all hazards"*, the Rough Riders, contrary to the popular myth of horse mounted troops charging up the hill guns a' blazing, led the charge up Kettle Hill on foot, without the aid of horses. They had been left behind because of transportation difficulties. The Rough Riders took Kettle Hill none-the-less, with a contingent of black soldiers of the 9th and 10th Cavalry regiments. They then turned their attention on San Juan Hill, which was taken soon after.

History is still alive with Roosevelt and his Rough Riders famous charge up San Juan Hill in a blaze of glory, but sadly, that wasn't the case. Instead, it was an on-foot-slug-fest against the Spanish stronghold, but a heroic bit of history anyway.

From the vantage point of the heights the Americans could look down into Santiago, and from there began a siege of the city the next day. On July 3rd, the Spanish fleet was destroyed off Santiago by U.S. warships and on July 17th the Spanish surrendered the city, thereby sealing the fate of the Spanish possession and ceding control to the U.S.

The United States was victorious, and the victory was very important in making the nation what it is today. In retrospect, the justification for attacking Spain was not there, though few in the country realized this at the time.

Historians have noted that the Spanish-American War was the beginning of the U.S. becoming a world power, and from which all citizens of the country, and many non-citizens have benefited.

Chapter 4 - Wars fought for the freedom of others

"In the long history of the world, only a few generations have been granted the role of defending freedom in its hour of maximum danger. I do not shrink from this responsibility - I welcome it."
John F. Kennedy

World War I (1914–1918) Rivalries over power, territory, and wealth led to the "Great War" as it has become known. In 1917, the U.S. joined the Allies (Britain, France, Russia, Italy, and Japan), who were at war with the Central Powers (Germany, Austria-Hungary, Bulgaria, and Turkey), after German submarines began sinking unarmed ships.

The war actually began in 1914, when Archduke Franz Ferdinand, heir to the throne of the Austro-Hungarian Empire, and his wife were assassinated in Sarajevo. This began a series of events that led to U.S. involvement. The American people were dead set against the U.S. becoming involved, but like a snowball rolling down hill, we eventually were sucked in.

It was the German's unbridled U-Boat aggression sinking ships that created such an uproar, President Woodrow Wilson asked Congress to declare war. By the time we entered the war nearly every country on the globe was involved. Participation in the war was widespread.

The factions were divided into the Allies (based on the Triple Entente of the United Kingdom, France and the Russian Empire) and the Central Powers of Germany and Austria-Hungary. The U.S. came in on the side of the Allies.

Though the U.S. entered the war late, it was the catalyst that was needed to bring victory for the allies. Our involvement lasted from 1917 to 1918, but our loses were shocking. 177,000 of our youth were either killed, wounded or missing in the two years we were fighting. Virtually every family had someone involved.

13

John Gunther last soldier
to be killed in World War

For the first time a tremendous number of American men - 1.2 million - were sent overseas to be separated from their families for a long period of time. Though the war has not remained as strong in the memory as the Civil War, the terror of the war, with its use of chemical weapons (nerve and mustard gases) is still burned into the collective minds of historians.

By the war's end an estimated 37 million people had been killed. Henry Nicholas John Gunther [28], an American conscript was the last soldier killed, dying on November 11, 1918, one minute before the Armistice was signed.

World War II (1939–1945) World War II began with Japanese and German expansionism in the late 1930's. Japan waged a series of conquering campaigns throughout Asia to expand their access to natural resources which were scarce on their island nation. Each campaign was more brutal than the next, and ended in the surprise attack on the Americans at Pearl Harbor, HI, December 7, 1941.

Germany on the other side of the world began their expansion campaign with the rise of Adolph Hitler in the mid 1930's aided in part by elimination of the opposition by Hitler's henchmen. Hitler openly began building a military arsenal in direct violation of the treaty Germany signed ending WWI, and invaded Poland in 1939. Joseph Stalin, who had signed a non-aggression pact earlier with Germany, gave a *tacit nod of approval* not to intervene. England and France declared war on Germany in 1939, as Germany went on through 1940 expanding its territory with hostile action against Finland, Norway, Denmark, Netherlands, Belgium, and Luxembourg.

The famous Flying Tigers flew in support of the Chinese as the First American Volunteer Group to thwart the Japanese.

In 1940 the United States began its "Lend-Lease" policy allowing President Roosevelt to send ammunition and other war supplies to England. This meant that the U.S. was no longer "neutral" and as such, gave England all the help possible "short of war."

Also during 1940 Germany defeated Greece and Yugoslavia and then in June, Hitler sent more than 3 million troops to the Eastern Front to invade the Soviet Union. In October a German submarine torpedoed the U.S. Navy destroyer DD-254, *Reuben James* [54] in the North Atlantic. It was the first U.S. warship sunk in the European War. Only 45 of the ship's 160 crew members survived.

At this point in history and following the memories of the "War to End all Wars", Americans were still debating the "War in Europe", but continued to oppose taking sides between the Germans and the English while Roosevelt's unflinching support of England was mainly "kept under the covers". Many Americans however, in partnership with many Canadians, did go off to war to fight the Axis Powers with England and fight the Japanese in China wearing uniforms other than the uniforms of American military.

The Flying Tigers [29], or the First American Volunteer Group (AVG) of the Chinese Air Force, was an all-volunteer pilot corps recruited from the United States Army military services. It was rumored to have been secretly authorized by President Franklin Roosevelt in the spring of 1941, but no such *document of authorization* has ever been found.

The Flying Tigers unit was commanded by Lt. General Claire Lee Chennault, who convinced 95 pilots and 185 ground crew to volunteer. Since the United States had not yet entered the war against Japan, the pilots flew to a British airfield in Burma for training and became an unofficial mercenary corps to support China's war against Japan.

Just two weeks after the Japanese attacked Pearl Harbor on December 7, 1941, the Flying Tigers flew their first missions. They flew combat sorties against the Japanese to ensure that the Burma Road would remain open to resupply China's Nationalist Army in its fight against Japan.

In addition to keeping the supply lines open for the Chinese army, the Flying Tigers flew missions against Japanese bombers that were hitting Kunming, China, and Rangoon, Burma. When the Japanese overran Burma in February of 1942, the Flying Tigers had to pull out of the area.

The Flying Tigers then became part of the Chinese Air Force until July of 1942, when they were absorbed into the US Army Air Corps as the 23rd Fighter Group. In the seven months that they fought as mercenaries, they are credited with destroying 299 Japanese aircraft, with 229 of those shot down in flight.

Even after they officially joined the American Air Force, the Flying Tigers kept their signature shark-jaw nose cones. Their losses in combat were four pilots killed in the air, one killed while strafing ground targets and one taken prisoner despite being outnumbered by 8 to one. News of the Americans' achievement electrified the world and gave courage to the faltering Allied forces, which had been repeatedly defeated by the Axis powers.

On the European front and prior to the United States' entry into WWII, many Americans also volunteered for service in the RAF (Royal Air Force) and RCAF (Royal Canadian Air Force). As the Battle of Britain raged on from May through October 1940, many Americans who were following the war in Europe knew that in time the US would more than likely become involved.

The stories of the RAF pilots flying their Hurricanes and Spitfires inspired many to join the RAF. The RAF was short on pilots so a call went out across America for pilots to replace the RAF's depleted ranks.

American aviators of the 71st Eagle Squadron flew for Canada and Britain

An organization named the Knight Committee was responsible for recruiting nearly 90 percent of the volunteer pilots. Thousands answered the call and volunteered to come to the aid of Britain. 244 Americans became pilots who made up a special flight wing called the Eagle Squadrons[30] - the 71st, 121st, and 133rd Squadrons of the Royal Air Force Fighter Command. It was the RAF's policy to pick Englishmen as squadron and flight commanders and 16 of these British pilots served with the Eagle Squadrons.

From the time the first Eagle Squadron was formed in September 1940 until all three squadrons were disbanded and incorporated into the U.S. Army Air Corps in September 1942, they destroyed 73 German planes. 77 American and 5 British members were killed.

Under American law, it was illegal for United States citizens to join the armed forces of foreign nations. In doing so, they lost their citizenship, although Congress passed a blanket pardon in 1944. These were acts of exceptional Americans. They boosted a world morale that was in the tank and came at the right time in history with the Axis powers running roughshod over the Allies in every theater of the war.

World War II ended in Europe on May 8, 1945. The losses were beyond belief. Hitler had committed suicide, as a way to keep from being held accountable for his actions. European cities had been leveled to the ground, and millions of people displaced. Millions had been killed and wounded and Europe faced starvation because most of the farmland lay in waste.

Posting the colors on Mt. Suribachi on the island of Iwo Jima

Cowards, and Hitler surely was a coward, often deprive a civilized society to exact their judgment. That was unfortunate in that today there are many who deny the evils of Nazism, and some even praise the goals of their Aryan ideals.

The victory over the Japanese occurred on August 15, 1945, following the bombing of Nagasaki and Hiroshima with the world's first nuclear weapons. The U.S. over the years has faced criticism for using the first weapons of mass destruction, but following so many losses in our *island hopping* campaign to drive the Japanese out of the territory they aggressively took leading up to our involvement, plus their sneak attack on Pearl Harbor, history has agreed with President Truman that The Bomb was the only solution.

Hindsight is almost always 20-20 in some people's eyes, but criticism of Truman's decision is unwarranted.

As American troops moved closer and closer to the Japanese homeland, it was apparent that having to make a beach invasion would cost possibly hundreds of thousands of lives of American and Allied troops. The bloody battle of Iwo Jima, Tarawa, and the battle of Okinawa [31] which proved to be the bloodiest battle of the Pacific War, was the *handwriting on the wall* as to what would be in store if we hadn't ended the war.

The losses in securing Okinawa were in excess of 38,000 wounded for the U.S. and 12,000 dead. For the Japanese, losses were an amazing 107,539 made up of Japanese troops and Okinawan conscripts who were forced to fight. It is estimated an additional 100,000 civilians of Okinawa were killed though an exact count is impossible due to the unbridled carnage.

The U.S. repeatedly encouraged the Japanese to surrender and each time our requests for *unconditional surrender*[32] were ignored. Even following the first bomb which fell on Hiroshima, our demand went unanswered.

It is important for those with hindsight...those liberal scholars and critics who spent the war and thereafter in the safety of their homes on the mainland of the U.S. and who do not know the meaning of *unconditional surrender*, to pay attention.

Many revisionist historians claim Truman only wanted to use the atomic bomb to show the Soviets the superior power and technology we possessed; that The Bomb was totally unnecessary; and that the Japanese had asked about surrender on August 3rd, three days before we dropped the first bomb on Hiroshima. "The Japanese offered to surrender on 3 August, but their offer was rejected because it wasn't an *unconditional* surrender", according John Clare [33].

According to historian, Herbert Bix[34], The Korean Broadcasting System, which did extensive research on Japan's rejection of the Potsdam Conference's call for unconditional surrender, looked at the issue, with a thorough understanding of Asian culture and mindset, which do not always parallel Western culture . . .

> *"The leaders of the imperial armed forces clung to the idea that as Allied lines of supply and communication lengthened, their own forces would do better on the homeland battlefields. But by this time Japan had virtually no oil, its cities were in ruins and its navy and naval air capability*

virtually non-existent. It is unclear at what point Hirohito abandoned the illusion that his armed forces remained capable of delivering at least one devastating blow to the enemy so that his diplomats could negotiate a surrender on face saving terms.

"But six months of intensive U.S. terror bombing of the Japanese civilian population had forced Hirohito, the Court Group, and the

government to take into account not only their huge losses of men and materials, but also food shortages and the growing war-

17-The first Atomic Bomb dropped on Hiroshima, Japan

weariness of the Japanese people. How could they lead and preserve their system of rule after peace returned?

"That question weighed on their minds when the Potsdam Declaration arrived (July 27-28), which called on them to surrender unconditionally or face immediate destruction. They rejected the four-power ultimatum (U.S., Great Britain, France, Soviet Union), feeling as former prime minister and navy 'moderate', Admiral Yonai Mitsumasa, said to his secretary on July 28, 'There is no need to rush'."

During the war, able-bodied Americans went to do the fighting (men and many women), while at home the War Production Board (WPB) ramped-up manufacturing as never before seen anywhere else in the world. Women were doing the jobs heretofore filled by men...welding, fabricating, assembling, supervision, and inspection, as Americans provided the Allies with more production than any other country to help win the war.

> *"Powerful enemies must be out-fought and out-produced. It is not enough to turn out just a few more planes, a few more tanks, a few more guns, a few more ships than can be turned out by our enemies. We must out-produce them overwhelmingly, so that there can be no question of our ability to provide a crushing superiority of equipment in any theatre of the world war."*

President, Franklin Roosevelt - 1942

When the the U.S. entered the war American military wasn't yet equal to the Germans or the Japanese in terms of head to head combat, but true to our American spirit, our workers could build ships and planes faster than the enemy could sink them or shoot them down.[35] America launched more vessels in 1941 than Japan did in the entire war.

Shipyards turned out tonnage so fast that by the autumn of 1943 all Allied shipping sunk since 1939 had been replaced. In 1944 alone, the United States built more planes than the Japanese did from 1939 to 1945. By the end of the war, more than half of all industrial production in the world was taking place in the United States. This set the stage for America's rise to the greatest economic power the world has ever seen.

The Korean War (1950-1953) The Korean War was a war that should never have occurred. There are many reasons why countries go to war [36]. Free capitalistic countries are less apt to go to war than totalitarian countries. In a capitalistic country, one with limited central planning by government, resources are allocated on the basis of supply and demand. When there are ample resources, the selling price for access to those resources is low.

When supplies are scarce, the cost rises. There is also less chance for wars when freedom of the country's people is assured by rule of law, and where the citizens have open, free and honest elections.

In closed societies, where the government restricts freedoms; where the citizens have few rights and limited access to capital; and where the government is in total control of allocating of a country's resources there are often shortages. When the citizens of a country are not free to chose how, where, and when to spend their money, there is unrest when they are face with limited choices.

This competition for resources may prompt a government to gain access to what is needed, by seeking to fulfill the need by aggressively taking it from another country, or the shortage may create internal strife by the citizens aggressively taking from one another. We saw this in World War II when Japan invaded its Asian neighbors to fill its need for natural resources.

We find a war may be started by a country wherein part of the population wants to secede from the other, most often for political ideology or religious beliefs. The opposite might be the basis for war if a country is looking to unify with a country with similar ethnicities, religions, geographic heritage or ideologies.

In the cases of both Korea and Vietnam, the wars incorporated the desire for unification by one side while the other side was against such a move. In both cases, the aggressor countries were totalitarian rule wanting to subject the other country which was under democratic rule, to submit to their will.

In both Korea and Vietnam the citizens had different perspective on what constitutes the governance under which they chose to live. While both countries saw a benefit in unification the two political parties could not compromise or resolved their political differences through diplomacy, so a war ensued. They often say use of physical strength is the final option, but since those who have elected freedom seldom chose to submit to a totalitarian form of government, force became the *first option*.

As with many international events following World War II, the stage was set for war in Korea by the way the peace process was handled. In the many conferences held by the Allies during WW II, the subject of conversation was the Post-War period. The British and Americans had a tenuous relationship with Stalin who never minced words.

Stalin had his designs on the countries his armies had "liberated" from the Germans and that included *the spoils of war*. Occupying those countries after the war was his principal goal while the Allies were focused on rebuilding Europe. With the surrender of Germany followed by the surrender of Japan the Allied countries agreed that Japan would be stripped of all its colonies including Korea.

The U.S. was partly responsible for setting the stage for the Korean War by proposing that the Soviet Union take responsibility for accepting the surrender of Japanese troops in the part of the Korean peninsula north of the 38th parallel, while the U.S. would receive the surrender south of that line. This decision resulted in the division and separation of the country along the 38th parallel splitting families with ties in both the South and the North.

The U.S. should have handled the Japanese surrender for all of Korea. Letting the Soviets participate had a disastrous effect on what was supposed to have been a temporary division of the country until the United Nations could supervised elections.

As with most events in which the UN was involved, politics and ineptness prevailed, and since the UN had little or no power, the Soviets knew they could do as they pleased in North Korea. When the UN called for free elections, the Soviet Union blocked the elections in the North killing any chance for a reunification of Korea.

Instead, Russia installed Kim Il Sung as the leader of the Democratic People's Republic of Korea (DPRK). Stalin's view[37] of elections was that it was enough that people knew they had an election, but *it's the one counting the vote that matters.* This allowed the Soviets to install a puppet government much as they had done in most of Eastern Europe.

The elections in the South were fair and open and with the backing of the U.S In the South, Syngman Rhee was elected leader of the newly founded Republic of Korea (ROK). Kim Il Sung and Rhee were nationalists and both wanted reunification, but both had different views as to the political system that should govern.

The Soviet controlled North obviously wanted a collectivism/Marxist style communist government, and the South wanted a democratic-republic form of government... two polar opposites.

Both North and South Korea initiated fire fights across the 38th parallel, but neither made any major advances until war broke out when the North invaded the South on June 25, 1950[38] supported by the Soviets, who thought it would be a swift and easy victory. Early-on it looked as if the Soviets were correct and by September, the South had been pushed back to a small area around Pusan.

When the invasion began the United States immediately called for a meeting of the United Nations Security Council which passed a resolution condemning the actions of the DPRK and demanded that North Koreans pull back. When the North Koreans refused, the UN sent forces composed of troops from 15 nations to the peninsula to stop the communist advance.

While the war began as a civil war of reunification between North and South Korea, the conflict soon escalated into an international conflict with the South backed by the coalition of countries under U.S. leadership.

The People's Republic of China (PRC) entered to aid North Korea[39]. The U.S. government emphasized that this joint military action by the UN was imperative to prevent the conflict from spreading outside Korea.

The defense of the Pusan Perimeter went on for nearly a month and a half aided by U.S military troops sent in from Japan. The North Korean army was extended beyond its supply capabilities and was in a prime position for being cut off with the right tactical maneuver.

That maneuver was brilliantly designed by Gen. Douglas MacArthur when a detachment of the First Marine Division and 7th Army Division landed at the western port city of Inchon[40], near Seoul, and began to move inland to retake the capital and decisively cut the already tenuous North Korean supply lines. On the 29th of September, after days of hard fighting, Seoul the capital, was returned to the South Korean government.

With Seoul now back in the hands of the U.S. troops, a hundred miles to the southeast, the Pusan Perimeter's defenders went on the offensive pushing out of the Pusan Peninsula. The North Korean resistance collapsed after a few days and retreated during the rest of the month of October. The Army and Marine units moving southwards from Seoul met those coming up from Pusan.

MacArthur's forces then moved north[41] above the 38th Parallel, but they miscalculated the threat from the Chinese. As they nearly reached the Yalu River, which marks the border between China and North Korea, the Chinese sent forces into North Korea.

The U.S. and UN had also grossly underestimated the size, strength, and determination of the Chinese forces. As a result, MacArthur's troops were quickly forced to retreat behind the 38th parallel. The heat of the Korean summer and the frigid winter weather made the war almost unbearable for the U.S. troops as they battled back and forth with neither side gaining the upper hand.

The Korean War was a war of wills between the communists and the U.S lead forces. Armistice negotiations held in Panmunjom lasted over two years while the armies of both sides continued fighting over one worthless piece of ground after another. It was not until a new regime took over in the USSR and a final battle at Outpost Harry that negotiations concluded and fighting ended.

Most of those who fought in Korea would agree it was nothing more than a waste land with hot summers and ice cold winters . . . not worth the life of one fighting soldier, but when duty called, they all went; 54,246 never returned[42]. In four years of war, 136 Medals of Honor were presented, 98 of them posthumously.

18-Battle for Outpost Harry raged on as peace talks went on for more than 2 years in Panmunjom

Bay of Pigs (1961) When Fidel Castro overthrew the Cuban Government of Fulgencio Batista Zaldívar, American businesses fled the island nation. The story of Cuba is not a simple one as Castro has managed to stay in power with his grip on the political system in Cuba for more than five decades, despite alienating many Cubans with his iron-fist rule.

The story really began with the election of Fulgencio Batista Zaldívar to serve as president from 1940 to 1944. After finishing his term he lived in the United States, returning to Cuba to run for president in again 1952.

Facing certain defeat, he led a military coup that preempted the election and declared himself dictator which lasted from 1952 to 1959 before being overthrown during the Cuban Revolution[43], headed by Fidel Castro. Castro found himself without a legitimate political platform and little income with which to support his family when Batista seized power.

As dictator, Batista set himself up, solidified his power with the military and Cuba's economic elite, and got the United States to recognize his government as legitimate. Castro was no dummy and though Batista had the wealthy and the military on his side, they would be no match for the majority of the Cuban people if they were to revolt. Castro recognized this and along with fellow members of the Ortodoxo Party, which had been expected to win in the 1952 election, organized an insurrection.

On July 26, 1953, Castro and approximately a couple of hundred of his supporters attacked the Moncada military barracks in an attempt to overthrow Batista. The attack failed, Castro was captured, and instead of being shot, which was customary in Latin American countries, was tried, convicted, and sentenced to 15 years in prison. Big mistake by the Batista Regime . . . the incident fostered an ongoing opposition to the government and made Castro famous throughout Cuba.

In May of 1955 the Batista government, yielding to international pressure as well as pressure from the U.S. to make reforms, released many political prisoners, including those who had taken part in the original failed Moncada assault. Fidel and Raul Castro went to Mexico to regroup and plan the next step in the revolution. In Mexico the Castros organized a coalition of many disaffected Cuban exiles who formed the new "26th of July Movement," named after the date of the original Moncada assault.

When the 26th of July Movement brigade returned to Cuba, they were ambushed by Batista's men and the survivors took refuge in the Cuban highlands where they prepared for another overthrow of Batista. Following a series of guerilla attacks against government troops, the Castro band of rebels gained members, weapons and stockpiled supplies and was ready to move on to Havana in 1958.

Batista and members of his government and followers, seeing that Castro's victory was inevitable, took what loot they could gather up and fled. Batista authorized some of his subordinates to deal with Castro and the rebels. Castro entered Havana to cheering crowds on January 9.

Though the Cubans thought they were getting freedom, Castro set-up a communist government with him as the head and began trying and executing the remnants of the dictatorship who had tortured, murdered, and imprisoned the opposition to the Batista government. When the United States saw that Castro was setting up a communist government, they imposed sanctions and a trade embargo which went into effect in 1962.

The Castro government gained support of the Soviet Union, meddled in the affairs of countries in Africa as a stooge of the Russians, and allowed Moscow to set-up, train, and deliver missiles to the island nation, to *thumb his nose* at the America government and those Cubans who fled Cuba when Castro came to power. This lead to the *Cuban Missile Crisis*[45].

Seeking to gain a foothold in the Americas when it was apparent the Soviets and United States would be vying for nuclear superiority to become the

19-Fidel and Raul Castro . . . Past and present dictators of Cuba

dominant superpower, the Soviets began a confrontation with President Kennedy, and moved close to 40,000 troops into Cuba, evidently to see who would back down first. As far as the U.S. was concerned, the Cuban-Soviet link was also a violation of the Monroe Doctrine[46].

The U.S. had tried to thwart Soviet expansion in the Western Hemisphere by using the CIA to stage an invasion of expatriate Cubans of the island country. *The Bay of Pigs* [47] as it was called, was ill-advised and poorly planned. Vowing to provide air cover by the U.S. military, the invasion went forward. Unfortunately, there was no air support and everything fell apart. This brought about the next chapter in the U.S. confrontation with Cuba.

When the invasion failed, the Castro regime feared the U.S. would surely launch another attempt, and asked for Soviet support. That brought about the missile crisis. Kennedy could not let the build-up go unanswered and put a stop to the action with a blockade of Havana bring the two sides to the brink of a possible nuclear war.

Soviet Premier Nikita Khrushchev, eventually backed down and the Soviets withdrew from Cuba. In exchange for the Soviet pull-out, the U.S. agreed to never invade Cuba, and as it was found out at a later date, the U.S. would secretly remove our missiles from Turkey, which the Soviets viewed to be as much a threat as the Cuban missiles were to the U.S.

Vietnam War (1961 -1973) The Korean War Armistice was only a ceasefire agreement, not a formal peace treaty ending the war. A final peace treaty was supposed to be on the agenda at the Geneva Conference of 1954, but by the time that conference began, the French colonial war in Indochina broke out and once again the march of communism was on.

The Korean *Conflict* as it is called, was a tragic loss of American lives and started the United States down a dangerous path of fighting wars, not to win, but more for political posturing, with politicians, not the military, calling the shots. The contrast to the all-out effort in World War II, the war which was fought on nearly every continent in the world, makes for an amazing study in government malfeasance, which would require volumes to cover.

With the exception of the first Gulf war to remove Saddam Hussein from Kuwait, the other U.S. wars since 1946, have been examples of political malaise. **The war in Vietnam was next on the list of American tragedies.**

As to the facts, which are directly traceable to the mindset created by the Korean Conflict in 1955, Communist North Vietnam invaded non-communist South Vietnam in an attempt to unify the country and impose communist rule, much the way the Korean debacle began. The United States had a treaty with Vietnam and joined the war on the side of South Vietnam in 1961.

The classic sound of the whirl of a helicopter propellers represented the most poignant sound of war in Vietnam, and brings flashbacks to those who served there. Here was a classic case of politics run amuck. There was really no fixed beginning for the U.S. involvement, as the United States entered incrementally in a series of steps between 1950 and 1965.

In May 1950, President Harry S. Truman authorized a modest program of economic and military aid to the French, who were fighting to retain control of their Indochina colony, including Laos and Cambodia as well as Vietnam. When the Vietnamese Nationalist (and Communist-led) Vietminh army defeated French forces at Dienbienphu in 1954, the French were compelled to accede to the creation of a Communist Vietnam north of the 17th parallel while leaving a non-Communist entity south of that line.

The United States refused to accept the arrangement. *"The administration of President Dwight D. Eisenhower undertook instead to build a nation from the spurious political entity that was South Vietnam by fabricating a government there"*, taking over control from the French, dispatching military advisers to train a South Vietnamese army, and unleashing the Central Intelligence Agency (CIA) to conduct psychological warfare against the North.

The key observance of Andrew Rotter [48], from Colgate University, as quoted in the above passage, was that the U.S. attempted to build a nation from the fabricated government of

South Vietnam in an effort to stop the spread of communism throughout Southeast Asia.

In early 1961, President John Kennedy secretly sent 400 Special Operations Forces (Green Beret) to teach the South Vietnamese how to fight what was called *counterinsurgency* war against guerrillas in South Vietnam, who were trying to overthrow the South Vietnamese government in collaboration with communists of North Vietnam.

When Kennedy was assassinated in November 1963, there were more than 16,000 U.S. military advisers in South Vietnam, and more than 100 Americans had been killed.

President Lyndon B. Johnson, Kennedy's successor, committed the United States to support South Vietnam in a full effort, though non-declared war. In August 1964, he secured from Congress a functional (not actual) declaration of war: the Tonkin Gulf Resolution[49], which gave broad congressional approval for expansion of the efforts to support South Vietnam.

During the spring of 1964, military planners had developed a detailed design for major attacks on the North, but at that time President Lyndon B. Johnson and his advisers feared that the public would not support an expansion of the war. By the summer of 1964 rebel forces (Viet Cong) had established control over nearly half of South Vietnam.

In the Spring of 1965, Johnson authorized the sustained bombing, by U.S. aircraft, of targets north of the 17th parallel, deep into North Vietnam and on 8 March dispatched 3,500 Marines to the airbase at DaNang, South Vietnam, to free-up South Vietnam troops to engage the Viet Cong. Legal declaration or not, the United States was now at war. Politics would govern the next eight years of an unpopular war.

President Johnson thought the bombing of North Vietnam would limit the war on the ground and the communists could be bombed into submission. Unfortunately, the North Vietnamese had a much decentralized economy and the bombings were not as effective Johnson hoped.

Additionally, U.S. policymakers and General Westmoreland's staff never managed to fit a real military strategy into the U.S. plans for victory in the war, and did not set any measure as to what were the goals and end-point in the war.

While President Kennedy had favored counterinsurgency warfare meeting the enemy in the South Vietnamese countryside, Johnson endorsed a strategy of massive bombing. The goal to win the hearts and minds of the South Vietnamese people was probably doomed at the start, and with the Johnson Administration's reluctance to mobilize the American people to get behind the war effort, the Vietnamese War looked to be a long drawn out and possibly futile effort.

20—Vietnam signaled the extended use of helicopters to take troops into battle and transfer the wounded to MASH surgical hospitals

As the war dragged on most of the insurgency battles were small skirmishes involving guerilla tactics, while the bombing of the North Vietnam kicked into high gear.

During the early months of this campaign, which started in 1965, there were restrictions against striking targets in or near Hanoi and Haiphong, but in July 1966, the air campaign known as Rolling Thunder, was expanded to include the bombing of North Vietnamese ammunition dumps and oil storage facilities. The three-year bombing strategy, in which President Johnson personally selected some of the targets, dropped about 643,000 tons of bombs on North Vietnam.

Those who served in Vietnam and those who were part of the logistical support team throughout Southeast Asia, are familiar with the defoliant, Agent Orange and other chemicals, which were innocently called "Rainbow Herbicides". Even after having been declared a *weapon of mass destruction*[50] by Congress and shown to be toxic as far back as World War II, the U.S. opted to use defoliant agents to deprive the enemy the coverage of the jungle and to destroy their food supplies.

> *"Between 1962 and 1971, Operation Ranch Hand*
> [51] *sprayed about 19 million gallons of herbicide,*
> *11 million of which consisted of Agent Orange.*
> *The spray fell mostly on the forest of South*
> *Vietnam, but some was used in Laos, and some*
> *killed crops to deprive Vietcong and North*
> *Vietnamese troops of food. The military purpose*
> *for using herbicides on non-cropland was to*
> *remove the vegetation cover used by Vietcong and*
> *North Vietnamese forces for concealment."*

Unfortunately, regardless of the intent to only destroy the jungle vegetation and not to spray directly on farmland crops, once Agent Orange was sprayed, it was impossible to control where the wind would carry it. Additionally, when our troop's missions took them into the jungle in pursuit of the enemy, they were exposed to the chemicals by contact, in their drinking water, and in their food supplies.

The long lasting effect of exposure to Agent Orange is still a hot topic today throughout the Veterans population as they continue their battle with the Veterans Administration for medical disability. The effect is also seen in the population of the Vietnamese people which suffers from horrific birth defects and far more cancer than a normal sampling of a country's population.

During the Vietnam War, the U.S. military released body counts of enemy and friendly dead to the media, and reported them on a daily basis. Invariably, the military data showed far more enemy dead than friendly dead and was designed to give the

71

illusion that the United States was winning the war. Ironically, despite those who in hindsight will never be convinced that the U.S. was winning the war up until 1968, The Tet Offensive [52] should have been the end for the North Vietnamese attempt to take over South Vietnam.

All you have to do is read the memoirs of Vietnamese General Vo Nguyen Giap [53], the brilliant North Vietnamese military leader of the Vietnam War. His memoirs confirmed what most Americans knew. The Vietnam War was not lost in Vietnam, but lost at home. In his memoirs Giap exposes the enormous power of a biased media in the U.S. which *"cut out the heart and will of the American public".*

General Giap was ready to call it quits following the Tet Offensive, so there is much blame to place on the doorsteps of Jane Fonda, John Kerry, and the *uber* liberal media:

> *"What we still don't understand is why you Americans stopped the bombing of Hanoi. You had us on the ropes. If you had pressed us a little harder, just for another day or two, **we were ready to surrender! It was the same at the battles of TET. You defeated us!** We knew it, and we thought you knew it.*
>
> *"But we were elated to notice your media was definitely helping us. They were causing more disruption in America than we could in the battlefields. We were ready to surrender. You had won!" "A truism worthy of note: Do not fear the enemy, for they can take only your life. Fear the media far more, for they will destroy your honour".*

21—58,220 U.S. military were killed in action during the Vietnam War

During the Vietnam War, the U.S. military suffered 58,220 killed in action, but the heroes stood tall with 248 Medals of Honor awarded, 156 (62.9%) of them posthumously. Soldiers of the Army received the most with 161, followed by 57 to the Marines, 16 to the Navy and the remaining 14 to the Air Force. The Vietnam War also sent American homes to a lifetime of illness and death by exposing them to the defoliant Agent Orange.

Dominican Republic (1965) The Dominican Republic is an island country in the Caribbean. The island is shared with Haiti and sits just off the coast of Florida to the east of Cuba. President Lyndon Johnson sent marines and troops to quash a leftist uprising in 1965, fearing the island nation would follow in the footsteps of Cuba and turn communist. That is the short version of this military, or more correctly, the short version of this political story.

On 28 April 1965, U.S. military forces found themselves in the Dominican Republic protecting U.S. interests for the fourth time in five decades. The *Good Neighbor Policy* of Franklin Roosevelt's and the actions of three U.S. administrations (Eisenhower, Kennedy and Johnson) resulted in the eruption of hostilities in the Dominican Republic in April 1965.

The trouble actually began in 1961, when dictator Rafael Trujillo was assassinated. While Trujillo had been a brutal tyrannical leader, he was very anticommunist which endeared him to the United States. With the death of Trujillo, the people elected a reform minded government headed by Juan Bosch in 1962. The Dominican military would have none of this and overthrew Bosch in 1963 because of his liberal slant on politics.

The ensuing chaos threatened to break out in an all-out civil war as the military became divided with each group vying for power. In 1965, one of the military groups demanded reinstatement of the Bosch Administration and began attacking factions of the military-controlled government. President Johnson feared another Cuba was in the making and several of his administration officials feared that Fidel Castro of Cuba was behind all the unrest.

On April 28, more than 22,000 U.S. troops, supported by forces provided by members of the Organization of American States, which was an organization much like the United Nations dedicated to matters solely related to the Americas and the Western hemisphere, landed in the Dominican Republic. The calming effect took several weeks, but they were able to put an end to the fighting and installed a civilian, conservative government.

The political consequences[54] of the Dominican Republic effort set President Johnson up for ridicule by the American press which was already questioning our involvement in Vietnam's internal struggle. The Johnson Administration lost the faith of the American media, and raised the suspicion of the American people.

This started the public reassessing the role of America in conflicts that involved internal matters in other states including the involvement in Vietnam. For the people of Latin America, they looked at the invasion as an example showing that President Johnson was not concerned with their welfare only American goals and interests.

Johnson ordered the invasion of the Dominican Republic to thwart, what he claimed to be, a Communist threat inspired by Cuba. Instead of gaining support from all the countries in the Western Hemisphere however, it was Castro who derived most political profit. He had nothing to do with the civil war . . . yet the spectacle of American troops fighting the Dominicans was a great propaganda value for Fidel's *anti-imperialist strategies* at home and abroad.

The President's staff, in an effort to minimize controversy over the invasion, decided to omit from public statements any reference to a *Communist threat*. Ambassador Adlai Stevenson argued that the President should not go beyond the need to protect American lives in explaining his decision, fearing a backlash from other countries over America's gunboat diplomacy[55]. To present it as an . . . *intervention 'to restore order' and prevent a Communist victory"* would most likely have been condemned, even at home.

The word became that the U.S. was simply conducting operations to protect Americans. However, as reporters started to look into the story, they became aware of the real reason behind the conflict. *"When the reporters went aboard the [USS] Boxer to be briefed by Commodore James Dare, the commodore told them that marines would stay ashore as long as necessary to 'keep this a non-Communist government.'"* [56]

The decision to cover-up the truth resulted in the media's distrust of the administration for the rest of the crisis. There has also been speculation that it was this breaking of trust that caused the media to report on Vietnam so aggressively.

22—U.S. Troops on patrol in Dominican Republic on May 5, 1965

The outcome of this joint military effort however was that the people of the Dominican Republic saw the return of democracy. On June 1st, 1966, the Dominican people were able to elect their leader. Balaguer and Bosch, both who had gone into exile, returned home and faced each other off at the ballot box. Balaguer was the undisputed winner with 57% of the vote.

Although some members of the Inter-American Peace Force (IAPF) had strongly objected to the intervention and chose not to participate, six countries volunteered. The countries consisted of Brazil, Honduras, Nicaragua, El Salvador, Paraguay and Costa Rica.

The significance of these countries participating and the official participation of the OAS were critical in this first real effort at supporting democracy in the Western Hemisphere. Although skeptics would argue that the OAS was simply responding to the U.S. in legitimizing the invasion, historians today interpret the outcome differently.

> *"Despite the cost and loss of prestige among our neighboring countries south of the U.S. border, the invasion of the Dominican Republic did produce some benefits. The Organization of American States (OAS) illustrated its ability to function as a multi-national body and democratic rule was eventually attained in the Dominican Republic."*

Salvador Gomez, University of Pittsburgh

Lebanon (1982–1984) For every president since the Sixties, the Middle East has posed treats to international security. This is a seemingly never-ending situation. The Lebanon of 1982 was, however, far different from that of 1958. U.S. troops formed part of a multinational peacekeeping force to help the fragile Lebanese government maintain power, but Lebanon chose to enter into an agreement with the Palestinian Liberation Organization (PLO) to provide *security* for the government.

The PLO, on the basis of this agreement, took the liberty to recruit, arm, train, and employ fighters against Israel. This prompted an Israeli invasion of Lebanon in 1982.

Along with a besieged set of Palestinian fighters, a Syrian expeditionary force on the ground, and dozens of separate armed Lebanese factions already

23—Lebanese soldiers prepared for clashes with Sunni Muslim gunmen in Beirut. U.S. could do little to restore the peace.

embroiled in lethal contests and active warfare fighting for control of the country, the entire region appeared to be ready to explode into uncontrollable warfare. This was no place for well-meaning strangers.

The Reagan administration feared that all the conflict among the factions backed by Syria and Israel, and with unending clashes between Israel and the Palestine Liberation Organization, an Arab-Israeli war was a heartbeat away. In the U.S. our government policymakers had differing views on how to prevent another all-out Arab-Israeli War, with many legislators calling for a commitment of U.S. troops to restore the peace and try to seek a diplomatic solution.

The advocates of military intervention won out and Reagan in 1982, sent 800 U.S. Marines to Lebanon [57] as part of an international peacekeeping force to the region. Later a suicide bomber attacked the Marine barracks in Beirut by driving a bomb-filled truck through the make-shift barricades blocking the roadway. The attack killed 241 Americans.

But by 1984, terrorist attacks, a lack of diplomatic progress, and congressional opposition led President Ronald Reagan to withdraw U.S. forces from Lebanon. It is reasonable to conclude that Saddam Hussein of Iraq also reached some views on American resolve from the Lebanon debacle, which was probably the motivating factor which fueled his appetite for his invasion of Kuwait.

"In Arlington National Cemetery, across the Potomac River from Washington, there is a Cedar of Lebanon. It stands over a small memorial. The Cedar marks the graves of some of the more than 300 American military, embassy, and civilian personnel who were killed in Beirut in the 1980s. On October 23 each year there is a remembrance service on the anniversary of the bombing of the U.S. Marine barracks.

"I have had the sad honor of speaking at two of these remembrance services. Just as we remember our dead, it is worth remembering why we sent the Marines to Beirut and what we did wrong so that we can try to avoid the same mistakes in the future.

24-Marine Barracks were destroyed by a terrorist truck blast killing 241. The attack caused U.S. to withdraw.

"The particular tragedy of the Marine barracks, like the repeated bombing of our embassies, was the result of negligent and poor security measures. Even without the loss of 241 dead Marines in one day, support for the Marine presence would have evaporated over time as casualties continued, even if it took a few more months. The result, I believe, would have been the same.

A token military force with a vague mission was probably a recipe for failure. The responsibility rests finally with the leaders who made the decisions".

John Kelly, U.S.
Ambassador to Lebanon from 1986 to 1988

With the failure of the international community to bring about a diplomatic solution, which is more often than not, the end result of *"feel good intentions that usually are visible after many lives are lost"*, President Reagan decided to withdraw our Marines.

Those advocating the deployment of troops in the first place scattered like cockroaches when the lights came on, with most quickly shrinking from the spotlight on the TV news programs. Few of the senior decision makers were as completely forthright or truthful in their reports to Congress or the public compared to that of President Reagan in his diary.

Grenada (1983) This year in American history was a mixed bag with political celebration over a victorious military action, and one of abysmal failure. President Reagan invaded the Caribbean country of Grenada to overthrow its socialist government, which had close ties with Cuba in the same month of as the Beirut bombing. Reagan ordered U.S. forces to the Caribbean island of Granada to rescue U.S. medical students at the university, while welcoming home the coffins of 241 U.S. Marines.

Unlike the deployment to Lebanon, President Reagan, citing the threat posed to American nationals on Granada by that nation's Marxist regime, ordered the Marines to invade and secure their safety. There were nearly 1,000 Americans in Grenada at the time, most of whom were students at the island's medical school. In little more than a week, Grenada's government was overthrown.

The situation on Grenada had been of concern to American officials since 1979, when the leftist Maurice Bishop seized power and began to develop close relations with Cuba. In 1983, another Marxist, Bernard Coard, had Bishop assassinated and took control of the government. Protesters clashed with the new government and violence escalated.

When the Marines landed they soon found themselves facing opposition from Grenada armed forces and groups of Cuban military engineers who were there to repair and expand the island's airport.

Dubbed Operation Urgent Fury, our Marines, again were sent into harm's way not knowing much about the situation and with faulty intelligence.

25 -U.S. Marines personnel, armed with M16A1 rifles, observe a C-141 Starlifter aircraft upon its arrival to evacuate American students during Operation URGENT FURY. Date: 3 Nov 1983.

Since we have allowed presidents to conduct acts of war without Congress' *formal* declarations of war as required by the U.S. Constitution, there has been a growing accumulation of questionable military adventures. In Grenada U.S. forces had to rely on old tourist maps, but in the tradition of the U.S. Marine Corps, the mission was completed in just a few days.

Reagan's timing was called into question by many Americans who were skeptical of the president's defense of the invasion, noting that it took place just days after a disastrous explosion in a U.S. military installation in Lebanon killed 241 Marines. Nevertheless, the students were returned to the States safely, so the Reagan administration claimed a great victory, calling it the first "rollback" of communist influence since the beginning of the Cold War.

Reagan's decision to occupy the country and replace the government with one more to his liking proved to be quite popular in the United States, with polls indicating that 63% of the public supported the invasion[58].

Casualties[59]: U.S. forces sustained 19 killed and 116 wounded; Cuban forces sustained 25 killed, 59 wounded, and 638 combatants captured. Grenadian forces casualties were 45 killed and 358 wounded. At least 24 civilians were killed, 18 of whom were killed in the accidental bombing of a Grenadian mental hospital.

Panama (1989) President George Bush, the elder, sent troops to Panama to put an end to the drug-trafficking business of Panamanian dictator Manuel Noriega. Noriega was indicted in the U.S. on drug trafficking charges and was long felt to be suppressing democracy in Panama. Furthermore there was fear U.S. citizens in Panama were at risk.

The story of Manual Noriega began in 1970. He was a standout in the Panama military and was enlisted by the Central Intelligence Agency (CIA) in our attempt to stop the spread of communism in Central America primarily in Nicaragua with Daniel Ortega and his Contra rebels, with support from Fidel Castro in Cuba.

The deal was a good one from Noriega's point of view, because he not only got paid by the CIA, they looked the other way when it came to his drug business. The CIA was keenly aware of the Noriega's drug connections when they enlisted his help to fight the Contras in Nicaragua, but in 1977 he was removed from the CIA payroll when the American public got wind of the Noriega-CIA drug situation.

26—The 40th President of the United States, Ronald Reagan. President Reagan brought conservatism and prosperity to the country which was in dire economic straits.

When Ortega and the Sandinistas Marxist government gained control of Nicaragua, there was no more need for the Noriega alliance. After the Marxist Sandinista government came to power in 1979, this was an opportunity for the U.S. government to score a political victory in America's war on drugs. Noriega was indicted on drug charges and the U.S. government decided to extradite him physically by use of military force.

U.S. military forces invaded Panama on December 20,1989. Noriega sent his Panama military to repel the U.S. military forces, while he tried to flee the island from Punta Paitilla Airport, a coastal airport in *Panama City* in his private jet. The U.S. military had anticipated this move and had destroyed the airplane soon after landing on the island.

Noriega's defense forces were no match for the superior American force and were quickly dispatched. With nowhere to run and nowhere to hide his next desperate move was to seek asylum with the Vatican Anuncio in Panama City.

Two weeks later Noriega was in American hands when he surrendered on January 3, 1990. In 1992, Noriega was found guilty on eight counts of drug trafficking, racketeering, and money

27—Panamanian army civilian atrocities. 25 Years later the death toll was still unknown

laundering. This was the first time in history that a U.S. jury convicted a foreign leader of criminal charges. He was sentenced to 40 years in federal prison.

Again, gunboat diplomacy charges were leveled at the United States, and the Organization of American States as well as the European Parliament both protested the invasion as a violation of international law. The federal government felt the international condemnation was worth the price for a victory in the war against drugs. Perhaps the families of the 23 U.S. soldiers who were killed in the fighting that ensued might just disagree with them, as would the estimated 500 Panamanian citizens caught in the middle of the gunfire who were killed.

Gulf War (1991) Iraq invaded Kuwait, and a U.S.-led multinational force came to Kuwait's aid to drive out the forces of Iraqi dictator Saddam Hussein's.

In May of 1990, Iraq accused Kuwait of over-producing oil from the oil field that runs along the border between the two countries. They claim the action was equivalent to an economic war between the two countries. Within a couple of months Iraq further accused Kuwait of actually stealing oil from the Rumaylah, Iraq's oil field near Kuwait, and began deploying mechanized troops along the Kuwait border.

28-The old USS Wisconsin—Re-outfitted with modern missiles technology was the perfect weapon for Gulf War I in supporting the invasion.

Following meetings between Iraq and U.S. Secretary of State, James Baker, over the oil dispute with Kuwait, the U.S. did not leave a strong enough impression that Iraq's moves toward the Kuwait border would not be tolerated, and Iraq's dictator president Saddam Hussein, felt confident he was free to take whatever means necessary to deal with Kuwait. Certainly, Iraq's superior military was enough to intimidate Kuwait, and Saddam believed his million man army had the same effect on America.

On August 2, emboldened by little action by the U.S. about 100,000 Iraqi troops crossed the border and invaded Kuwait, initiating the Gulf War. The U.N. Security Council passed Resolution 661[60] imposing a trade embargo on Iraq in a 13-0 vote, with Cuba and Yemen abstaining. Even the Russians voted in favor of the resolution.

As was to be suspected of usual UN resolutions, Saddam Hussein paid it no attention as his troops went about plundering Kuwait's treasures and terrorizing the Kuwaiti population. It was up to the United States to develop a coalition of forces to oppose Iraq's aggression and physically remove Iraqi forces from Kuwait.

The sanctions called for in Resolution 661 included shutting down the Iraqi revenue stream from petroleum exports, but many of the signers of the resolution violated the sanctions under the table.

President Bush was able to form the largest coalition of forces[61] since World War II and included the countries of: Australia, Argentina, Bahrain, Bangladesh, Belgium, Canada, Denmark, Egypt, France, Greece, Italy, Kuwait, Morocco, Netherlands, New Zealand, Niger, Norway, Oman, Pakistan, Portugal, Qatar, South Korea, Saudi Arabia, Senegal, Sierra Leone, Singapore, Spain, Syria, the United Arab Emirates, the United Kingdom, to join the effort to oust Iraq.

Most of America and a narrow majority of the Congress supported President Bush's actions to rid Kuwait of Iraqi troops. Daily reports were received from Kuwait about the pillaging by the Iraqi forces and it is a wonder that any American would oppose military intervention, but there was a substantial number who bought into the slogan, "no war for oil" . . . there are always those who will submit to aggression and hide their collective heads in the sand.

U.S. Army General Norman Schwarzkopf, Jr.[62] the Commander of U.S., Central Command - CENTCOM, was tasked to develop the plan of action to protect the Saudis in case Iraq expanded their aggression into Saudi Arabia. This became known as Operation Desert Shield. The plan called for the

29 - Gen. Norman Schwarzkopf. A soldier's general who pulled off an amazingly quick victory over Saddam's "Million-Man Army" in Operation Desert Storm.

deployment of 500,000 U.S. troops along the Saudi border.

The next step in the organizational plan was to develop an attack plan should Saddam not be persuaded to leave Kuwait, using the coalition of troops from the above list of countries. This became known as Operation Desert Storm. As the coalition forces began preparation for what was potentially a major battle with Iraqi troops, the U.S. and United Kingdom began softening the opposition with an air campaign, the likes of which the world hadn't seen since the Second World War.

The air campaign began on January 17, 1991. Much of the action was broadcast live on CNN and on the nightly news by tape delay. The public watched in awe at the devastating display of military might . . . it seemed surreal to most. The coalition flew over 100,000 missions[63], dropping more than 88,500 tons of bombs, widely destroying military and civilian infrastructure.

Virtually the entire arsenal of U.S. weaponry, from Tomahawk Missiles to depleted uranium tank munitions were used in the shock and awe display of U.S. might. The air campaign was largely finished by February 23, 1991, when the coalition tanks and troops moved across the border into Kuwait. By February 27th, the rout of Iraqi troops was completed with nearly the entire occupational army either destroyed or in complete disarray.

On the last 2-days of hostilities the *Highway of Death* [64] occurred on the six-lane highway out of Kuwait heading toward Basra,

30-As many as 10,000 Iraqi soldiers were killed as they fled Kuwait after being ousted by Coalition Forces in Operation Desert Storm. American gunship helicopters and A-6 aircraft had a "turkey shoot" as the Iraqis were trying to make-off with goods stolen from the Kuwaiti people.

Iraq. U.S. helicopter gunships and A-6 aircraft had a violent *turkey shoot* in which as many as 10,000 Iraqi soldiers were caught in the open fleeing with the spoilage of what they had stolen from the Kuwait people. The Iraqis were killed in one of the most brutal incidents ever seen in war which most thought was justifiable payback for the atrocities they committed on the Kuwaitis.

Although hostilities ceased[65] with Iraq's defeat, it was not until April 11, when Saddam Hussein agreed to the terms of the U. N. Security Council Resolution No. 678, that the conflict was declared officially over.

Somalia (1992-1994) After World War II, it became apparent the American government had lost focus on the meaning of the word "war" and what it was all about. War was no longer looked at as a mission with a stated objective and knowing when an end-point had been reached. Instead, political expediency became the governing factor on how a war would be fought, with politicians instead of military generals determining rules of engagement. Fighting to win became secondary to global opinion and political posturing on the home front. The end result is what anyone with an IQ above a single digit could figure out . . . an inordinate number of casualties, and a never-ending drain on the country's financial resources . . . which may sound a bit cynical but true.

31 -Somali Warlords ruled Somalia, stealing everything from the civilian population and destroying everything of value in the country.

The East African country of Somalia was no different than other uses of force following WWII. Like in Korea, the federal government turned over supervision of the mission to the bureaucrats of the United Nations in order to seek an end to the slaughter of innocent civilians by *interclan* tribesmen seeking control over the county.

Instead of sending troops to remove the threat of genocide among the warring tribes, which probably would have meant real fighting would have been necessary, the UN, with their usual *feel-good intentions*, sought to bring all sides together without firing a shot. They instead laid out ill-defined plans for nation building. Seeming to never learn a lesson from history, this mission like most other tasks undertaken by the UN, was headed for trouble from the start.

The United States Military has a long tradition of humanitarian relief, but such a tradition was developed in far different situations and not in the middle of a hot-fire war zone. Before hostilities would cease, no such operation has proven as costly or shocking, as the one undertaken in Somalia from August 1992 to March 1994.

Initially the Somalis were happy to be saved from starvation, but as the U.S. soldiers were slowly drawn into power struggles between the warring sides, dozens of our soldiers were killed or wounded in fierce fighting in the streets of the capital city Mogadishu. A graphic display of the violent fighting was exhibited in the movie, Blackhawk Down, and shown on the evening news when some of our killed military personnel were

32 -U.S. military successfully provided food and medical care for Somali people but got bogged down in the street fighting with the warlords. Here a Blackhawk helicopter was downed and became the basis of the box office hit movie Blackhawk Down. The fighting eventually turn the people against the street fighting and the U.S. troops withdrew.

dragged through the streets of Mogadishu by cheering Somali

88

mobs-the very people our soldiers thought they had rescued from starvation.

As quoted from the Center for Military History[66] (CMH Pub 70-81-1):

"The United States had entered Somalia in December 1992 to stop the imminent starvation of hundreds of thousands of people. Although it succeeded in this mission, the chaotic political situation of that unhappy land bogged down U.S. and allied forces in what became, in effect, a poorly organized United Nations nation-building operation.

"In a country where the United States, perhaps naively, expected some measure of gratitude for its help, its forces received increasing hostility as they became more deeply embroiled into trying to establish a stable government. The military and diplomatic effort to bring together all the clans and political entities was doomed to failure as each subelement continued to attempt to out-jockey the others for supreme power.

"The Somali people were the main victims of their own leaders, but forty-two Americans died and dozens more were wounded before the United States and the United Nations capitulated to events and withdrew. American military power had established the conditions for peace in the midst of a famine and civil war, but, unlike later in Bosnia, the factions were not exhausted from the fighting and were not yet willing to stop killing each other and anyone caught in the middle. There was no peace to keep.

"The American soldier had, as always, done his best under difficult circumstances to perform a

*complex and often confusing mission. But the best
soldiers in the world can only lay the foundation
for peace; they cannot create peace itself. All
attempts to reconcile the Somali factions had
proven futile, and the international community
gradually lost its patience with the total lack of
political results.*

*"Operation UNITED SHIELD, the final UN
withdrawal from Somalia, was completed on 3
March 1995. The United States, as part of the
international community, had made major
contributions to the Somalia humanitarian
operations for over two years. Starvation had been
stopped and hundreds of thousands of lives saved.
The U.S. had accomplished much in the initial
stages of the operation, but the political situation
had unraveled even as the food supplies increased,
allowing Somalia to slide backwards into disorder
and anarchy."*

Bosnia (1992–1995) During the Bosnian civil war,
which began shortly after the country declared independence in
1992, the U.S. launched air strikes on Bosnia to prevent "ethnic
cleansing," primarily by Serbs against Bosnians. The U.S. became
a part of NATO's peacekeeping force in the region.

Yugoslavia would be an excellent study in the concept of
diversity and the damage it can do to a country. What has made
America great throughout our history is that the people who have
come to our shores have left their *diversity* at the door step, and
assimilated into an *American way of life.* They learned the
language, moved into mixed ethnicity communities, adopted the
clarity of mind that they can be successful with hard work, and that
their families would have a much better life in this country than the
country from which they came.

Yugoslavia came into existence[67] as a result of World War I. A movement for unification of the Slavic peoples of eastern and east central Europe - simply called Pan-Slavism[68], became a 19th-century movement to recognize "the common ethnic background among the various Slav peoples

33 -The Kingdom of Yugoslavia after World War II and prior to the many wars the split the country into ethnic

and sought to unite those peoples for the achievement of common cultural and political goals". The movement was led by Serbia and was the major cause of World War I.

When a Serbian nationalist assassinated Austrian Archduke Francis Ferdinand[69], nephew of Emperor Franz Josef and heir to the Austro-Hungarian Empire, in Bosnia, on his wedding anniversary, Austria declared war on Serbia. This signaled a series of other events that brought about World War I.

In 1914 only Serbia, which included today's Republic of Macedonia and Montenegro, were independent states. The countries of Croatia, Slovenia, and Bosnia - Herzegovina, were part of the Austro-Hungarian Monarchy. The Paris Peace which ended World War I recognized the new state of Yugoslavia, called the Kingdom of Yugoslavia, and enlarged its territory at the expense of the Austro-Hungarian Monarchy adding Bosnia, Croatia, Slovenia, and other territories.

The 1920's Yugoslavia saw the rise of Josip Broz Tito[70] who was somewhat of a hero after he was drafted into the Austro-

Hungarian army where he fought against Serbia after the outbreak of World War I. In 1915 he was sent to the Russian front, where he was captured. According to History.com, *"In the prisoner-of-war camp, he converted to Bolshevism and in 1917 participated in the Russian Revolution".* *Marshal* Tito, as he became known, and his communist partisans emerged as the leaders of the anti-Nazi resistance when the Germans occupied the Kingdom of Yugoslavia in 1941.

In 1944, as the Germans were rapidly losing territory it had occupied, Soviet forces liberated Yugoslavia. Following the war, with Stalin seizing most of the countries of Eastern Europe, Tito was installed as head of a new federal Yugoslav government. Meanwhile the Russians were seeking all the *spoils of war* they could find, and extending their sphere of influence through intimidation. The people of the region were exhausted by war and had no spirit left to resist the communists. They were willing to sacrifice their freedom for Russian security. As Ben Franklin said, *"Those who would sacrifice freedom for security, deserve neither".*

While Tito was a communist, he was a fiercely *independent* communist. The Russians were hand-picking *controllable* leaders for each country they were bringing into the Soviet Union, but Tito was different having a history of surviving Soviet/Russian leadership purges over the years. His government began to pursue an independent course in foreign relations. Economic and military assistance was received from the West. This brought the wrath of the Soviet government down on Yugoslavia. In 1948 Stalin ordered Yugoslavia expelled from COMINFORM, which the Soviet Union had established in 1947 to serve as a coordinating body for the world's communist parties.

After its expulsion, Yugoslavia continued to be a communist country, but maintained its independence in its domestic and foreign policies. The U.S. actively sought a relationship with Tito and offered economic and military aid in the late-1940s and 1950s. Tito however, refused to be the puppet of any government, and following Yugoslavia's expulsion from COMINFORM, the Soviet Union officially dissolved the organization by 1956. Tito died in May 1980, just a few days before his 88th birthday.

After the collapse of communism in 1989, ethnic tensions resurfaced. In 1991, the Yugoslav federation broke apart, leaving only Serbia and Montenegro remaining in the Socialist Federal Republic of Yugoslavia. Slobodan Milosevic was the President of Serbia from 1989 to 1997 and President of the Federal Republic of Yugoslavia from 1997 to 2000. Civil war broke out in 1992 when Milosevic attempted to keep ethnically Serbian areas in the other Yugoslav republics under Yugoslav rule, even if by use of military force.

34—There was seldom any peace after Yugoslavia president Tito died in 1980. The country returned to the centuries old ethnic hatred.

President George H. W. Bush and his advisors considered the situation in the Balkans to be primarily a European issue[71] to be addressed by the European Union.

According to the U.S. State Department, "The lack of U.S. response became an issue in the 1992 presidential campaign, as candidate Bill Clinton advocated a *lift and strike* policy—lifting the arms embargo, which was operating at the disadvantage of the Bosnian Muslims and Croats, and conducting airstrikes against Bosnian Serb forces."

The European Union was critical of Milosevic's policies and from 1992 through 1998. In December 1995, NATO sent an unprecedented 60,000 troops to ensure that all sides would abide by the Dayton accords[72], which was replaced by a smaller force of 32,000 troops a year later. The peacekeeping force had to be used to keep some semblance of order in the region. These *Accords* put an end to the 3- ½ year-long Bosnian War, but was just one of the Yugoslav Wars which lasted until June 1999.

35 -Ethnic cleansing drove whole populations of Albanians out of the country

While Bosnia settled down, unrest in Kosovo began. Kosovo had been historically recognized as the home of Serbian nationalism with population of Kosovo being mostly Albanians. The government of Slobodan Milosevic reduced the autonomy of Kosovo and initiated a process to increase the proportion of Serbs in the territory. After a half decade of tension and fighting - disputes among the separatists - a war broke out in Kosovo in 1999, and pitted Milosevic's Yugoslavia army against the NATO peacekeeping troops, which had to give support to the Kosovo Albanians.

Again, it took the leadership of the United States to call for NATO intervention. The Europeans were very slow to move, fearing the unrest might become global but in March 1999, NATO began airstrikes against the Milosevic regime in an attempt to end genocide in Kosovo and enforce the area's autonomy. In October 2000, Milosevic was ousted in a popular revolution. He was then arrested and charged with crimes against humanity and genocide. He died on March 11, 2006, in prison in the Hague, before his trial ended.

The Second Persian Gulf War - Afghanistan to Iraq (2003 - 2006) If President George H. Bush had not ceded to public pressure by stopping Operation Desert Storm following the *Highway of Death* incident, there might not have been the need for this Second Persian Gulf War. Hindsight is usually 20-20 and it appears we are in a never-ending campaign that has turned into a more than fifteen year battle with terrorism with no end in sight.

After the attack on the United States on September 11, 2001, when Al-Qaida terrorists hijacked and flew passenger airliners into the twin towers of the World Trade Center in New York, and the Pentagon in Arlington, Virginia, President George W. Bush declared the U.S. would take revenge with military action against the terrorists whose sanctuary was located in Afghanistan.

There were naysayers who claimed the attack was not as it appeared, but more than 3000 American were dead, and Osama bin Laden was proudly taking the credit.

Many Americans were not aware of the difficulty the Russians had fighting in Afghanistan in support of the Soviet-backed Parchamites led by Babrak Karmal[73]. Karmel came to power through the assassination of Hafizullah Amin by the Russian military. While still engaged in the arms race with the U.S., the Soviet Union became embroiled in Afghanistan when they sent troops to aid and prop up the illegal Afghan government which was having an internal struggle fighting off several different radical Muslim groups, among them were the followers of Osama bin Ladin.

After staging the coup of Amin and installing a pro-Soviet government under Karmal, Amin's bitter rival, Kamal began suppressing any opposition from the traditional Muslim Afghans, and arrested thousands while executing thousands more. By April 1979, outside the major city of Kabul, much of the rest of the country was in open rebellion and before the end of the year the government had lost control.

The Soviet–Afghan War [74]lasted over nine years from December 1979 to February 1989, until the Soviets had reach unsustainable losses fighting "insurgent groups", collectively called the *Mujahidin* who were Jihadists. They were under severe pressure back home having Russian citizens comparing Afghanistan to America's war in Vietnam. The war was a drain on Soviet resources and coupled with the cost of supporting the arms race of the Cold War, the Soviet Union collapsed in 1990.

As we have said before, those who fail to learn a lesson from history are doomed to repeat it. The Afghanistan adventures which helped bring down the Soviet Union are eerily familiar to those of us who follow history. The Mujahidin received aid from both Christian and Muslim countries, and fought against the Soviets for nine years, in which between 850,000–1.5 million civilians[75] were killed.

Millions of Afghan refugees fled the country mostly to Pakistan and Iran. When President Bush wanted to avenge the 911 tragedy, they took little heed from the failure of the Soviets and the determination our

37-Russians went into Afghanistan to support the government of Babrak Karmal, only to become their "Vietnam", eventually costing many lives and losing the faith of the Russian people. The tremendous financial cost helped drive the final nails into the coffin of the Soviets ability to win the Cold War.

troops would face with the radical Muslims.

So, go into Afghanistan we did to hunt down Osama bin Laden and his band of Al-Qaeda followers. Our noble goal was to dismantle Al-Qaeda and to deny it a safe base of operations in Afghanistan. To do that we had to remove the Taliban from power because they refused to extradite Osama bin Laden under a three year old standing request made by the United Nations..

The United Kingdom, under the leadership of Prime Minister Tony Blair, supported our efforts from the start, and even today as fight continues, the U.K. still maintains some support though this has cooled down substantially with the election of a liberal Parliament in the UK. This phase of the War is the longest war[75] in United States history.

By ousting the Taliban, NATO established an interim government until formal elections could be held. Unfortunately, Afghanistan is one of those countries that seemingly has always had a problem with a corrupt government because it has a single major industry - heroin.

Protecting the poppy fields was the most important role of whoever would become the leader of the country. Hamid Karzai won the popular elections of 2004, and country changed its name to the Islamic Republic of Afghanistan.

While some semblance of stability could be seen initially, the Taliban went underground to regroup. To reassert its rule in the countryside and maintain control of the poppy fields from which to produce the cash-crop of heroin, the Taliban began reappearing to fight a guerilla war with ambushes and killing anyone who supported the newly elected government. Suicide attacks against city targets, intimidation of village populations and recruitment of government forces to kill coalition forces, allowed the Taliban to exploit every weakness of the Afghan government.

Much like the failed strategy of the U.S. involvement in Vietnam, NATO's International Security Forces sought an increase in troops for *counterinsurgency operations* against the Taliban. This premise always fails because the citizens know that if they cooperate with the occupying troops, there will be reprisals once the government is left to fend for itself and the insurgents return. No one can predict just how many times these kinds of programs have failed to win the hearts and minds of the citizens, but *nation building* is just a flat-out losing proposition.

With NATO operations in Afghanistan winding down President George W. Bush asked members of his administration to develop a strategy to move into Iraq to confront the growing *Axis of Evil* which dictator Saddam Hussein represented. Hussein's refusal to cooperate with the United Nations inspectors, who were beginning to look a lot like the bumbling *Inspector Jacques Clouseau,* Blake Edward's farcical character of *Pink Panther* fame, was just the excuse needed to finish the *takedown* of Iraq.

In January of 2002, the Bush Administration raised the public's level of awareness regarding Iraq's failing to abide by the terms of the 1991 cease-fire which ended the First Gulf War. The Administration contended that Saddam was ramping up instead of dismantling his WMD program and being overly evasive to UN inspections.

The Administration was adamant that Iraq was not only a partner of the *Axis of Evil,* but the number one supporter of terrorism in the world. So began a campaign wherein government officials began suggesting that the *War of Terror* should be expanded to include Iraq.

The beefed up rhetoric insisted on a *regime change* in Baghdad and issued warning to Iraq that if they continued to interfere with UN inspectors, the U.S. intended to take military action. As a result, Iraq announced in September 2002, that UN inspectors could return to their inspection routine. As expected, nothing really changed Iraqi compliance as they continually stalled the inspection process.

In October of 2002, Congress approved the use of force against Iraq, and in November the UN Security Council passed a resolution offering Iraq a "final opportunity" to

38 -The fall of Baghdad in 2003. U.S. tanks enter the city to take control

cooperate on the WMD inspections. As 2002 rolled to a close no headway had been made in locating WMD's, so in spite of much international opposition from our NATO allies France, Germany, with additional apprehension from Russia, the United States and Britain continued their military buildup near the Iraq border.

Most of the UK and American forces were in place in Kuwait and other locations by March of 2003, however the UN Security Council refuse to authorize the use of force to make Iraq comply. Since the British Parliament did not want to move forward without the UN authorization, the Bush Administration issued an ultimatum . . . "comply or else" . . . to Iraqi president Hussein on Mar. 17.

Two days later, without UN sanction, the air war began with strikes against government targets in Baghdad. The ground war began simultaneously with its sights on Bagdad, the oil fields in the southern part of Iraq, and port facilities that would seal-off Iraqis from escape and/or resupply efforts. A second front was opened in Kurdish territory by American and British airborne forces before the end of March.

Much like the First Gulf War, Iraqi troops proved to be no match for the well-disciplined coalition forces primarily consisting of British and American forces. By the middle of April the allied troops were in control of all the major cities in Iraq, and Saddam had disappeared from sight. In Baghdad, widespread looting broke out, with government offices being looted, banks being broken into, and the monuments of Saddam being knocked down and vandalized. The coalition force let the citizens have their way, seeing no reason to intervene.

On May 1, Bush declared victory in the war against Iraq. No WDM's were used or uncovered in the blitzkrieg-like handling of the war. The international community cried "foul" and claimed the U.S. and Britain had exaggerated the WMD situation to finish the job start by the First Gulf War.

Although Saddam initially escaped capture, he was eventually captured in December 2003; found hiding in a hole on a rural farm, with a stash of U.S. currency. In 2004, he was transferred to Iraqi custody, was tried and convicted of crimes against humanity, and was executed in 2006.

This ended the Second Gulf War and closed the chapter of the book that deals with the Gulf Wars, however it must be noted, it only marked the end of the chapter with the rest of the story yet to be written.

War Against the Islamic State (ISIS) (2014 - ?) -With President Barack Obama's political decision, against the advice of his military commanders, to remove troops from Iraq, he created a vacuum in U.S. leadership in the Middle East. It was quickly filled by The Islamic State of Iraq and Syria (ISIS) - also called the Islamic State of Iraq and the Levant (ISIL).

One does not have to have a long memory to remember how the President described Al Qaeda as having been *decimated, on the path to defeat,* or some other variation at least 32 times[76] since the attack on the U.S. consulate in Benghazi, Libya.

ISIS began immediately upon the removal of U.S. troops when they seize upon the opportunity and took advantage of the poor military defense forces that Iraq had assembled prior to the U.S. pull-out. Without any back-up or reserve force of U.S. military to lend support to the fledgling Iraq police and military force, Iraq became quickly dominated by the much better trained insurgences who had been biding their time waiting for the U.S. to withdraw.

Unwilling to admit his mistake going into the 2012 Presidential election cycle, Obama laughed off the threat of ISIS as he was warned by his best military advisors, calling them the *Junior Varsity* compared to Al Qaeda. Aided by a very uninformed media on all levels who failed to challenge the president's assertion, Obama was swept into office for a second term over a very lackluster campaign run by Republican candidate, Mitt Romney. Immediately thereafter, the world woke up to the Middle East and North Africa erupting in flames set ablaze by the ISIS terrorists.

Even as late as of the writing of this book, the president refuses to even acknowledge the true threat posed by this well-fund band of terrorists . . . he cannot even utter the words, "Radical Islamic Terrorists", and therefore has relegated his administration to be simply biding its time until he is out of office in 2016.

39—President Obama referred to ISIS – the Islamic State—as nothing but a Junior Varsity, even as they proceeded to rout the Iraq military and gain control of the Iraqi oil field, which is making this terror organization the most powerful and well-financed terror group ever seen in history.

This does not bode well for the people of America or for the military which is becoming a ghost of its former self with major cut-backs in every area, from troop strength to fighting vehicles, ships, planes, and material. The military morale, on the wane since the public was made aware of the disrespect handed the veterans by an almost non-existent Veterans Administration, who seemingly could care less about the care promised to those who have given so much and *volunteered* to serve.

The politicians in Washington along with President Obama, promised to make fixing the VA, its highest priority, yet with the aging population and more and more military personnel being booted from the military roster, the demand for medical care by the growing veteran population, seems to be going totally out of control with waiting lines for even the most basic of services.

With the Veterans Administration's dismal track record dealing with our *all-volunteer* military, many of us now question whether or not we will be able to muster the forces necessary to take the fight to ISIS even with the election of a new president, without reinstating the Draft.

The War on Terror[77] has entered an entirely new phase, and ISIS has literally captured control of most cities in Iraq in which they were defeated, giving them a substantial base of operation, and allowing unfettered access to the rich oilfields

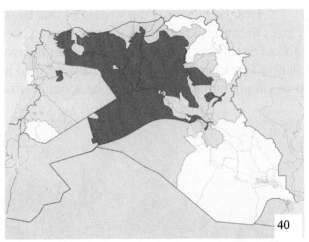

40

In spite of many warnings from our military leaders, President Obama refuses to take ISIS seriously as they grow in number, strength, and financial power, and the land they have captured. Map courtesy of http://www.foreignpolicyjournal.com

which allow them to finance their operations.

With such resources at their disposal they have become the most well-financed terror organization every imagined, able to purchase weapons, and establish research programs for developing weapons of mass destruction (WMD's) with support from Iran, North Korea, and others with a vendetta against the West.

We have seen ISIS's treatment of those under their domain, and the treatment of prisoners provided by the instant media of the Internet . . . Facebook, Twitter, and other websites. They have become masters at recruiting a large number of losers and ne'er-do-wells, societal dropouts, and useful fools, who cannot find meaning in their lives, using the social media, while the world stands around and is powerless to intercede.

Most of the civilized world has yet come to grips with the dangers we face, and too many Americans are more interested in *Dancing with the Stars*; one has to believe most are totally clueless.

Recent terror strikes in France and the U.S. are but a minute sample of the isolated terror attacks that are beginning to rain down on our homelands. There have been hundreds around the world as civilized countries become mere shooting galleries for the uncivilized world. The freer the country, the more apt there will be unbridled terrorism, as the people simply don't want *security* if it means a reduction in their rights. At least in the U.S. many of our people own weapons giving our citizens a fighting chance

Perhaps an all-out war against terrorism will become a priority for civilized countries and they will join a coalition to once and for all, go after ISIS in Iraq, Syria, and other operations in the Middle East, and then hit Boko Haram in Somalia and elsewhere in Africa. With the U.S. *kid-glove* handling of Iran on nuclear weapons and financing global terrorism, the hapless response to the saber rattling of the North Koreans, and the intimidation of the Russians and Chinese play out on the world stage, the world needs to pay attention and take action before it is too late.

Chapter 5 - The U.S. Patent Office and how it has protected the genius of man to further the concept of entrepreneurial enterprise

"Everything that can be invented has been invented."

Charles H. Duell, Commissioner of
US patent office in 1899

Though Charles Duell is credited with the above utterance, an 1899 edition of Punch Magazine[78] that had been donated to Harvard University by the Pulitzer family must make us reconsider the source of the quote. According to Dennis Crouch[79], *"in that edition, the comedy magazine offered a look at the 'coming century'. In colloquy, a genius asked 'isn't there a clerk who can examine patents?' A boy replied 'Quite unnecessary, Sir. Everything that can be invented has been invented'."*

Be that as it may, the importance of the U.S. Patent Office, is as vital to the progress of civilization as any invention devised or discovered by modern man, and any thought as to its demise is, as was said by Mark Twain[80], *"The reports of my death have been greatly exaggerated"*. Yet the myopic nature of man in this day and age of a population which knows who the winner of *American Idol* is, but can't name the Vice President of the United States, should not surprise us.

Yet, even in jest, some will point to various statements and take them to heart. In 1843, Patent Office Commissioner Henry Ellsworth made a report to Congress in which he said facetiously, *"the advancement of the arts, from year to year, taxes our credulity and seems to presage the arrival of that period when human improvement must end"*. But let's face it — that was rhetorical bloviating, not a serious proposal to close down the Patent Office.

What exactly is a patent[81]? A patent is the grant of a *property right* to the inventor, excluding others from making, using, offering for sale, or selling" the invention. What is granted **is not** the right to make, use, offer for sale, sell, or import, but the *right to exclude* others from making, using, offering for sale, selling, or importing the invention.

King Henry II of France introduced the concept of the patent by publishing the description of an invention called a Holometer, an instrument for making of angular measurements for surveying, in 1551. The King granted Abel Foullon a 10 year exclusive (patent) monopoly in exchange for publishing a description of it.

The United States got into the business of patents when Congress established the United States Patent and Trademark Office to issue patents on behalf of the government. From the Patent Office website we read:

> *"The Patent Office as a distinct bureau dates from the year 1802 when a separate official in the Department of State, who became known as "Superintendent of Patents," was placed in charge of patents. The revision of the patent laws enacted in 1836 reorganized the Patent Office and designated the official in charge as Commissioner of Patents.*

> *"The Patent Office remained in the Department of State until 1849 when it was transferred to the Department of Interior. In 1925 it was transferred to the Department of Commerce where it is today. The name of the Patent Office was changed to the Patent and Trademark Office in 1975 and changed to the United States Patent and Trademark Office in 2000."*

41-U.S. Patent Office established by Congress in 1790. Since its inception, there have been more than 8 million patents filed, with Americans owning about 80% of them. Because of the ability to patent a concept America has lead the world in the march of civilization by spurring entrepreneurial enterprise.

The first Patent Act of the U.S. Congress was passed on April 10, 1790, titled *"An Act to promote the progress of useful Arts."* The first patent was granted on July 31, 1790 to Samuel Hopkins[82] for a method of producing potash (potassium carbonate). This was before Congress passed the law establishing the U.S. Patent Office.

The earliest Patent Act law in 1790, required that a working model of the invention be submitted with the application, which was then examined to see if an inventor was entitled to the grant of a patent. In 1793, the requirement for a working model was dropped, and revised so that patents were granted automatically upon submission of the description.

In addition to patents the Patent office deals in a number of other property-protecting issues, including copyrights, which deal with written works to protect "original works of authorship" including literary, dramatic, musical, artistic, and certain other intellectual works, both published and unpublished. The patent office also provides for protection through the use of trademarks and service marks. A *trademark* is a word, name, symbol, or device that is used in trade with goods to indicate the source of the goods and to distinguish them from the goods of others, while a *service mark* is the same as a trademark except that it identifies and distinguishes the source of a service rather than a product.

There are three types of patents:

1) **Utility patents** may be granted to anyone who invents or discovers any new and useful process, machine, article of manufacture, or composition of matter, or any new and useful improvement thereof;
2) **Design patents** may be granted to anyone who invents a new, original, and ornamental design for an article of manufacture; and
3) **Plant patents** may be granted to anyone who invents or discovers and asexually reproduces any distinct and new variety of plant.

The history of the U.S. Patent Office is vital to the entrepreneurial spirit of the United States and we believe its importance supersedes many of the great discoveries of mankind. You see, the Patent Office is at the very heart of the free enterprise, capitalistic economic system.

Since its establishment the U.S. Patent Office has issued more than 8 million patents. According Matt Williams, Associated Editor of Government Technology[84], *"Patent No. 8,000,000 was issued on Tuesday, August 16, 2014 to Second Sight Medical Products Inc., 'for a visual prosthesis apparatus that enhances visual perception for people who have gone blind due to outer retinal degeneration. The invention uses electrical stimulation of the retina to produce the visual perception of patterns of light'."*

In 1970 the U.S. entered into The Patent Cooperation Treaty (PCT) which was developed to assist applicants in seeking patent protection internationally for their inventions. Instead of having to file separately the treaty made it possible to make one blanket filing and thereby seek patent protection in all 148 countries that have signed on to the treaty.

As there is no such thing as an "international patent" that would provide protection against violation in one central international court, the treaty simply minimizes the paperwork of having to file 148 separate applications. Violations would still require the patent holder to seek relief in the country in which the violation occurred and to go through the court process in that country. Making applications in every country, helps patent Offices with their patent granting decisions, and facilitates public access to a wealth of technical information relating to those inventions.

Most all inventors end up filing for a patent in the United States, because of our vigorous prosecution of patent, trademark, service mark, and copyright infringements. It is not uncommon to attend a football tailgate party and see someone having their merchandise being hauled-off by law enforcement officials because they were dealing in counterfeit merchandise. It is strong enforcement that has protected America's free economic system and the inventors that continually feed the system with new ideas and products.

The patent system is not without its critics. Many people believe that inventions should become public domain, because the inventor had to use public assets in order to develop his invention. Perhaps the inventor used public roadways or the ingredient to make the invention were delivered by vehicles on public roads and highways.

The most adamant critics to patents seemed to have come out of Europe in the 19th century which has a long history of socialism. Its most prominent activists were - Isambard Kingdom Brunel[85]; an English mechanical and civil engineer; William Robert Grove[86]; a Welsh judge and physical scientist; and William Armstrong[87], an English industrialist, who were inventors and entrepreneurs, and supported by radical laissez-faire[88] economists. Historian Adrian Johns, summarizes some of their main arguments as follows:

"Patents projected an artificial idol of the single inventor, radically denigrated the role of the intellectual commons, and blocked a path to this commons for other citizens — citizens who were all, on this account, potential inventors too. [...] Patentees were the equivalent of squatters on public land — or better, of uncouth market traders who planted their barrows in the middle of the highway and barred the way of the people."

One can see how such thinking can discourage an individual from his natural curiosity to discover new ideas and create new inventions. The central-planned governments throughout history would still be languishing today some hundred or more years behind the current state of civilization had they been able to exert their tyrannical government over the rest of the world. When you take the profit motive off the table in a Marxism style government, everyone is forced to accept mediocrity.

6. Inventions - Putting the thought process to work

"Twenty years from now you will be more disappointed by the things that you didn't do than by the ones you did do. So throw off the bowlines. Sail away from the safe harbor. Catch the trade winds in your sails. Explore. Dream. Discover."

Mark Twain

Early inventions of mankind that benefited the world.

Prehistory man's contribution to civilization - Inventors, be they scientists funded with grant money, on the payroll of major corporations, or everyday "handymen" working out of their garage, barn, or home, have made significant contributions to the lives of everyday people. One does not have to be a genius to come up with new ideas . . . they happen every day. Some helpful inventions even allow the

42-Early man came into this world with nothing and had to learn to survive. This meant inventing shelter, clothing, weapons, and learning to hunt

inventor to reap great financial rewards for his or her effort. And you know what . . . this phenomenon has been going on since man first began inhabiting this world.

When the first man walked on this earth, whether he was a Neanderthal or Cro Magnon or Early Modern Humans by whatever name we assign him, by nature he had to adapt to his environment in order to survive. He came into this world with absolutely nothing, bare naked, and no shelter, and therefore had to be more than *creative* or would have become food for other creatures. So

111

we believe the proper place to start when looking at what man has had to do to advance civilization to our current level, the best place to start is with what we can call "cavemen".

Anthropologists have readily documented Modern Humans dating back some 100,000 years or more, yet Scientists have unearthed the jawbone of what they claim is one of the very first humans[89]. Carbon dating tells us the 2.8 million-year-old specimen is 400,000 years older than researchers originally pegged as when "mankind" first emerged.

According to Sciencemag.org[89-1], Arizona State University (ASU) anthropologists stated, *"the partial lower jaw is the oldest known member of the genus* Homo. *Radiometrically dated to almost 2.8 million years ago, the jaw is a window on the mysterious time when our genus emerged"*.

Modern Humans of 100,000 years ago is early enough for us to start in recognizing what these early humans did to advance the cause of civilization. That being said, just what did these early inhabitants bring to the table in way of *creative imagination* . . . our term for *invention.*

We can start with being *stark naked* which is the way everyone comes into this world. Imagine the plight of this first person. Obviously, for people back then to endure the elements and not be eaten by some animal or other creature or die from exposure, the first humans had to come up with solutions for the basic elements needed for survival:

1. Shelter
2. Clothing
3. Food
4. Self-Defense

There are many theories about early humans, but the best bet is that they originally were tree dwellers[90], and were not knuckle-dragging creatures. As tree dwellers they would have had some protection against other creatures by seeking the safety of "high ground" in the trees where they lived. Trees didn't do much to protect against the elements -wind, rain, snow, and temperature, so it is a good bet life expectancy was rather short-lived.

When they came down from the trees, the most logical shelter would have been caves, because tools hadn't been invented and there were not too many ways they could have built much in the way of shelter.

Self-defense would have also been a big problem as would killing something to eat because they had yet to discover weapons. Keep in mind . . . These early humans, our forefathers, were carnivores just as we are today.

To survive they had to become ingenious. So looking at these folks it's safe to conclude they soon found that a sharp pointed stick would make a good weapon for self defense and might possibly allow them to kill a creature for food. Somewhere in those early days they found they could use the skin of their prey for clothing and warmth.

They say *necessity is the mother of invention*, which is the primary driving force for most new inventions. These early needs of the caveman are the prime examples of how true that statement is.

43-The first recorded history can be found on cave walks of early man, which tell his story and is the first known communication

Those *tree dwellers* soon became *cave dwellers*, and while these events couldn't have happen overnight, many accounts of their inventions and evolution on the path to civilization were recorded by drawings done on the walls of their caves dating back more than 40,000 year ago[91].

We can credit early humans, with coming up with shelter, self-defense weaponry, clothing, and killing other species for food. We can see that from

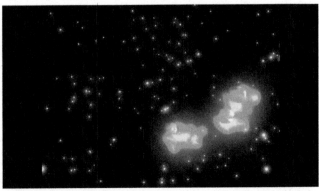

44-Early man became the first astronomers as they gazed into the sky in the dark of night. Perhaps what they saw led them to believe in a spiritual world or just frightened them can only be conjecture.

their first accounts they recorded by their artwork on cave walls.

We can also give them credit for discovering fire and the benefits it had for warmth and giving them the ability to cook what they killed. We can be sure they also found that fire provided light at night and became a defense weapon against predators.

The origins of human language[92] will perhaps remain forever obscure, but the origin of individual languages has been the subject of very precise study over the past two centuries. Communication between members of any species of animals has been known since we have begun to think, so it stands to reason that the early humans developed some form of communication besides hitting each other over the head with clubs to make a statement or get their point across.

Probably the primary motive to develop words was to place names on things that were discovered or perhaps invented, which ties right into the subject we are discussing in this book. So we can safely credit early man with the advent of communication.

The cave drawings are fascinating in that while the cavemen left no written documentation of life all those years ago, they did leave us with pictures of what they went through and often the challenges they faced. Included in the recording of events is their fascination with the stars at night making them the first astronomers. One can only imagine how bright the stars must have been in the absolute darkness that engulfed them when the sun went down. No light would have emanated from ground sources like we see today from towns and cities.

It would have been impossible not to turn their attention to the heavens at night, as they must have starred at wonderment at the universe that surrounded them. What were they thinking as the moon went through its phases? Was there sheer terror when an eclipse occurred?

Could this have given rise to a belief that perhaps there were spirits or even a God that should be worshiped when these and other natural occurring lunar events took place. Asteroids shooting across the sky, meteor showers, and other phenomenon had to give them some food for thought and could easily have been the basis for a superior being or a Divinity to worship. We probably need to credit them with being the first *spiritualists*.

Chapter 7 - Individual versus the team approach

"Over the years, I have learned that every significant invention has several characteristics. By definition it must be startling, unexpected, and must come into a world that is not prepared for it. If the world were prepared for it, it would not be much of an invention".

Edwin Land

Cognitive thinking relates to the mental processes of perception, memory, judgment, and reasoning, and is probably all that is really needed to become an inventor or make a startling new discovery. Many would disagree, but it really is that simple.

Most of us, when we think of inventing something new or improving on an old concept, perhaps envision a lone individual sitting by himself in a laboratory conjuring up some brilliant new idea or device, and then jotting down a bunch of notes or drawings, piecing together the idea into a working model, and then experimenting and redesigning it until the idea worked perfectly. It is easy for us to create such a stereotypical person, but in reality, most new discoveries or inventions come about by accident.

Roy Plunkitt - Well, maybe not all inventions are by accident, but we stumbled upon a case that would typify the way things are discovered while looking for solutions to totally unrelated problems. We found this gem about the invention of Teflon® on the Chemical Heritage Foundation[93] website:

"Roy J. Plunkett's first assignment at the DuPont Company's Jackson Laboratory was researching new chlorofluorocarbon refrigerants— then seen as great advances over earlier refrigerants like sulfur dioxide and ammonia, which regularly poisoned food-industry workers and

people in their homes.

"Plunkett had produced 100 pounds of tetrafluoroethylene gas (TFE) and stored it in small cylinders at dry-ice temperatures preparatory to chlorinating it. When he and his helper prepared a cylinder for use, none of the gas came out—yet the cylinder weighed the same as before. They opened it and found a white powder, which Plunkett had the presence of mind to characterize for properties other than refrigeration potential.

"He found the substance to be heat resistant and chemically inert, and to have very low surface friction so that most other substances would not adhere to it. Plunkett realized that, against the predictions of polymer science of the day, TFE had polymerized to produce this substance— later named Teflon—with such potentially useful characteristics."

45-DuPont researcher, Roy Plunkett, who discovered Teflon®... The by-product of an accident while working on a project with *tetrafluoroethylene gas (TFE)*

Enrico Fermi - On the other hand, a whole lot of inventions have required team work, multiple partners, huge sums of money, and years of redesigning and experimenting with a lot of trial and error failures along the way. Sometimes the lone genius scenario just can't get the job done by himself. A case in point is the development of the atomic bomb.

The atom bomb was on the minds of governments looking for the ultimate weapon of war. Not satisfied with simply blowing people and things up with normal explosives, the most devious of minds wanted to do it bigger and faster.

Fortunately for the world, it was the United States which unlocked the secret of the atom first. Our scientists found a way to package it into an explosive device that not only brought a war to an end with its awesome destructive power, but put fear into hearts and minds that it could eventually destroy the world.

46-Physicist Enrico Fermi has been called the "architect of the nuclear age", and the "architect of the atomic bomb", working with other renown physicists, Albert Einstein and Robert Oppenheimer.

America was not the first country and it certainly will not be the last to want to possess such a devastating weapon. Thank God such a project is not easy to accomplish. Its secrets are detailed in the records of the Manhattan Project dating back to just before World War II. It has been summarized and encapsulated by the credible U.S. History website[94] owned by the Independence Hall Association in Philadelphia, and reads as follows:

> *"Early in 1939, the world's scientific community discovered that German physicists had learned the secrets of splitting a uranium atom. Fears soon spread over the possibility of Nazi scientists utilizing that energy to produce a bomb capable of unspeakable destruction.*
>
> *"Scientists Albert Einstein, who fled Nazi persecution, and Enrico Fermi, who escaped Fascist Italy, were now living in the United States. They agreed that the President must be informed*

of the dangers of atomic technology in the hands of the Axis powers. Fermi traveled to Washington in March to express his concerns to government officials. But few shared his uneasiness.

"Einstein penned a letter to President Roosevelt urging the development of an atomic research program later that year. Roosevelt saw neither the necessity nor the utility for such a project, but agreed to proceed slowly. In late 1941, the American effort to design and build an atomic bomb received its code name — the Manhattan Project.

"At first the research was based at only a few universities — Columbia University, the University of Chicago and the University of California at Berkeley. A breakthrough occurred in December 1942 when Fermi led a group of physicists to produce the first controlled nuclear chain reaction under the grandstands of Stagg Field at the University of Chicago.

"After this milestone, funds were allocated more freely, and the project advanced at breakneck speed. Nuclear facilities were built at Oak Ridge, Tennessee and Hanford, Washington. The main assembly plant was built at Los Alamos, New Mexico. Robert Oppenheimer was put in charge of putting the pieces together at Los Alamos. After the final bill was tallied, nearly $2 billion had been spent on research and development of the atomic bomb. The Manhattan Project employed over 120,000 Americans during the project.

"Secrecy was paramount. Neither the Germans nor the Japanese could learn of the project. Roosevelt and Churchill also agreed that the

Stalin would be kept in the dark. Consequently, there was no public awareness or debate. Keeping 120,000 people quiet would be impossible; therefore only a small privileged cadre of inner scientists and officials knew about the atomic bomb's development. In fact, Vice-President Truman had never heard of the Manhattan Project until he became President Truman.

"Although the Axis powers remained unaware of the efforts at Los Alamos, American leaders later learned that a Soviet spy named Klaus Fuchs had penetrated the inner circle of scientists.

47-The Atom bomb was first used on the Japanese bringing the Second Word War to an end. It took two bombs, one on Hiroshima the other on Nagasaki to get Japan to agree to an unconditional surrender.

"By the summer of 1945, Oppenheimer was ready to test the first bomb. On July 16, 1945, at Trinity Site near Alamogordo, New Mexico, scientists of the Manhattan Project readied themselves to watch the detonation of the world's first atomic bomb. The device was affixed to a 100-foot tower and discharged just before dawn. No one was properly prepared for the result.

"A blinding flash visible for 200 miles lit up the morning sky. A mushroom cloud reached 40,000 feet, blowing out windows of civilian homes up to 100 miles away. When the cloud returned to earth it created a half-mile wide crater

121

metamorphosing sand into glass. A bogus cover-up story was quickly released, explaining that a huge ammunition dump had just exploded in the desert. Soon word reached President Truman in Potsdam, Germany that the project was successful ...The world had entered the nuclear age."

The two examples cited above are proof that there are many ways to skin the proverbial cat. Each patent sitting in the U.S. Patent Office has its own story to tell. The remarkable fact is that while each story may be different, the evidence is clear to those who have witnessed the contributions Americans have made through new discoveries and inventions, that without the free market, entrepreneurial, capitalistic economic system we have in America, we would never have made such extraordinary achievements in advancing civilization.

Additionally, we have put into force a system that protects one's ideas under our free market system, which prohibits others from copying or stealing the idea. Such protection has made it possible for our country to become a great economic powerhouse, and enabled fortunes to be made.

When we say, ***"America is not a country but a concept"***, we refer to America being a country of exceptional people who have the freedom to risk everything in their quest for success. America is a place where opportunities happen every day and where hard work and good fortune will be rewarded as in no other country.

It is the *concept* of America that separates the United States from central-planned Marxist countries of the world where there is little or no reward for excellence and where new discoveries often go unrewarded and unnoticed. This was one of the most evident observations that we alluded to in our introduction when comparing the growth of America's gross domestic product to the communist Soviet Union.

Chapter 8 - Other great American inventors

"As we enjoy great advantages from the inventions of others, we should be glad of an opportunity to serve others by any invention of ours, and this we should do freely and generously".

Benjamin Franklin

When you read about these world-changing inventions, you will find that most inventions are not the result of *original* thought and are certainly not created in a vacuum. You'll see many great discoveries began when others failed in their efforts. *Discoveries*, and that's what inventions are, generally are sought to meet a need.

Most are built on previous inventions created by other inventors years, decades or even centuries before. Often something works relatively well but it isn't fast enough, is too costly, or the quality of the end product is just not sufficient, so it motivates others to carry on for something that works better.

Every invention has problems. Anything man can produce, another man can, in most cases improve upon. It might be some other inventor who comes along and sees a way to make things better, and in many instances one change can lead to many changes, losing track of the person who invented it in the first place. Many of the stories in this book fit into that mold.

Suppose Henry Ford has simply settled for developing the concept of the automobile moving assembly line and left it at that? To confuse things further, it usually isn't the original inventor who gets the credit, but rather the inventor or inventors who made the crucial improvement that walks away with the honors.

It has been said that "war" has been responsible for the majority of discoveries or inventions. That might be factual or just conjecture. Since man discovered ways to communicate we find they didn't always to a good job at getting their point across and war became an alternative solution.

It is sad but true that the military has come up with better. faster, and easier ways to destroy everything in its path We have learned to kill in ways the caveman never dreamed off, but it is also true that when we put our thinking-caps on, we will see many things developed for destruction, have an even greater benefit when used for peace. This is particularly true in transportation, communication, and other technologies.

Where we go from here is to summarize what we feel are American's greatest contributions to the advancement of civilization. We can't cover them all in one book, so inevitably we will have to do additional volumes to make sure we eventually cover the real genius of America, and those who came here to make it all possible.

The list of discoveries presented herewith is a good start. We chose inventions that really had big impacts on not just American lives, but have been gladly shared for the benefit of all. We list them, not in any particular order of importance, but randomly just as they would have occurred in real life. Some names are probably recognizable, though long forgotten, and some you may read about for the first time. The importance to show you here is that there is no end to man's imagination and no end to man's needs.

Reality starts with dreamers

Alexander Graham Bell & Thomas Watson- Bell was born on March 3, 1847, in Edinburgh, Scotland. His education was received through numerous experiments in sound and working with his father on *visible speech* for the deaf with more hands-on learning rather than a formal education at a major university.

48-Alexander Graham Bell

49-Thomas Watson

His father moved the family to Brantford, Ontario, Canada in 1870, because both of his brothers had died[95] from tuberculosis and felt North America would provide conditions for better health for the entire family. Alexander moved down to Boston, Massachusetts in 1871, and began working on a "communication device".

History notes Bell as a great inventor with his foremost accomplishments being the telephone[96] (1876) and the refinement of the phonograph[97] (1886).

Working with Thomas Watson who became intrigued by Bell's idea that it might be possible to transmit human voices over distance by wire, was the added "voice" needed in the project. Together they labored on a harmonic telegraph and a voice transmitting devices until they came up with a revolutionary "talking machine" which became the telephone.

Needless to say, the telephone has been one of the most important discoveries of all time, allowing people all over the world to communicate without having to be within sight of each other.

Folklore over this exciting invention has it that Bell knocked over a container of transmitting fluid and shouted, "Mr. Watson, come here. I want you!". Be that fact or fiction we will never know, but those famous words have been credited as being the first words transmitted by telephone. They filed for patent protection in 1876, and though a far cry from the portable *smart telephones* we have today, was a giant step toward the future. Bell went on to develop other inventions and filed 18 additional patents.

Benjamin Franklin - Benjamin Franklin is best known as one of the Founding Fathers of the United States and the negotiator of the 1783 Treaty of Paris, which ended the Revolutionary War. Long forgotten is his work as an inventor, and the important discoveries he made, such as *bifocal glasses* which eliminated the need to carry two sets of glasses around - one for reading, the other to assist distance vision.

50– Benjamin Franklin

Additionally most people have no idea that it was Ben Franklin who came up with the concept of book rentals in Philadelphia in 1731, and is considered the father of the today's library.

Franklin, was always one to pursue new ideas. He published the famous *Poor Richard's Almanack*[98] for twenty-five years from 1732-1757, selling an average 10,000 copies a year. The almanac was a collection of periodicals written by Franklin and contained humor, general information, new ideas he ran across, and proverbial wisdom, such as "Early to bed and early to rise, makes a man healthy, wealthy, and wise."

He was known for his wit, wisdom, and intelligence, but it was his curiosity with lightning and electricity that led to lasting principles of electricity. *"It was in Boston, Massachusetts, in 1746 that Franklin first stumbled upon other scientists' electrical experiments, and he quickly turned his home into a little laboratory, using machines made out of items he found around the house"*, states Ideafinder.com.

Keeping precise records, he documented his work in collaboration with Peter Collinson, a fellow scientist and friend in London who found Franklin's work fascinating, and felt the information should be published to eliminate redundancy by other scientists. Franklin was the first person working with electricity to use the terms *positive* and *negative* (plus and minus) and actually came up with the concept of the battery though he had no idea what someone would want that for.

Franklin was the first to notice the similarities between lightning and electricity and believed, like other scientists, that lightning was electricity, though no one had ever been able to prove that yet. Lightning was of interest to the scientific community because many homes and buildings were struck by it. The natural correlation between fire and lightning was pretty much established by a million eyewitnesses . . . When a building was struck by lightning, it went up in flames. While conventional wisdom thought that lightning might be electricity, Franklin was determined to find a method of proving it.

Franklin believed that it would be possible to protect homes and buildings from fires caused by lightning strikes, but he needed to first prove the relationship between lightening and electricity. His idea was to put a metal key on the string of a kite and fly it into a lightning storm to see if it would attract a bolt of lightning.

Not a very brilliant idea knowing what we know about lightning today, but sometimes a near-death situation can be a good teacher. No one understood the power of a single electrical jolt carried in a bolt of lightning and Franklin could have easily been fried to a crisp by electrocuting himself. He was fortunate that it was a mild lightning storm the night he confirmed his belief, but he did get the results he anticipated.

With the knowledge that iron did indeed attract the *flash,* he believed a simple iron rod could be used to "direct" the lightning away from a building. Placing an iron rod in the ground near a building and connecting the building to the iron with a cable, it might just direct the lightning away from the building, or strike the rod and go directly into the ground. If it struck the building then it would be directed through the cable attached to the rod and go into the ground.

Franklin described his theory of the rod being 8-10 feet long and pointed on the end sticking out of the ground. He wrote, *"the electrical fire would, I think, be drawn out of a cloud silently, before it could come near enough to strike". . .* But instead of starting a fire by striking a building the electrical charge would be directed into the ground, hence the term *grounding*. Franklin's lightning rods could soon be found protecting many buildings and homes.

Samuel F. B. Morse - Samuel Morse invented the single-wire telegraph system and was co-inventor of the Morse code communication language, named in his honor. Probably just as important, Morse was also an American artist best remembered for his wonderful and critically acclaimed artistic talent as characterized by his *Dying Hercules, I Am a Child, Gallery of the Louvre*, and others, some of which hang in the Louvre in Paris, and in the Smithsonian Institute.

51-Samuel B. Morse

In 1838, Morse formed a partnership with another inventor Alfred Vail, who financed the development of the Morse Code . . . a *language* system which consisted of a series of dots and dashes for sending signals that would print out a message.

No one knows for sure whether or not Morse knew of other inventors in Europe who were working on a similar system, but he was the first to develop a working prototype that transmitted signals over lengthy distances, and was able to secure his patent in 1847.

Prior to applying for his patent, Morse and his partner

Alfred Vail received a grant from Congress for $30,000 to construct an experimental 38 mile telegraph line between Washington DC and Baltimore, Maryland, which was completed in 1844. The first message that was tapped out over this line was his now-famous, "What hath God wrought!"[99].

The telegraph helped open the west, paving the way for rapid communication and became essential for newspapers, government

52-Samuel Morse's Dying Hercules

messaging, and to spread the news of emergencies and disasters. It also assisted the expansion of the Pony Express mail delivery service.

Almost as soon as Morse received his patent for the telegraph in 1847, he was hit with litigious claims from partners and rival inventors. The legal battles[100] culminated in the U.S. Supreme Court decision *O'Reilly v. Morse* (1854), that stated Morse had been the first to develop a workable telegraph. In spite of the court's clear ruling, Morse received no official recognition from the U.S. government. Samuel Morse died of pneumonia on April 2, 1872, at his home in New York City at age 80.

Thomas Alva Edison - One of the most recognizable names in America is the name, Thomas Edison. People immediately associate his name with electricity, but his accomplishments are beyond most mortal men, and his ability to see people's needs were on a completely different level than most inventors, past or present.

According to History.com[101], *"Thomas Edison acquired a record number of 1,093 patents (singly or jointly) and was the driving force behind such innovations as the phonograph, the incandescent light bulb and one of the earliest motion picture cameras. He also created the world's first industrial research laboratory. Known as the "Wizard of Menlo Park," for the New Jersey town where he did some of his best-known work. Edison had become one of the most famous men in the world by the time he was in his 30s. In addition to his talent for invention, Edison was also a successful manufacturer and businessman who was highly skilled at marketing his inventions–and himself–to the public.*

52-Thomas Alva Edison

"By the time he died on October 18, 1931, Thomas Edison had amassed a record 1,093 patents: 389 for electric light and power, 195 for the phonograph, 150 for the telegraph, 141 for storage batteries and 34 for the telephone."

One of Edison's most important inventions was the phonograph, which came about as a result of the work he was doing on voice transmission and amplification (for clarity over the telephone line) It was a lengthy undertaking but made an immediate splash once produced and sold commercially. People were so amazed that the press labeled him "the Wizard of Menlo Park."

54-The Edison light bulb which revolutionized the ability to see at night or any place where little light was available. It literally brought us out of the dark ages!

With so many inventions to his credit, there probably isn't any inventor more important, though it is almost a coin toss as the order of importance Mr. Edison's inventions played in advancing civilization, with the probable exception of the *light bulb*.

The ability to light a room without the use of dangerous oil or gas lamps was a commercial success for Edison, and in 1881, he established an electric light company in Newark, New Jersey. He moved his family to New York, from his home in Menlo Park that same year. Though Edison's early incandescent lighting systems had their problems, they were used at such prestigious events as the Paris Lighting Exhibition in 1881 and the Crystal Palace in London in 1882.

His list of accomplishments ran the gamut from the initial work he did in the film industry, to developing alkaline batteries, which the government took an interest in for the emerging war industry and its production of submarines. His ability to see needs where others would simply take the status quo for granted, placed Edison front and center before many of America's industrial giants, including Henry Ford, where he pioneer the work for an electric starter for Ford Automobiles.

Just imagine the thousands of industries Edison was able to help along the way, and the thousands of start-up business and millions of jobs his inventions were able to provide for those living in America. As to important American inventors, one would have to place Thomas Alva Edison at the top of the list, and most probably, the most important inventor of all-time except perhaps the one who invented "the wheel", whoever that might be.

Henry Ford - Ford did not invent the automobile or the assembly line, though many people attribute such production methods to Ford Motor Company. What Henry Ford did do was come-up with *the moving assembly line*, in which parts are added as the *work-in-process* assembly moves from work station to work station. In this manner parts are added to the assembly in a specific sequence until the end product is produced.

55-Henry Ford

Ford observed how other manufacturers at the time were mass producing products in which workers often were employed to numerous task in the assembly process. He viewed those methods as an antiquated process which left plenty of room for errors to occur. Additionally, workers wasted time having to redo work already completed. Ford understood that one person doing a job repetitively, would enable the worker to get really proficient at his job, and improve overall productivity of the assembly team.

Ford's answer was in moving the parts to the area for each

57-1914 Ford Model T touring car

phase of the assembly process and move the semi-finished assembled component from work station to work station. In this *repetitive* manner of building a product, it can be assembled much faster with less labor than by having workers carry parts to a stationary *work-in-process* product for assembly.

Applying his principles to the development and manufacturing process of building an automobile, reduced costs so drastically, in spite of paying higher wages than what was considered *the norm* for the day, Ford Motor Company was the first car company to produce an automobile that was affordable for most middle class Americans.

Building a car cheap enough for all, the automobile went from an expensive curiosity to a practical convenience that profoundly changed the way people traveled and commercially, the way goods could be shipped. Additionally, the automobile changed everything in America, and provided millions of jobs building the infrastructure of highways, gasoline service stations, energy production to produce fuel, and automobile maintenance facilities, across the country.

With the advent of improved methods of travel, consider the ramifications Henry Ford had and the giant steps Americans could take in the march of civilization.

Automated travel powered our industrial revolution and the millions of jobs created by the industrial growth improved the quality of life for everyone. Ford's dealership franchise system that put dealerships throughout most of North America and in major cities on *six continents*, gave the world the ability to improve their standard of living as well. This is the power generated by the *Concept of America.*

In short, what Henry Ford did, was to create an *employment machine*, that helped build America. The United States became the *immigrant destination* of the world's population - jobs, opportunity, money, financial security became available to all who applied themselves.

Without the improvement in transportation Ford provided, it is safe to say that America could never have handled the population growth that occurred after the turn of the century. Is it any wonder that such innovation spurred the most rapid increase in the standard of living ever seen.

What has gone overlook by those who promote the Marxist theories as an alternative to America's free market capitalistic system, there is no *collectivist* system that can measure up to the economic growth America has seen since 1900. . . They don't even come close.

56-Mr. & Mrs. Henry Ford in his first produced automobile

Henry Ford provided the world his manufacturing concepts which were matched only by his marketing genius at selling cars and trucks. It is unfortunate that America has forgotten to relay these facts to our children.

Had the United States not taken a leadership role during two world wars with our industrial might modeled after Ford's approach to manufacturing, in most likelihood the world would be under the dark cloud of some tyrannical regime today.

Whereas many discoveries made in developing new weapons of war, in time have been adapted to peaceful endeavors, Henry Ford's peaceful manufacturing endeavor was adapted to help supply the free world with material to wage war . . . an interesting turn of events.

On a final note about Henry Ford and his great company; Ford systematically revolutionize lower cost business innovations which have become the model for many industries in many countries. They have even been adopted by collective societies, and have been proven to increase production and better quality products there as well.

Eli Whitney - Whitney was born on December 8, 1765, in Westboro, Massachusetts. For a northern Yankee, it might appear unlikely that someone living more than a thousand miles from the heart of the cotton harvest region, would be the person that revolutionized the processing of cotton. In an age when cotton was harvested by hand, and in which more than 60% of those involved in the harvesting were slaves, the fact that a Yankee invented a product that changed an entire industry doesn't seem plausible.

58-Eli Whitney

Whitney, like many American inventors who invented or discovered a product as a way to do something better, happened to be at the right place at the right time in history. After leaving his home near Yale University where he studied law, he headed to the Carolinas to take a position as a tutor only to find upon his arrival, the job paid about half of what he was promised. Once Whitney found out about his tutoring salary he decided tutoring wasn't in the cards for him.

On the boat down to the South Carolina from Massachusetts he met Catherine Greene who was from Georgia, the widow of a Revolutionary War general. After telling her of his plight, he accepted a position from Ms. Green to "read law" (in the 1800's the term was used to imply studying the law[102]) at her Mulberry Grove plantation in Georgia.

Good fortune was to be the luck of Whitney because while at the plantation he met Phineas Miller, another Yale alum, who was Greene's fiancé and manager of her estate. This would come in handy in very short order.

The market for tobacco[103] was declining, and Ms. Greene learned the agricultural community in Georgia was in need of a *money crop*. Additionally, tobacco growing did not allow full use of a plantation's property as growing tobacco utilizes most of the soil's nitrogen so fields had to be alternated.

Farmers wanted a year-round crop they could grow over the entire plantation. Cotton was an option but even though green-seed cotton was widely available, it took hours of manual labor to properly clean the seed and extract the fiber . . . this was not an attractive alternative to those accustomed to growing tobacco. It required very little processing and could be easily handle by slave labor.

During the mid-1800s, Southern cotton production was in high demand all over the world. Production could not meet the demand. More than a million bales of cotton were being produced by 1840, and the call for more was out of the question for such a labor intense product. The big delay was in separating the seeds from the cotton fiber, a process which had to be done by hand. There simply weren't enough slaves to increase production.

59-Whitney's Cotton Gin

With Greene's support, Whitney worked through the winter to devise a machine that was able to quickly and efficiently clean the cotton using a system of hooks, wires and a rotating brush. Miller assisted him. Some historians believe Catherine Greene devised the cotton gin and Eli Whitney merely built it and applied for the patent, since at that time women were not allowed to file for patents. Others believe the idea was Whitney's but Greene played an important role as both designer and financier.

Whitney and Miller showed their cotton gin to a group of farmers who exhibited much enthusiasm. The gin looked like it would be very profitable, so many people tried to copy it.

With the cost of litigation to protect their patent, it was years before any profit was really seen even though the machine was a success. Not to be discouraged about designing products where there was a demand, Whitney moved on to a new concept.

His next big venture would involve the production of muskets[104] for the federal government. He felt he could manufacture them faster than the competition by developing a system so that they could be mass-produced using interchangeable parts.

With the possibility of a war with France the government agreed to allow Whitney to supply firearms when he promised to manufacture 10,000 rifles within a two-year period of time. That followed with another contract for 15,000 more muskets.

S. 290

60-Whitney's mass-produced 1763 French Charleville model musket

Such quantities of weapons would have been difficult to produce using the then current method of muskets being assembled entirely by individual craftsman and by hand with each rifle having its own distinctively made parts. Applying his mass-production ideas, Whitney set-up milling machines to produce parts using templates or patterns from which the laborers who assemble the weapons did not require the skill of a *craftsman*, but rather the skill of an *assembler*.

They set-up the manufacturing plant in Connecticut, and typical of all new ideas, they were unable to perfect the process and complete the contract for 10,000 muskets for about 10-years. Even with the delays the government reward him with the additional contract for 15,000 more guns. The second order only took a couple of years to complete.

The concept developed by Whitney is still the model for mass producing most large quantity of products and continues to influence modern assembly lines. Most historians agree he earned the title, "the father of *American technology*."

A lasting tradition also established by Whitney in his manufacturing plant was the attitude he had for his employees. He built a number of worker residences that became known as Whitneyville, and is still part of the Connecticut landscape today as part of Hamden, Connecticut.

The ethical guidelines however, he used to build harmonious employee relations, were based on his Puritanical upbringing, but sad to say, they did not survive the industrial revolution he helped to further, and were lost over the years to the harsh reality and competitive nature of manufacturing.

Levi Strauss - *"Anyone can make a pair of blue jeans, but Levi Strauss & Co. made the first blue jeans — in 1873."*

Levi Strauss was born in Buttenheim, Bavaria on February 26, 1829 to Hirsch Strauss and his wife, Rebecca Haas Strauss. Strauss' claim of being a *great* American inventor was his ability to see the need for rugged men's work pants that just didn't wear out.

61-Levi Strauss

Not only did Strauss invent and manufacture, at a cost anyone could afford, a garment of clothing that was almost indestructible, but Levis (as we all know them) were the pants that literally, "won the

West". According to the Nashville Scene.[105] In fact, Levis are the best selling *garment* of all time.

Levis typifies the true American *rags to riches story* of which folklore is made. Levi had three older brothers and three older sisters. The brothers proceed to America before Levi arrived on our shore. From the Levis home page we learn the history behind the product that changed America and was so unique it even developed its own *culture*. Two years after his father died of tuberculosis in 1846, Levi and his sisters emigrated to New York, where they were met by his two older brothers who owned a New York city based wholesale dry goods business called *"J. Strauss Brother & Co."*.

Levi soon began to learn the trade himself, and when news of the California Gold Rush made its way to New York, *"Levi journeyed to San Francisco in 1853 to make his fortune, though he wouldn't make it panning gold. He established a wholesale dry goods business under his own name and served as the West Coast representative of the family's New York firm. Levi eventually renamed his company 'Levi Strauss & Co'.*

"Around 1872, Levi received a letter from one of his customers, Jacob Davis, a Reno, Nevada tailor. In his letter, Davis disclosed the unique way he made pants for his customers, through

the use of rivets at points of strain to make them last longer. Davis wanted to patent this new idea, but needed a business partner to get the idea off the ground. Levi was enthusiastic about the idea. The patent was granted to Jacob Davis and Levi Strauss & Company on May 20,

62-Levi Strauss and Company Circa 1870's

1873; and blue jeans were born.[105-1]

With success of his patented, *and now riveted* jeans, Levi Strauss became involved in numerous other businesses. With his headquarters in San Francisco he became a charter member and treasurer of the San Francisco Board of Trade in 1877, and accepted a prestigious position on the Board of Directors of the Nevada Bank; the Liverpool, London and Globe Insurance

Company; and the San Francisco Gas and Electric Company. Business was booming, so Levi and two associates purchased the Mission and Pacific Woolen Mills.

63-The Jeans that won the West

Later in life he was one of San Francisco's greatest philanthropists, helping to finance numerous Jewish humanitarian ventures, almost before such undertakings were fashionable. He supported the Pacific Hebrew Orphan Asylum and Home; the Eureka Benevolent Society; and the Hebrew Board of Relief[105-2]. But his generosity didn't stop with just helping foundations, he helped people in need - In 1897 Levi provided the funds for twenty-eight scholarships at the University of California, Berkeley, all of which are still in place today.

By the turn of the century you could say he was going like the Energizer Bunny and was still actively involved in the day-to-day operations of his company. Reading from the Levis Foundation[106] website it is interesting to note that the best selling Levis jeans, the 501's, actually has a "history" and is not just a model number.

In 1890 The *rivet patent* went into the *public domain,* which meant that Levi Strauss & Co. would no longer be the exclusive manufacturer of riveted clothing.

With Strauss Company, *"lot numbers are first assigned to the products being manufactured. '501' was used to designate the famous copper-riveted waist overalls."* . . . *"We don't know why this number was chosen. We also made a 201 jean, which was a less expensive version of the pants, as well as other products using other three-digit numbers, because we loss of our records in 1906".*

The reasons for the many of the changes in Levis overall's numbering system are unknown, but 501® will remain forever, as it was registered with the trademark office when the rivet *patent protection* ended. 1890 also marks the year Levi and his nephews officially incorporated the company.

Levi Strauss passed away on Friday, September 26, 1902. His personal estate amounted to nearly $6 million, the bulk of which was left to his four nephews and other family members, and additional donations were made to local funds and associations. Today Levis Strauss and Company is the 86th largest private corporation in America with an estimated value of $8.4 billion and annual sales of $4.74 billion . . . not too shabby for a family of immigrants who made it to America.

This is another bit of American history they don't share with our children in our school systems, and another success story you will never see in a Marxist country!

Granville T. Woods -Woods has been compared to the *Black Thomas A. Edison,* having held more than 50 Patents . . . more than any African-American in history. His name surely belongs on this impressive list of great American inventors, as he truly typifies the Concept of America where one is only limited by his dreams, and confirms Martin Luther King's dream that we should all be recognized by the content of our character.

"Before the Civil War, slavery and racial sentiments did much to hamper the recognition of black inventors," Michael C.

Christopher explained in the "Journal of Black Studies"[107]. *"Slaves were not allowed to receive patents or assign them to others. Because slaves were not citizens, they were not allowed to enter into contracts with the government or private citizens."*

64-Granville T. Woods

The end of the U.S. Civil War in 1865 provided black inventors legal recognition, but it failed to foster complete social acceptance. This anti-Black sentiment, had many African-Americans refusing to acknowledge their race for fear of jeopardize the commercial value of their inventions, nevertheless Granville was still successful . . . a tribute to his perseverance.

To grasp the importance of many of his discoveries, you should know a little railroad history[108], which spans the last two hundred years relating to modern rail travel, but actually has a history dating back to ancient civilizations of Greece and Egypt.

Industrial Europe (1600s -1800s) used trains with horses or bulls as primary sources power but were much simpler in design and far slower than the trains which appeared in America. These forerunners of modern rail systems generally traveled in two directions and used rails because it required less force to move the cargo cars loaded with coal, iron and other goods.

While early trains were indeed simple, they did pave the way for far more sophisticated rail service beginning in the 1800's, when faster travel was needed to cover great distances, particularly in industrialized England to transport people and manufacturing raw materials. One of the problems with early rail systems was that safety never seemed to be a concern and disasters of trains crashing into one another happened on a regular basis. NOTE: Stopping a heavily loaded train once it gets rolling, requires a long distance.

144

65-Advertisement for shares in the Union Pacific Railroad, Harper's Weekly, August 10, 1867. (Gilder Lehrman Collection)

When steam powered trains came into being, they changed the manufacturing landscape as larger capacity loads could be carried and more passengers could be transported over greater distances. With a decrease in the time it took to get material more products could be built, and once products were built, delivery time to the consumer was dramatically reduced, and greater production capacity could be accomplished.

By the time America began developing a rail system in the nineteenth century, the undertaking became a high government priority to facilitate a more rapid expansion and settlement of The West. To a government that was still technically in the development stages as the U.S. certainly was, financing such an undertaking was a problem that took American ingenuity to solve.

According to The Journal of the Gilder Lehrman Institute[110]

" The first transcontinental railroad, built between 1864 and 1869, was the greatest construction project of its era. It involved building a line from Omaha, Nebraska, to Sacramento, California, across a vast, largely unmapped territory.

"To most Americans the West was as remote as the moon, its terrain as alien and forbidding. Like the moon project of a later generation, its conquest required immense resources. Unlike the moon project, the building of the railroad was undertaken by private interests, but only after Congress passed legislation to help finance the work."

While history has coined the term, "transcontinental railroad", making it sound like the venture of a single rail company, the United States has never had a railroad under one ownership that went from Atlantic Coast to the Pacific. The distance and cost would have been too large for one company and so the undertaking involved two groups: The Union Pacific and Central Pacific Railroad Companies. Both companies, one coming from the East, the other from the west, met in Promontory Point, Utah, to drive the last spike linking the two systems together.

To reward investors the unique financing scheme wherein, *"each railroad company received its right-of-way along with a land grant of ten alternating sections on both sides of every mile of track (about 12,800 acres per mile); the*

66-East meets west at Promontory Point, Utah where the last spike in America's Transcontinental Rail System was driven into the ground.

government retained the sections in between. In addition, the companies received government bonds totaling $16,000 a mile for each twenty-mile section of track completed on the plains" .

"The project was dominated by the so-called "Big Four"[110]: Collis P. Huntington, Mark Hopkins, Leland Stanford, and Charles Crocker of the Central Pacific Railroad, which for their willingness to gamble their fortunes, provided unbelievable wealth as they developed their individual land grants once the project was completed.

67-The train opened up a new opportunities in the wild west for the outlaws, and provided jobs for the Pinkerton Detectives tasked to chase them down. Legends were made out of train robbers like Jesse James and Butch Cassidy and the Sundance Kid.

The implementation of the U.S. rail system drastically reduced the size of the country, opened-up business opportunities for *outlaw train robbers* and gangs of lawmen to chase them; and enabled travel across country in just a couple of days versus more than a month by horse back and wagon train. It also facilitated the establishment of towns and cities which grew up along the rail route, and in turn, became supply centers for industry and farming which serviced and fed America.

While America was not the birth place of railroads, it was America that provided improvements to *the system* and were adopted world-wide. Thanks to great inventors like Granville, the safety issue was soon minimize by one of his most notable inventions which was a system for letting the engineer of a train know how close his train was to other trains on the track. This device helped reduce accidents and collisions between trains.

From the Brooklyn Historic Railway Association[111] we learn that Granville was responsible for other safety inventions like the *induction telegraph system* which allowed messages to be sent to and from moving trains. This enabled train conductors and engineers to avoid collisions, report hazards on tracks ahead, or about other emergencies the train personnel might observe in its travel. Granville's vision was so far ahead of his time the induction telegraph system was the predecessor of today's wireless LAN Network (Local Area Network) idea. The technology he used was a multiplex wireless cab signal system which he called the "synchronous multiplex railway telegraph".

Most inventors would have been satisfied with these contributions to the railroad systems of America, but trains are trains, and not the only mode of transportation to run on rail systems. Woods developed many of his inventions for use on electric trolley and electric train systems, the predecessors to today's *light rail systems* found in many major cities in the U.S. and across Europe.

The Transport Workers Union Black History Committee & Brian Kassel provides much history on Granville Wood's contribution, and credit his inventions for allowing the New York city subway system to be built to help shape modern society. The following was researched and written by David L. Head, Chairman of the committee:

> *"Granville T. Woods invented an innovative field shunting speed control system for trolleys and electric rail cars; this system would replace the resistor based speed control systems then in use. The earlier resistor based systems controlled train speed by reducing the electrical energy being supplied to the traction motors through the application of resistors. This system was not only inefficient but also produced a great deal of heat, since excess energy would be converted to heat.*
>
> *"The excess heat was problematic when combined with the wooden trolleys and rail cars in use at that time; resistor based speed control systems could (and occasionally would) cause the wooden rail cars to spontaneously ignite.*
>
> *"Granville Woods' invented an electric rail car speed control system that used field shunting instead of resistors. In this system, the field coil in the electric motor would have a portion (step) of its field coil added or removed from the circuit thereby supplying the motor with more or less*

energy allowing the car to accelerate, maintain speed or coast (and decelerate by using a regenerative braking system).

The electric railway power distribution systems invented by Granville T. Woods

"On Saturday February 13th 1892 (roughly a year after Woods' arrival in New York) Woods' 'Multiple Distributing Station System' was tested by the American Engineering Company and demonstrated to the public at Coney Island, Brooklyn. The Demonstration amazed the crowd and made a very favorable impression with the electrical experts and surface railway magnates of that period.

"This system was a dramatic departure from any previous distribution system for electric railway power. It allowed for the wireless transmission of electric power, utilizing principles of 'electro-magnetic induction' instead of overhead wires, a 3rd rail or any physical contact point.

"Unfortunately, Wood's dream of widespread implementation of the 'Multiple Distributing Station System' would be derailed by the scurrilous tactics of Mr. James S. Zerbe of the American Engineering Company. Woods eventually resorted to litigation after Mr. Zerbe and the American Engineering Company attempted to market his patented invention. A newspaper article from that period states: 'Mr. Woods asserts that he never received one penny compensation for the work done, while the American Engineering Company is preparing to reap a rich harvest'.

149

"Woods would eventually succeed in court, but this particular invention would not see widespread implementation. Interestingly enough this invention was 100 years ahead of its time.

"Wood's 'Multiple Distributing Station System' bears a striking resemblance to today's experimental linear induction railroad propulsion systems, while the three other electric railway power distribution systems invented by woods would see widespread implementation.

"During the 1890's and Early 20th Century Woods' invented the 'Electric Railway Conduit System' in 1891, which was used extensively on Washington D.C. and Manhattan's Streetcar systems (see patented drawing and description). Granv ille T. Woods also invented a 3rd Rail Power Distribution system. The patent for third rail (Patent #687,098) was issued to Granville T. Woods in 1901.

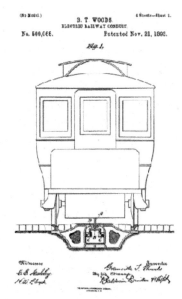

68-Granville Woods' *Electric Railway 3rd Rail Conduit System'* 1891 Patent

"This extremely durable and low maintenance system of power collection and distribution allowed for the electrification of 'Heavy' rail operations such as passenger and freight railway lines. The third rail system also allowed for more efficient tunnel

150

*construction and underground train operation.
This type of power distribution system was
implemented on Subway, railway and rapid transit
lines around the world. Third rail systems have
been used in the New York City Subway System
since its inception and continues to be used
today.*

Woods' other inventions included an improved air
brake (a patent he sold to Westinghouse), and an
improved telephone transmitter. In recognition of
Granville T. Woods and the contributions his inventions
made to the NYC Subway System, a *Granville T. Woods
Award for Excellence* has been established by the city of
New York to be awarded annually to an MTA employee
for innovation and excellence.

Elias Howe - Elias was born on July 9, 1819,
in Spencer, Massachusetts. In his early days he apprenticed in the
textile industry[112] at a manufacturing plant in Lowell at the age of
sixteen. When the plant went out of business during the Panic of
1837, he had to move to Cambridge, Massachusetts with his
cousin, Nathanial Banks, to work as a mechanic in another textile
facility

As a mechanic his job was to
operate and maintain a carding
machine, which is a mechanical
process that disentangles, cleans and
intermixes fibers to produce a
continuous web or sliver which is a
process that combs fiber, which is
then drawn into long strips where
they are positioned parallel, suitable
for subsequent processing. This
process breaks up locks and
unorganized clumps of fiber and then

69-Elias Howe

151

aligns the individual fibers to be parallel with each other, and is used in preparing wool fiber for spinning.

It was a laborious job, but it did acclimate him to the textile industry, and became essential in the background needed to create his inventive spirit. Like most Americans, many are born and weaned on entrepreneurial spirit, so inventing *things* became natural ways around time consuming tasks. Howe was hungry to put his creative ideas to the test to solve many of the time consuming and painstaking tasks involved in the textile industry.

His first moment came in 1838 when he was apprenticing under a master mechanic in Cambridge who specialized in the manufacture and repair of chronometers and other precision instruments, named Ari Davis. While employed by Davis, Howe envisioned the idea of the sewing machine, but contrary to popular belief, Howe was not the first to put his ideas for a such a machine down on paper. Many others had formulated ideas but ran into difficulty in developing a needle that allowed thread to be secured from the bottom of the cloth. This process was called the "lock stitch".

For one of the most important machines ever devised in elevating civilization and making it possible for the world to clothe itself, it took many years from the time since Charles Weisenthal first took out a patent for a needle to be used for mechanical sewing in 1755.

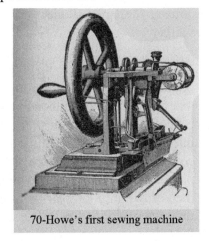

Weisenthal was a German immigrant who lived in London. His mechanical needle had an eyelet on one end and a point on the other for penetrating the cloth to be stitched together, and he was awarded a British patent for his idea.

70-Howe's first sewing machine

An early design in 1790, was one of the first such stabs at solving the automated sewing problem and the design was even rewarded a patented. There were possibly many dozens of inventors who produced working machines, however, locking the stitch from the underside proven to be the biggest hurdle to overcome. According to Graham Forsdyke, researcher at the International Sewing Machine Collectors Society:

"America's first real claim to fame came in 1818 when a Vermont churchman John Adams Doge and his partner John Knowles produced a device which, although making a reasonable stitch, could only sew a very short length of material before laborious re-setting up was necessary.

"One of the more reasonable claimants for inventor of the sewing machine must be Barthelemy Thimonnier who, in 1830, was granted a patent by the French government. "He used a barbed needle for his machine which was built almost entirely of wood. It is said that he originally designed the machine to do embroidery, but then saw its potential as a sewing machine.

"Unlike any others who went before him, he was able to convince the authorities of the usefulness of his invention and he was eventually given a contract to build a batch of machines and use them to sew uniforms for the French army. In less than 10 years after the granting of his patent Thimonnier had a factory running with 80 machines, but then ran into trouble from Parisian tailors. They feared that, were his machines successful, they would soon take over from hand sewing, putting the craftsmen tailors out of work".

That brings us back to Howe who originated significant refinements to the design concepts of all the predecessors, and on September 10, 1846, he was awarded the first United

States patent (U.S. Patent 4,750) for a sewing machine using a lockstitch[113] design. His machine contained the three essential features still used on sewing machines today - a needle

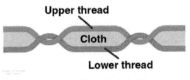

Upper thread
Cloth
Lower thread

71-Howe's lockstitch design

with the eye at the point, a shuttle operating beneath the cloth to form the lock stitch, and an automatic feed . . . the first *practical* sewing machine.

In 1867, Howe was awarded the French Légion d'honneur, and received the Gold Medal at the Paris Exposition, and then went on to design another very important concept for the textile industry, yet after receiving his patent, decided the effort to bring it to fruition was a waste of time. The invention was the ZIPPER!

Between 1865 and 1867, Elias established *The Howe Machine Co* in Bridgeport, Connecticut. He turned operation of the facility over to his sons-in-laws, the Stockwell Brothers. The plant was later run by his son, Benjamin Porter Howe, and his older brother, Amasa Bemis Howe, but continued under the name of 'The Howe Sewing Machine Co'.

72-Elias Howe Stamp

A lasting recognition of Elias Howe was a tribute by the U.S. government when they commemorated him with a 5-cent stamp in the Famous American Inventors series issued October 14, 1940. In 2004, he was inducted into the United States National Inventors Hall of Fame[114] The Hall of Fame documented the struggles he had in defending his unique patent:

" Years of disappointment and discouragement followed before he was successful in introducing his invention, and

154

several imitations which infringed his patent, particularly that of Isaac Merritt Singer (1811-1875), had already been successfully introduced and were widely used.

"His rights were established after much litigation in 1854, and by the date of expiration of his patent (1867) he had realized something over $2,000,000 out of his invention. During the Civil War, he used his wealth to underwrite and equip an infantry regiment for the Union Army, and served in that regiment. He died in Brooklyn, New York, on the 3rd of October 1867."

Chester F. Carlson - Chester Floyd Carlson was born on February 8, 1906, in Seattle, Washington. While he was in his teens, family illness and poverty forced him to become the family's key financial supporter. With no family help for funding a college education, Carlson worked his way through school, earning a Bachelor of Science Degree in physics from California Institute of Technology in 1930.

Unable to find job in California after graduating from Cal Tech, he decided to try the New York market. He landed his first job out of school with P. R. Mallory Company, an electrical manufacturing company working in its patent department. Working with Mallory proved to be an education unto itself and would become the foundation for his future as an inventor.

73-Chester Carlson and his electrophotographic machine

Mallory introduced him to what patents were all about and the procedures one must go through to protect his ideas. When filing for patents it is essential to carefully document inventions, produce drawings, and validate every step of the process, but most importantly to duplicate patent drawings and specifications. In the Forties, he became acutely aware of the inadequacies of the existing photo static copy process, and then later, of thermofax copying processes which tended to fade and have short "shelf lives".

Working at Mallory, allowed Carled a second degree in law in 1939. A year later he was admitted to the New York Bar. While attending NY Law he spent his free time studying possible ways to produce clean copies quickly and make duplicate copies without the use of chemicals, film, and special paper, and possibly ways to increase the life of copies once produced.

His research led him to believe that all the current methods of producing copies posed little prospect for success and that his solution was to think "outside the box". He believed that only *dry coping* would produce satisfactory results. He final came to the conclusion that it might be possible to duplicate documents by making use of *photoconductivity*, and coined the phrase "electrophotography."

Carlson stayed at Mallory until 1945, and eventually became head of the patent department. While at Mallory, Carlson had joined forces with an unemployed German physicist and engineer named Otto Kornei, who offered to help him. Carlson and Kornei, had few funds to put into their project but were able to cover the costs on a modest budget of $10.00 a month. In October 1938, they succeeded in making the first *electrophotographic* copy. The document produced simply read "10-22-38 Astoria".

Through trial and error the copy was produced[115] in a primitive manner. First, Carlson found that if cotton cloth was rubbed vigorously over the surface of a zinc plate coated with a layer of sulfur, the rubbing charged the plate with static electricity.

Whether it was a joke or not, Carlson stated that the same effect would happen by using a rabbit's foot indicating rabbit's fur could be used instead of cotton cloth . . . perhaps that was inferring the rabbit's foot doubled as a lucky charm as well as creating the needed static electricity.

He took a glass slide on which he'd written "10–22–38 ASTORIA" in India ink, pressed it against the charged plate, and placed both the slide and plate under a lamp. After 10 seconds, he removed the plate and dusted it with a fine powder. When he blew on the powder, the image 10–22–38 ASTORIA shone on the plate. In effect, the intense illumination produced an invisible electrostatic image of the material being copied.

74-The first copied image by Carlson

In order to make the fragile powder image permanent, Carlson carefully pressed a piece of wax-coated paper over the prepared plate. The powder adhered to, and fixed upon the surface of the waxed paper.

This innovative method would form the foundation for Carlson's subsequent research and for the industry that grew out of it. The American inventor Chester F. Carlson (1906-1968) had invented the process of xerography which became "the" operation of the office copying machine business first introduced by the Xerox Corporation in 1959, and became *the standard* in the document duplicating business.

75-Modern document processing machine

Carlson retired from Mallory and as *xerography* became too much of a complex technical business, he withdrew from active involvement in the company, but continued on as a consultant. From his xerography patents Carlson became a multi-millionaire, and in later life he engaged in many philanthropic endeavors.

By 1945 his invention brought him sufficient financial security so that he could retire from consulting with Mallory-Royalties from Xerox secured Carlson wealth.

Leo Hendrik Baekeland - Leo was born on November 14, 1863, in Ghent, Belgium. He received his doctorate *maxima cum laude* from the University of Ghent at the age of 21 and taught there until 1889. After graduation, Baekeland and his wife took advantage of a travel scholarship to visit universities in England and America. While in New York, he met Professor Charles F.
Chandler of Columbia University and Richard Anthony, owner of E. & H. T. Anthony & Company, which was the largest supplier and distributors of photographic supplies in the United States during the 19th century.

76-Leo Hendrik Baekeland

Chandler was influential in convincing Baekeland to stay in the United States. Anthony was impressed with Baekeland and his graduation class ranking of *maxima cum laude,* the highest possible honor in doctorate degrees, and offered him a job should he decide to stay in New York.

Baekeland had already received a patent in Belgium in 1887 for his work in photographic plates using water instead of chemicals, and the fit looked to be good for all concerned. The

158

employment opportunity with Anthony provided a financial foundation for he and his wife in the U.S.

Baekeland soon established his own company however, to manufacture his new invention, *Velox*, a photographic paper that could be developed under artificial light. It was the first commercially successful photographic *paper*. In 1899 Baekeland sold his company and rights to the Velox to the U.S. inventor George Eastman for $1,000,000, who developed it into one of the leading products that launched the Eastman Kodak Company.

Baekeland's scientific mind continued to ponder new ideas and he was anxious to proceed in his American Dream. In 1905 he began to search for a synthetic substitute for shellac which eventually led to the discovery of Bakelite[116] (*polyoxybenzylmethylenglycolanhydride*). It is a thermosetting phenol [117] formaldehyde[118] resin, which formed when the mixture was subjected to high temperature and pressure.

Most discoveries are made when an inventor is looking to find a solution to a need. Baekeland's situation was just the opposite. He had discovered a product and needed to find an application. He found it could be used for electrical non-conductivity and heat-resistant properties in electrical insulators, which was a start.

Today the applications for Bakelite are almost too numerous to count, including radio and telephone casings, and such diverse products as kitchenware, jewelry, pipe stems, children's toys, and, because of its durability. . . to make firearms. Baekeland was also the first to find a method of forming it into the thermosetting plastic.

77-Over 15,000 different products have been made using Bakelite®

Baekeland received many honors for his invention and served as president of the American Chemical Society in 1924.

He has been called "The Father of the Plastics Industry" for his invention of Bakelite, which marked the beginning of the modern plastics industry. In 1917 Baekeland became a professor by special appointment at Columbia University.

With a portion of the money he made from the sale of his photographic film to Eastman and revenue from Bakelite, Baekeland purchased "Snug Rock", a house in Yonkers, New York, where he set up his own well-equipped laboratory. He often described himself[119], *"in comfortable financial circumstances, a free man, ready to devote myself again to my favorite studies... I enjoyed for several years that great blessing, the luxury of not being interrupted in one's favorite work."*

Baekeland received many awards and honors in life, which he credits to becoming an American citizen , including the Perkin Medal in 1916 and the Franklin Medal in 1940. In 1978 he was posthumously inducted into the National Inventors Hall of Fame at Akron, Ohio.

What makes America's immigrant population so successful? It has to be their assimilation into the American *Concept*, that even if they don't find success initially, like Baekeland, they truly believe they will eventually make-it here. At Baekeland's death in 1944, the world production of Bakelite, was in the neighborhood of about 175,000 tons, and has been used in over 15000 different products. As an inventor, Baekeland held more than 100 patents[120], including processes for the separation of copper and cadmium, and for the impregnation of wood.

George Washington Carver - In 1941, Time magazine dubbed Carver a "Black Leonardo", a complimentary referral to Leonardo DaVinci. To call someone a DaVinci is only done out of respect. For an African-American who was born into slavery and not even sure of his exact birthday; to live during the Civil War and Reconstruction, such accolades would be envied by any individual.

78-George Washington Carver

When you add-in being humbled by the very issue of slavery and the demeaning social injustice of the Jim Crow Laws; and be subject to the intimidation of the Ku Klux Klan, to rise to such admiration among his fellow man is absolutely an amazing accomplishment.

From the 1860's until his death on the 5th of January 1942 in the middle of World War II, Carver touched the lives of not only the Blacks, but he became an inspiration to all Americans, particularly those in rural America. He was born in Missouri, in the heartland of America, yet being Black he didn't enjoy the real benefits of freedom that white people did.

He was considered brilliant without any stretch of one's imagination based on his research into and promotion of alternative crops for cotton, such as peanuts, soybeans, and sweet potatoes, which became staple nutritional dietary products for farm families trying to survive the Great Depression.

He encouraged poor farmers to grow alternative crops both as a source of their own food and as a source of revenue producing products to improve their quality of life. He developed 44 practical bulletins for farmers which contained 105 food recipes just using peanuts. He found more than 100 products in which peanuts could

79-Professor Carver in his laboratory

be used for the house and farm, including cosmetics, dyes, paints, plastics, gasoline, and nitroglycerin.

His natural affinity for God and the natural order of things made him a leader in promoting environmentalism, well before it became the *"in-thing"* to do in the 21st century. He was honored for his work many times over, including the **Spingarn Medal**[121] of the **NAACP**[122].

As one would expect, understanding the fear and cruelty of slavery as well as the racial prejudice of his day, life was not easy. When George was only a week old, he, a sister, and his mother were kidnapped by **night raiders**[123] from Arkansas. George's brother, James, was rushed to safety from the kidnappers.

The kidnappers sold them just like you would do with any stolen *merchandise* in Kentucky, and it appeared Carver would be lost to his family forever. The story does have a somewhat happy ending. Carver's father hired **John Bentley**[124] to track down the night raiders and gain the return of his family. Unfortunately, only the young Carver was returned.

According to Carver's biography, *"After slavery was abolished, Moses Carver and his new wife Susan, raised George and his older brother James as their own children. They encouraged George to continue his intellectual pursuits, and 'Aunt Susan' taught him the basics of reading and writing"*.

Blacks were not allowed to attend the public school in Diamond Grove, Missouri, so he had to travel 10-miles to a school in Neosho before finally earning a high school diploma at **Minneapolis High School in Minneapolis, Kansas**. He then went on to study botany at Iowa State Agricultural College in Ames. He was the first Black student. Carver's Bachelor's [125] thesis was "Plants as Modified by Man", dated 1894.

Carver quickly gained national recognition and respect as a botanist, and a teacher. He was the first Black faculty member at Iowa State University, and then went on to a long career at Tuskegee Institute.

From the Tuskegee Website[126] we learn much about Carver's life at the University:

> *"As a botany and agriculture teacher to the children of ex-slaves, Dr. George Washington Carver wanted to improve the lot of "the man farthest down," the poor, one-horse farmer at the mercy of the market and chained to land exhausted by cotton.*

> *"Unlike other agricultural researchers of his time, Dr. Carver saw the need to devise practical farming methods for this kind of farmer. He wanted to coax them away from cotton to such soil-enhancing, protein-rich crops as soybeans and peanuts and to teach them self-sufficiency and conservation.*

> *"Dr. Carver achieved this through an innovative series of free, simply-written brochures that included information on crops, cultivation techniques, and recipes for nutritious meals. He also urged the farmers to submit samples of their soil and water for analysis and taught them livestock care and food preservation techniques.*

> *"In 1906, he designed the Jessup Wagon, a demonstration laboratory on wheels, which he believed to be his most significant contribution toward educating farmers.*

"Dr. Carver's practical and benevolent approach to science was based on a profound religious faith to which he attributed all his accomplishments. He always believed that faith and inquiry were not only compatible paths to knowledge, but that their interaction was essential if truth in all its manifold complexity was to be approximated.

"Always modest about his success, he saw himself as a vehicle through which nature, God and the natural bounty of the land could be better understood and appreciated for the good of all people.

"Dr. Carver took a holistic approach to knowledge, which embraced faith and inquiry in a unified quest for truth. Carver also believed that commitment to a Larger Reality is necessary if science and technology are to serve human needs rather than the egos of the powerful. His belief in service was a direct outgrowth and expression of his wedding of inquiry and commitment."

"It is not the style of clothes one wears, neither the kind of automobile one drives, nor the amount of money one has in the bank, that counts. These mean nothing. It is simply service that measures success."

George Washington Carver

George Washington Carver, throughout his academic Career until his death in 1942, set the standard in Agricultural education excellence[127]. He developed techniques to improve soils that become depleted of nitrogen by repeated plantings of cotton and tobacco.

Together with other agricultural experts, he urged farmers to naturally restore nitrogen to their soils by practicing systematic crop rotation; alternating cotton crops with plantings of sweet potatoes or vegetables like peanuts, soybeans and cowpeas. These crops both restored nitrogen to the soil and are good for human consumption. Following the crop rotation farmers began to see improved cotton yields and which gave them additional revenues. Before he had finished his life's work, Carver developed an agricultural extension program for Alabama that was similar to the one at Iowa State University.

Charles Richard Drew - Dr. Charles Richard Drew (1904-1950) was an African-American medical doctor and surgeon who came up with the idea of blood banking[128] and a system for the long-term preservation of blood plasma (he found that plasma kept longer than whole blood). His ideas revolutionized the medical profession and has been instrumental in saving many lives.

His story is inspiring to those minorities who believe "the deck is stacked against them", and that only those of *White Privilege* can achieve success in America.

80-Dr. Charles Richard Drew

Dr. Drew's story is like that of many who open their eyes and apply themselves, not make excuses, and persevere. He, along with the many African-Americans we have written about in this book, simply followed the path of those who are successful, and never looked back. This should remind everyone, regardless of ethnicity, the words of Satchel Paige, the great pitcher in the Negro Baseball League, with the moral that *nobody can defeat you but yourself -*

"Don't look back. Something might be gaining on you . . . Work like you don't need the money.

165

*Love like you've never been hurt. Dance like
nobody's watching. "*

The Charles R. Drew University of Medicine and
Science[129] is named in honor of this brilliant African-American
physician, famous for his pioneering work in blood preservation,
and founder of the concept of "blood bank storing".

The University of Michigan honored Dr. Drew by naming
it's Medicine and Science Program after him to be an inspiration to
others. In spite of his very short life, Drew touch many lives. Very
few of those he touched he actually knew, but those lives which
benefited from his life-saving idea of blood storage, number well
into the tens of millions and probably much greater than that. He
willing shared his knowledge to benefit mankind.

Charles Richard Drew was born June 3, 1904, in
Washington, D.C. He attended Amherst College in Massachusetts,
where he earned his undergraduate degree in science and where his
athletic prowess in track and football earned him the Mossman
trophy[130] as the man who contributed the most to athletics in his
four years on campus.

He taught biology and served as coach at Morgan State
College in Baltimore before entering Canada's prestigious medical
university, McGill University School of Medicine in Montreal. As
a medical student, Drew became an Alpha Omega Alpha Scholar
and won the J. Francis Williams Fellowship, based on a
competitive examination given annually to the top five students in
his graduating class. He received his MD degree in 1933 and
served his first appointment as a faculty instructor in pathology at
Howard University [131] from 1935 to 1936.

He then became an instructor in surgery and an assistant
surgeon at Freedman's Hospital[132], which was founded in 1862 in
Washington, DC. It was the first hospital of its kind to aid in the
medical treatment of former slaves. Later it became the major
hospital for the African-American community in the District of
Columbia and Capitol area.

From the University of Michigan website [133] we learn:

"In 1938, Drew was awarded a two-year Rockefeller fellowship in surgery and began postgraduate work, earning his Doctor of Science in Surgery at Columbia University. His doctoral thesis, 'Banked Blood' was based on an exhaustive study of blood preservation techniques.

"It was while he was engaged in research at Columbia's Presbyterian Hospital that his ultimate destiny in serving mankind was shaped. The military emergency of World War II had a demanding vital need for information and procedures on how to preserve blood.

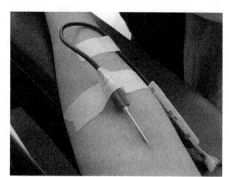

"As the European war scene became more violent and the need for blood plasma intensified, Drew, as the leading authority in the field, was selected as the full-

81-Donating blood at the local blood bank is a charitable contribution everyone can make. It is not just for catastrophic events.

time medical director of the Blood for Britain project. He supervised the successful collection of 14,500 pints of vital plasma for the British.

"In February 1941, Drew was appointed director of the first American Red Cross Blood Bank, in charge of blood for use by the U.S. Army and Navy. During this time, Drew agitated the authorities to stop excluding the blood of African-Americans from plasma-supply networks, and in 1942, he resigned his official posts after the armed forces ruled that the blood of African-Americans

167

*would be accepted but would have to be stored
separately from that of whites."*

Never one to seek publicity, Dr. Drew was such an exceptional surgeon that the NAACP awarded him the Spingarn Medal in 1944 in recognition of his work on the British and American blood banking projects which became the largest blood storages in the world. Honorary degrees followed from Virginia State College with an honorary doctor of science degree in 1945, as did his alma mater Amherst in 1947.

81A-Great American Commemorative Stamp issued in Dr. Drew's name.

On April 1, 1950, Drew was driving with three colleagues to the annual meeting of the John A. Andrews Association in Tuskegee, Alabama, when he was killed in a one-car accident. The automobile struck the soft shoulder of the road and overturned. Drew was severely injured and rushed to nearby Alamance County General Hospital in Burlington, North Carolina, where they had yet to adopt blood banking, and where he was pronounced dead due in part to loss of blood.

His untimely death, left behind his wife, Lenore, four children and a legacy of inspirational, unstinting dedication to service for all people. In 1981, the U.S. Postal Service paid tribute to Drew by issuing in his honor, a stamp in the GREAT AMERICANS Series.

George Eastman - Eastman was born on July 12, 1854, in Waterville, New York to George Washington and Mary Eastman. He was one of those outstanding American inventors with vision. How else could one explain such a statement, because he was largely self-educated, although he attended a private school in Rochester after the age of eight.

82-George Eastman

He must have inherited his business acumen from his father who started a business school, the Eastman Business College[134] in Poughkeepsie, New York, which was for a time one of the largest commercial schools in the United State until the Great Depression caused its closing in 1931.

The curriculum of Eastman's college offered eight business courses—spelling, business writing, correspondence, business arithmetic, bookkeeping, business forms, business habits, and banking, finance and actual business. There were three additional special courses in penmanship, telegraphy, and phonography/typewriting. Foreign students and students with deficiencies could opt to take courses in spelling, reading, arithmetic, grammar or composition.

It is interesting to note that the school required students to attend lectures in topics such as elements of success in business, advertising, manners *and morals*, and political economics. Perhaps our current day educational programs could take a page out of Eastman Business School's notebook, as such subjects are sorely lacking in today's business world.

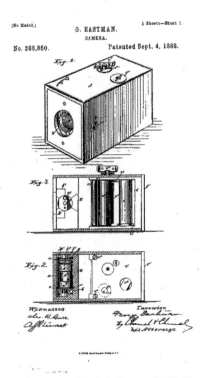

Eastman was truly an American innovator and entrepreneur . He founded the Eastman Kodak[135] Company, popularized the use of *roll film*; helped to bring photography into every household by making picture taking easy and simple; and might be best remembered by the older crowd by developing the *tagline*, "the Kodak moment".

His idea of making cameras that would take pictures from a roll of film helped lead to the invention of motion picture film[136] in 1888 by the world's first film-makers Eadweard Muybridge and Louis Le Prince. A few years later they were followed by Léon Bouly, Thomas Edison, the Lumière Brothers, and Georges Méliès.

In 1884, Eastman patented the first film in roll form which actually worked every time. He had been working at home to develop it, and in doing so he was able to build a camera as well. In 1888, he perfected, what became known as "the" Kodak camera, which was the first camera for everyday use designed specifically to use roll film. He quickly patented his "system", and in 1892, established the Eastman Kodak Company, with his first business location being

84-The most popular camera in the world during its day; The Kodak Brownie loaded with a roll of film.

in Rochester, New York.

From his new location he went about putting together a manufacturing facility and became one of the first firms to mass-produce standardized photography equipment. Like many American inventors, Eastman opened the *proverbial can of worms*, as he watched his fledgling company take off like a rocket. Because of its instant success, he was able to lockout much of the potential competition for years, and Kodak became a giant.

What aided the rapid growth was that the company also manufactured the flexible transparent film devised by Eastman in 1889, which proved vital to the subsequent development of the motion picture industry. Kodak quickly became the "in demand product" on every continent and a *household word* in every city.

In short order, it seemed everybody owned a "Kodak", which gave rise to the new business and subsequent employment of millions of people in the film development business, and opened the door for every media outlet, newspapers, magazines, and others to *bring life* to articles and books. Eastman Kodak put real meaning in the phrase, "a picture is worth a thousand words".

Success was not horded away like many of the industrial giants of the time. Eastman became a leading philanthropist[137], sharing his wealth generously with the schools of dentistry and medicine at the University of Rochester and in with schools in London. He contributed to the Rochester Institute of Technology (RIT) and the construction of several buildings at MIT's second campus on the Charles River.

In addition to donations to schools in the northern part of the U.S., he was also generous with traditional Black institutes, particularly the Tuskegee Institute and Hampton University in Virginia.

Eastman's biographers, estimates that Eastman donated $125 million to these charities. This level of giving made Eastman one of the four largest donors in history. Despite this level of giving, Eastman's philanthropy is largely unknown outside of the institutions to which he donated. With interests in improving the plight of others, he provided funds for clinics in London and other European cities to serve low-income residents.

In his final two years, Eastman had seen his health decline rapidly[138] due to what is now believed to have been spinal stenosis. He gathered a group of his friends at his home in order to witness a change of his will, and when he was done, he asked them to leave and retired to his bedroom. Moments later he was found dead with a gunshot wound to his chest. The following note was by his side: "To my friends: my work is done. Why wait?"

Otto Frederick Rohwedder - Have you ever heard of the saying, *"This is the greatest thing since sliced bread?"*[139] Ever wonder where that saying came from? Well, meet Otto Frederick Rohwedder.

85-Otto Frederick Rohwedder

Rohwedder was born in Davenport, Iowa in 1880. He was the son of Claus and Elizabeth Rohwedder, of German descent, and born into the family's second generation. Like most people who immigrated to the U.S., Rohwedder's father wanted to make sure his children fared better in life than himself when they settled in Iowa. This was the attitude of all those who arrived in America through Ellis Island in New York.

Otto lived with his family and attended Davenport public schools to get a basic education. He stayed at home until around the age of 21, and then at his father's urging, began looking to develop skills in a trade. He became an apprentice to a jeweler while studying optometry in Chicago at, Northern Illinois College of Ophthalmology and Otology[141], the largest optometry college in the country in its day. He graduated with a degree in optometry in 1900.

Rohwedder had a brief career as a jeweler, and became the owner of three jewelry stores in St. Joseph, Missouri. He used his spare time working with watches and jewelry to tinker with gadgets always on the look-out to invent new time-saving things.

He became interested in slicing bread while waiting at a bakery for the baker to slice a loaf of bread. Being done manually, and given the fact that the slices were not uniformly thick, caught his interest. He thought that it was time consuming to cut a regular loaf of bread manually, and the lack of uniform size simply was not really desirable. So he decided to see if he could design a machine to do a better job.

86-Rohwedder's first bread slicer machine

He built a prototype bread slicer which worked fairly well. Word spread quickly in the area about this new machine even if it wasn't tired and proven, so Rohwedder knew he was definitely on to something and decide to go all in. He sold his jewelry stores to fund the development effort and go into the manufacturing business of making bread slicing machines.

In 1917 a fire broke out at the factory where Rohwedder was manufacturing his machine. It destroyed his prototype and blueprints. With the need to get funding again, Rohwedder was delayed for several years in bringing the bread slicer to market.

In 1928 he was back in business and thought he was ready to go to market. His first bread slicing machine was installed at Bench's Bakery, in Chillicothe, Missouri. Unfortunately, with the daily use of the machine, it began falling apart after about six months, but he was not disappointed, because the bakery loved it and Bench's customers like the way it uniformly sliced their bread . . . it just need to be made more rugged.

By 1929, he had beefed-up the machine and he felt ready for business. Sales of the machine to other bakeries increased and his bread slicer slowly became available across the country. Gustav Papendick of St. Louis liked the slicer but wanted some way to mechanically wrap the loaf of sliced bread. He tried using rubber bands to hold the loaf together while it went through a wrapping machine, but that failed. Papendick finally invented a wrapping machine that worked and got his first patent. With bread now being able to be sold already packaged, people went crazy and bread sales increased by as much as 80% for the bakeries that automated their bread slicing.

Large bakeries jumped on the sliced-bread bandwagon. Holsum Bread, today one of the region's largest bread companies, began selling sliced bread. Holsum was the brand of bread marketed by the Campbell Taggart Co. The founder, Winfield Campbell, had started in 1925 in Kansas City, and his use of the slicer was an tacit endorsement for Rohwedder.

Rohwedder's goal was to develop a nationwide association of bakeries that could provide a brand of baked goods throughout the country. A.L. Taggart became his partner. Soon after the company had grown to 19 bakeries in nine states and all were turning out loaves of sliced and packaged bread.

Another success story for the books. Hard work and perseverance proved to pay off for Rohwedder, and those who purchased his bread slicing machine. By 1936 he had seven patents approved all having to do with bread slicing and handling.

The public loved the convenience of sliced bread and, by 1929, Rohwedder's Mac-Roh Company was feverishly meeting the demand for bread-slicing machines. By the following year, the Continental Baking Company was selling sliced bread under the *Wonder Bread* label. Having achieved success, Mr. Rohwedder had time to reflect on his invention. In the June 1930 issue of the Atlanta-based bakery trade journal, *New South Baker*, Rohwedder had this to say:

> *"I have seen enough bakers benefit in a big way from Sliced Bread to know that the same results can be obtained by any baker anywhere if he goes about the matter correctly. A good loaf, a proper presentation of Sliced Bread to the grocers and a truthful, clean advertising program based upon successful experiences and the baker can build his business far beyond what he could do without Sliced Bread . . . We are continuing our experimental and developmental work confident in the belief that the real possibilities of Sliced Bread have scarcely been scratched."*

His original bread slicing machine is in the Smithsonian Institution in Washington, DC.

Dr. John Stith Pemberton -

Dr. Pemberton was born on July 8, 1831, in Knoxville, Georgia. His father was James Pemberton, the brother of Confederate General, John Clifford Pemberton[141], who was noted for his defeat and surrender in the critical Battle of Vicksburg[142] in the summer of 1863. He entered the Reform Medical College of Georgia in Macon, which suspended operations during the Civil War and

87-John Pemberton

175

never reopened. He graduated in 1850, at the age of nineteen, and was licensed to practice pharmacy.

Pemberton married Ann Eliza Clifford Lewis in Macon in 1853, and served with the Confederate Army's Third Georgia Cavalry Battalion through the Georgia State Guard during the Civil War. Ironically his service to the Confederacy became the road down which Pemberton was able to develop the world famous Coca Cola, the most popular beverage of all time.

In April 1865, while serving as a lieutenant colonel, he was wounded in the Battle of Columbus (Georgia) and sustained injury from a saber when he was slashed across his chest. Like many of the wounded veterans, he became addicted to the morphine[143] which was used during the war to ease pain.

Back to civilian life after the war . . . As a pharmacist, Pemberton sought a cure for his morphine addiction. In 1866, he started working on painkillers that would serve as *opium-free alternatives to morphine*.

COCA-COLA
SYRUP ⟡ AND ⟡ EXTRACT.

For Soda Water and other Carbonated Beverages.

This "INTELLECTUAL BEVERAGE" and TEMPERANCE DRINK contains the valuable TONIC and NERVE STIMULANT properties of the Coca plant and Cola (or Kola) nuts, and makes not only a delicious, exhilarating, refreshing and invigorating Beverage, (dispensed from the soda water fountain or in other carbonated beverages), but a valuable Brain Tonic, and a cure for all nervous affections — SICK HEAD-ACHE, NEURALGIA, HYSTERIA, MELANCHOLY, &c.

The peculiar flavor of COCA-COLA delights every palate; it is dispensed from the soda fountain in same manner as any of the fruit syrups.

J. S. Pemberton;
⟶ Chemist, ⟵
Sole Proprietor, Atlanta, Ga.

88-CocaCola poster complying with non-alcohol temperance movement.

His first attempt, in reality the first Coke, was *Dr. Tuggle's Compound Syrup of Globe Flower*. It contained Cephalanthus occidentalis[144] which is considered toxic due to the presence of cephalathin[144-1]. Pemberton probably calculated just enough toxicity to dull the pain, but it wasn't very effective.

He next began experimenting with coca and coca wines, eventually creating his own version of Vin Mariani, containing kola nut and damiana, which he called *Pemberton's French Wine Coca*[145]. Whether or not these concoctions of what we now know as Coca Cola proved to be of any value in curing addiction, we can only surmise that they didn't get the job done.

The end of the Civil War brought about *Reconstruction* and an age of temperance in Fulton County, Georgia, so Pemberton had to find an alternative to his French Wine Coca, as it contained alcohol from the fermenting process. He relied on Atlanta drugstore owner-proprietor Willis E. Venable[146] to test, and help him perfect, the recipe for a new beverage, which he formulated by trial and error.

"With Venable's assistance, Pemberton worked out a set of directions for its preparation that eventually included blending the base syrup with carbonated water by accident when trying to make another glass. Pemberton decided then to sell it as a fountain drink rather than a medicine. Frank Mason Robinson came up with the name "Coca-Cola" for the alliterative(the repetition of similar sounding words) name, which was popular among other wine medicines of the time. This new beverage first went on sale to the public on May 8th, 1886."

Pemberton made many health claims for his product, touting it as a "valuable brain tonic" that would cure headaches, relieve exhaustion and calm nerves, and marketed it as "delicious, refreshing, pure joy, exhilarating," and "invigorating". With public concern about the drug addiction, depression, and alcoholism among war veterans, there was definitely a market among the male population.

89– CocaCola advertising sign from Tennessee

With the women of The South", a condition called *neurasthenia*[147] (an ill-defined medical condition characterized by lassitude, fatigue, headache, and irritability, generally associated chiefly with emotional disturbance) was widely diagnosed by doctors. Pemberton seized upon that opportunity to state in fact that his beverage would control the disease.

Pemberton's elixir being advertised as particularly beneficial *for all those whose sedentary employment causes nervous prostration"*, Coca Coke looked to fit the bill as a cure-all for any condition. Pemberton's claims helped to locally popularize the beverage. The old English Proverb spells it all out, "timing is everything".

Soon after Coca-Cola was on the market, Pemberton fell ill and nearly filed for bankruptcy. He was sick and desperate so he began selling his rights to his business partners in Atlanta. His financial difficulty stemmed from his continued addiction to morphine.

Pemberton was quoted[148] as saying he had a hunch that his formula *"some day it will be a national drink"*, so he attempted to retain a share of the ownership to leave to his son. But Pemberton's son wanted the money. So in 1888 Pemberton and his son sold the remaining portion of the patent to Asa Candler[149].

His son continued to sell an alternative to his father's formula, but sadly, only six years after Charles Pemberton died, his son also died - an opium user himself.

Orville and Wilbur Wright - Wilbur and Orville Wright were American inventors and pioneers of aviation. In 1903 the Wright brothers achieved the first powered, sustained and

controlled airplane flight. Getting a plane off the ground was one thing, but two years later when they built and flew the first fully practical airplane, it opened the

90-Orville and Wilbur Wright . . . "The Fathers of Modern Aviation"

door to man's ability soar with the birds, only higher, faster, and better.

Man has been infatuated with flight since he first saw birds fly. The thought of flying goes back thousands of years. Men on every continent had a vision to soar with the birds. People have long had an obsession with flight[150].

Characters from legends and fairy tales often have the surprising ability to take off from the solid Earth and glide effortlessly through the air. One of the earliest accounts of flight comes from Greek mythology. It is the story of Daedalus[151]:

> *"Daedalus managed to get out of the Labyrinth - after all, he had built it and knew his way around. Daedalus decided that he and his son Icarus had to leave Crete and get away from King Minos, before he brought them harm.*
>
> *"However, Minos controlled the sea around Crete: the king kept strict watch on all vessels, permitting none to sail without being carefully*

searched by his soldiers. Since Minos controlled the land and sea routes, and there was no route of escape there. Daedalus realized that the only way out was by air. **But only the gods could fly!**

75.   *Dædalus Icaro alta nimis ambienti orbatur.*

91-Ancient mythology and the flight of Daedalus

"To escape, Daedalus built wings for himself and Icarus, fashioned with feathers held together with wax. Daedalus tried the wings on himself first and was satisfied that his plan would work.

"Before taking off from the island, Daedalus warned his son to follow closely behind him. He sternly cautioned Icarus not to fly too close to the sun, as it would melt his wings, and not too close to the sea, as it would dampen them and make it hard to fly.

"They successfully flew from Crete, but Icarus grew exhilarated by the thrill of flying and began getting careless. The father and son passed the islands of Samos, Delos and Lebynthos, and the further away from Crete they flew, the more cocky became Icarus.

"Forgetting his father's stern advice, Icarus flew too close to the sun god Helios, pulling

180

the sun behind his chariot high in the sky. The wax holding together his wings softened and melted from the heat and, try as he might, Icarus could not prevent the feathers from falling off his body. Furiously he flapped his arms, but soon no feathers at all were left and he fell to his death, drowning in the sea, as his helpless father with anguish watched his son perish.

"His father cried, bitterly lamenting his own arts, and called the land near the place where Icarus fell into the ocean Icaria in memory of his child. The Icarian Sea, where he fell, was forever named after him and it is said that the great hero Heracles (Hercules), who was passing by, gave him proper burial."

The Wright Brothers, Wilbur and Orville accomplished what thousands of inventors set out to do. Many of those early pioneers of flight died believing they really could fly.

Wilbur Wright was born on April 16, 1867, near Millville, Indiana. He was the middle child in a family of five children. His father, Milton Wright, was a bishop in the Church of the United Brethren in Christ. His mother was Susan Catherine Koerner.

As a child Wilbur's playmate was his younger brother, Orville, who was born four years later in 1871. Neither boy attended college, and no, they were not engineers, mathematicians, or

92-Early vision of flight from every continent. Depiction here is India

181

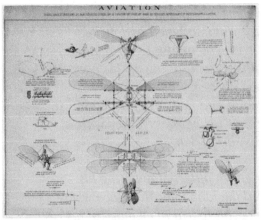

93-Through Europe man dreamed of soaring with the birds though commercial applications were probably not of paramount importance to those with such dreams.

displayed any signs of genius. They, like most Americans were simply *ordinary*.

Wilbur and Orville's infatuation with flying began in 1878,when their father brought back a small model helicopter toy for his boys. It was made of cork, bamboo and paper, powered by a rubber band to twirl its blades. The model was based on a design by the French aeronautical pioneer Alphonse Pénaud[151].

The boys were absolutely amazed that the toy actually flew and from that moment on Wilbur and Orville were hooked on aeronautics and flying.

Though neither of the brothers were college educated that does not mean they were dull or dumb. Wilbur was a bright and studious child, and excelled in all of his school subjects. He had an outgoing and energetic personality. He had planned on attending Yale University but in the winter of 1885-86, he was badly injured in an ice hockey game, when another player's stick hit him in the face. The accident changed the course of Wilbur's life.

The accident drove Wilbur into a state of depression and he did not graduate from high school choosing instead to drop out. He cancelled his plans for college and spent most of his time at home reading and caring for his mother who was sick with tuberculosis. She died shortly after he left high school.

The boys were entrepreneurs from the start. In 1889 they opened a newspaper called the *West Side News*, with Orville as the publisher and Wilbur doing the editing. They also took an interest

94-German aviator Otto Lilienthal

95-German aviator Otto Lilienthal died in a crash of one of his winged gliders shown here.

in bicycles and Orville decided he needed a bicycle repair shop to go along with his duties as publisher of the paper. Bicycling was a current fad at this point in time, much as it is today, so naturally the boys had to design their own bicycle.

Whatever venture the two close brother became involved in, they still maintained the idea of *manned-flight* on their minds. They would occasionally follow inventors who were looking to be the first in flight and paid particular attention to a German named Otto Lilienthal. When Lilienthal died in a self-made glider crash, the brothers decided they really needed to be involved in their own experiments with flight.

It looked as though most of those searching for the secrets

96-Preparing for the first flight . . . Primitive!

of flying were focusing on the principles of gliding, much the way birds did. So they started with gliders, determined to develop their own successful design. They knew that they would need to be in an area where there was strong enough wind to permit gliding and decided to move to Kitty Hawk, North Carolina, on the east coast near the Atlantic Ocean.

Wilbur, the avid reader of the two, read everything he could find on aeronautics, and Orville set to work trying to figure out how to design wings for flight. The first place to start involved a lot of bird watching and he noticed the correlation of balance and control,

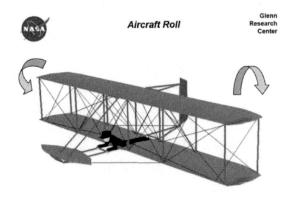

98-The problem with flight is the necessity to maintain 3-dimensional control of the aircraft's movement. Up and down, the tendency of the wings to "roll", and the need for directional control or turning right or left. The Wright Brothers mastered all three with the use of cables.

and tried to emulate this, when he developed a concept called "wing warping"[153].

It was the major breakthrough of the Wright brothers because it gave them the ability to control and maneuver their aircraft. That was followed by discovering a method to control "roll"[154]. The tips of their wings could be twisted relative to the rest of the wing by a series of cables.

When they added a moveable rudder, the Wright brothers found they had the magic formula - up and down, the ability to turn directions, and the ability to control roll. After much trial and error with gliding and several attempts to achieve flight with power, they finally achieve success.

On December 17, 1903, they accomplished their first free, controlled flight with a power-driven, heavier-than-air machine. Wilbur flew their plane for 59 seconds, at 852 feet. It was an extraordinary

97– Wright Brothers First powered flight in 1903

achievement, and began one of the greatest advancement in the course of human events . . . the ability of man to fly.

In all things there are naysayers, and as hard as it might seem to believe, the Wright Brothers found their fair share. The Americans of all people, seeing the great leaps of mankind through new inventions, scoffed at the "value" of the *contraption* the boys had built. Like most critics, they had no vision of what they were seeing.

The Wright brothers had accomplished what the greatest aeronautical minds of the time couldn't see . . . They found the secrets of flight, the actual THEORY of flying.

Not to be dispirited at the lack of enthusiasm in America, Wilbur set-off to Europe to find more success convincing the public about the future of flight, and of course, sell airplanes.

After America had gained its freedom from the England, and after defeating the French and Spanish in war, you would think the Europeans in general, would have little use for anything American. It was in France however, where Wilbur found a much more receptive audience. He was warmly received and made many public flights, giving plane rides to officials, journalists and statesmen,. He created an atmosphere like a hometown county fair fun zone called a "Midway"[154-1] .

In 1909 Orville joined his brother in Europe, as did their younger sister Katharine. Together they became huge celebrities and were hosted by royals, heads of state, and were constantly featured in the press.

The Wrights began to sell their airplanes in Europe, before returning to the United States in 1909, at which time Americans were prepared to listen. The brothers became wealthy businessmen, filling contracts for airplanes in Europe and the United States.

What made the Wright brothers successful was that they were almost eager to share the credit for their accomplishments. While they both had sharp business minds and were alive with entrepreneurial spirit, Wilbur was the business mind and executive of the operation, serving as president of the Wright company. Orville became the co-pilot, probably much due to yielding to the age of his older brother.

I don't know what is was about those who met the Wright brothers in Europe that was lacking from the American's they left standing on the shores down at Kitty Hawk. They had vision as to what air travel was all about while Americans just didn't see the whole picture. This was contrary to most advancements made in moving civilization forward by American ingenuity. It makes one want to scratch his head.

99-WWI planes were prepared to do battle

100-WWI planes could wipe out ground troops

101-WWII Bombers destroyed whole cities below

102-WWII Fighters could shoot down bombers

186

When America did finally come around, the world was headed toward the biggest event up to that time in history . . . World War I. Even with the onset of fighting it took a while before someone actually saw the value of airplanes, and when that finally happened there was a mad dash to build planes with a focus on maneuverability, power, and performance, and a "California Gold Rush mentality", to enlist and train pilots to fly them. Airplanes changed the face of war, and altered the entire focus over weapons superiority

103-B 2 Stealth Bomber over the Gulf

104-Stealth planes with laser guided missiles

Following the war, with their value firmly established, airplanes began to rapidly change the way companies and the government conducted business. The airplane could fly the mail to a destination long before any other mode of transportation could guarantee arrival. Coast to coast travel was reduced to hours instead of days - just what was needed to keep up with America's horse-race pace to industrialize the country.

By the time World War II arrived, the airplane became the most valuable weapon known to man. Planes could reduce the battlefield size, destroy whole armies, sink ships before any defensive maneuver could

105-Commercial airliners carry 500+ passengers

occur, and wipe-out battlefield armor more effectively than anything man had imagined up 'til now.

While most countries had spent unbelievable sums of money building battleships and cruisers, airplanes showed the world they could reduce the size of any navy in the world in the matter of minutes with superior air power. Airplanes made history during World War II and proved beyond any shadow of doubt that airpower would forever reign supreme in warfare. The Wright Brothers invention of manned flight showed the world that with the advent of the atomic age and with The Bomb and other weapons that could be delivered by airplanes, man had reached the point of possible total annihilation. Today we see the future of aircraft as being only limited by one's mind.

The death and legacy of the Wright Brothers will never be forgotten. Wilbur[155], had a life that was very short lived. He was diagnosed with typhoid on a trip to Boston in April 1912, and died on May 30 at his family home in Dayton, Ohio. Milton Wright wrote in his diary, "A short life, full of consequences. An unfailing intellect, imperturbable temper, great self-reliance and as great modesty". Orville[156] went on to develop technology for the U.S. Army and died in Dayton on January 30, 1948.

Willis Haviland Carrier - Carrier was born on November 26, 1876, to Duane Williams Carrier and Elizabeth R. Haviland. The first family member to reach America was Thomas Carrier in 1622, and who is said to have been a political refugee from the country of Wales. Because of his status as a refugee, there is evidence that Thomas assumed the last name of "Carrier".

Initially things didn't go well for Mr. Thomas Carrier. He married Martha

106-Young Willis Carrier

188

Allen, whose father was one of the first founders of the town of Andover, Massachusetts. Life kind of started downhill for Thomas when his wife Martha, was accused of being a witch[157]. She was arrested and her two sons testified against her after being tortured, which was a common occurrence during the Salem Witch Trials. Politically influential New England Puritan minister Cotton Mather denounced her and she was promptly hung on August 19, 1692.

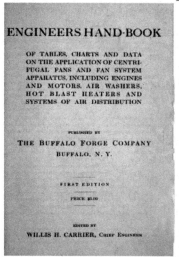

ENGINEERS HAND-BOOK

OF TABLES, CHARTS AND DATA
ON THE APPLICATION OF CENTRI-
FUGAL FANS AND FAN SYSTEM
APPARATUS, INCLUDING ENGINES
AND MOTORS, AIR WASHERS,
HOT BLAST HEATERS AND
SYSTEMS OF AIR DISTRIBUTION

PUBLISHED BY
THE BUFFALO FORGE COMPANY
BUFFALO, N. Y.

FIRST EDITION
PRICE $1.00

EDITED BY
WILLIS H. CARRIER, Chief Engineer

107-Engineers Hand-Book

Many of us have skeletons in our closet and thankfully people have short memories, but the Carriers continued to live in New England until 1799, when they headed west into the Mohawk Valley in western New York. 37 years later, they moved to Erie County, New York, where Willis Carrier was born. Willis' mother died when he was eleven years old.

He earned a degree in engineering from Cornell University, and went to work in Buffalo, New York, for the Buffalo Forge Company. While at Buffalo Forge, Carrier co-wrote and edited the *Engineers Hand-Book*, which became required reading for engineering students.

There are many among us that believe we Americans have it too easy. We are spoiled, and according to the liberal elite, American entrepreneurs have not accomplished much of anything without help from the federal government. "You didn't build it", was a refrain we heard often during the 2012 presidential elections.

So too, there are many people who live in America, that do not appreciate how the many discoveries and inventions developed here have made life better for not only the U.S. citizen, but for people the world over. Some have gone so far as to believe that the invention of things like air conditioning are bad and ruining our environment.

One example is Stan Cox, an environmentalist who advocated in the Washington Post[158], that Americans should abandon their air conditioners and that the residents of Washington DC should embrace the heat wave that hit the region here in 2016:

> *"Washington didn't grind to a sweaty halt last week under triple-digit temperatures. People didn't even slow down. Instead, the three-day, 100-plus-degree, record-shattering heat wave prompted Washingtonians to crank up their favorite humidity-reducing, electricity-bill-busting, fluorocarbon-filled appliance: the air conditioner.*

> *"This isn't smart. In a country that's among the world's highest greenhouse-gas emitters, air conditioning is one of the worst power-guzzlers. The energy required to air-condition American homes and retail spaces has doubled since the early 1990s. Turning buildings into refrigerators burns fossil fuels, which emits greenhouse gases, which raises global temperatures, which creates a need for — you guessed it — more air-conditioning . . .*

> *"Saying goodbye to A.C. means saying hello to the world. With more people spending more time outdoors — particularly in the late afternoon and evening, when temperatures fall more quickly outside than they do inside — neighborhoods see a boom in spontaneous summertime socializing.*

> *"Rather than cowering alone in chilly home-entertainment rooms, neighbors get to know one another. Because there are more people outside, streets in high-crime areas become safer. As a result of all this, a strange thing happens: Deaths from heat decline. Elderly people no longer die alone inside sweltering apartments, too afraid to*

venture outside for help and too isolated to be
noticed. Instead, people look out for one another
during heat waves, checking in on their most
vulnerable neighbors"

This notion of course, is crazy. I believe Mr. Cox's line of reasoning typifies what is wrong in our school systems and that serious discussions of America's contribution to the advance of civilization is simply never brought up. Many school teachers spend more time talking about political correctness than things that are really important. If we do not teach the historic facts about America, the *greatness* of our country will have as little meaning to our children as it does for Mr. Cox.

According to a reputable builder, Ivan Widjaya[159] (and he is definitely on the side of the vast majority of the people world-wide), *"An HVAC (air conditioning system) is expensive; however, while the upfront costs may seem phenomenal, the returns definitely outweigh the negatives. When an office environment is 30% more comfortable, the costs will be recouped over time. For example, if you have three office workers that are increasing their productivity by 30%, theoretically you'll be getting the value of a whole other worker; in addition, consider the salary, recruitment costs and equipment costs of hiring someone new".*

If one were to take Mr. Cox's *comfort argument* out of the debate, but concentrate if you will, on the health issues that air conditioning provides for those in hospitals; the storage of food, transportation of perishable goods, control of mold, mildew, bacteria, fungus and pests, his words lose their meaning very quickly. Properly conditioned air improves the learning ability of our school children, and makes any conjecture about supposed *adverse effects* on our environment seem more than ridiculous.

From Carrier's website history section, "In May 1922, Willis Carrier unveiled his single most influential innovation[160], the *centrifugal refrigeration machine* (or "chiller"). Over the next decade, the centrifugal chiller would extend the reach of modern air conditioning from textile mills, candy factories and pharmaceutical labs to the revolutionary work of ensuring human comfort in theaters, stores, hospitals, offices and homes". In short, when workers are comfortable, their productivity, as stated by Mr. Widjaya, is vastly improved.

Certainly the environmentalists are right about one thing in their rhetoric: America may create more pollution than the other 195 countries on earth. What they leave out is that to produce anything, it requires energy, and a by-product of energy generally creates some pollution. Those early cave dwellers produced little in the way of anything tangible and were basically *pollution free*.

So to those like Mr. Cox, perhaps their suggestion would be to go back to the Stone Age and give up on the pursuit of progressing civilization. No other country on the face of the earth has the production capabilities of the U.S., and in fact, it is our production capabilities that produce the goods for global consumption and the taxable revenue needed to support U.S. aid to countries in need.

Back to Willis Carrier - In 1902, in response to a quality control problem experienced at the Sackett-Wilhelms, a New York lithographing and publishing company located in Brooklyn, Carrier submitted drawings for what became recognized as the world's first modern air conditioning system. These were not the only drawings that Carrier had prepared for Buffalo Forge Company. He also created designs for heating plants, a lumber dry kiln and a coffee dryer, which were far advanced for the times.

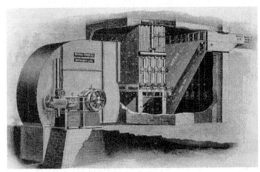

When Sackett-Wilhelms contracted with Buffalo Forge, the 1902 installation was the first air conditioning system and most unique because it allowed for *humidity control*, which is most essential in the printing business. The

108-First A/C System

192

system set the standards which still hold true today that air conditioning, which we think of as "cool air", must accomplish four things in *conditioning* the air:

1.) The most obvious is control temperature.
2.) control humidity.
3.) control air circulation and ventilation.
4.) cleanse the air.

From Page 41, of Margaret Ingels' book titled, **Willis Haviland Carrier: Father of Air Conditioning we read:**

> *"In December 1911, Carrier presented the most significant and epochal document ever prepared on air conditioning – his 'Rational Psychrometric Formulae'– at the annual meeting of the American Society of Mechanical Engineers (ASME). It became known as the 'Magna Carta of Psychrometrics.' This document tied together the concepts of relative humidity, absolute humidity, and dew-point temperature, thus making it possible to design air-conditioning systems to precisely fit the requirements at hand.*

109-First multi-story A/C System

> *"With the onset of World War I in late-1914, the Buffalo Forge Company, for which Carrier had been employed 12 years, decided to confine its activities entirely to manufacturing. The result was that seven young engineers pooled together their life savings of $32,600 to form the Carrier Engineering Corporation in New York on June 26, 1915. The seven were Carrier, J. Irvine Lyle, Edward T.*

Murphy, L. Logan Lewis, Ernest T. Lyle, Frank
Sanna, Alfred E. Stacey, Jr., and Edmund P.
Heckel. The company eventually settled on
Frelinghuysen Avenue in Newark, New Jersey.

"Despite the development of the centrifugal
refrigeration machine and the commercial growth of
air conditioning to cool buildings in the 1920s, the
company ran into financial difficulties, as did many
others, as a result of the Wall Street Crash in
October 1929.

"In 1930, Carrier Engineering Corp. merged
with Brunswick-Kroeschell Company and York
Heating & Ventilating Corporation to form the
Carrier Corporation, with Willis Carrier named
Chairman of the Board."

The company became a subsidiary of United Technologies
Corporation in 1980. The Carrier Corporation remains a world
leader in commercial and residential HVAC and refrigeration. In
2007, the Carrier Corporation[160-1] had sales of more than $15
billion and employed some 45,000 people.

Josephine Cochrane - We all know the drill. It has been this way since man became civilized enough to eat food from dish plates. It is the same everywhere in the world . . . *"It's your turn to do the dishes"*.

It is heard at the end of every meal, and it's a task nobody likes, but it always gets done; and done a lot quicker than doing dishes by hand, thanks to Josephine Cochrane's dishwashing machine.

110-Josephine Cochrane 1st dishwasher

Though her story doesn't mention it, I am sure she was finally tired of the dishwashing arguments herself in trying to get help with the dishes. Josephine was a wealthy woman, was always having dinner parties, and she wanted to find a faster way of cleaning up after one of her get-togethers. In 1886, she got tired of waiting for someone else to invent a dishwasher and proclaimed, *"If no one else is going to invent a dishwashing machine, I'll do it myself!"*

This is another of the great American inventions that we never tell our children about, yet when you want to hear kids *really scream*, tell them the dishwasher is broken and they have to do the dishes in the sink by hand. Oh, the things they take for granted!

The dishwasher . . . it's one of the first things on the purchase list when you build or purchase your home or remodel the kitchen. Thanks to Josephine's invention, the words we hear today is not so much about washing the dishes, but arguments over whose turn it is to empty the darn thing.

195

Josephine Garis Cochrane was born on March 8, 1839, Ashtabula County, Ohio, she was the inventor of the first commercially successful hand-powered dishwasher which was constructed with the help of a mechanic named George Butters.

Inventing "things" was not new to Josephine's family; her grandfather, John Fitch[160], was an inventor who was awarded a steamboat patent. I guess this would give the people who believe America is just another *run-of-the-mill countries* in relation to the other 195, and is nothing special, would probably attribute her invention prowess with pure luck or something to do with the "gene pool".

She was raised in Valparaiso, Indiana, and attended private school until the school burnt down. Her father sent her off to live with her sister in Shelbyville, Illinois. After high school graduation, Cochrane's life took a traditional turn. She married 27 year old William Cochran at age 19. In 1857, her husband took off for the California Gold Rush like many others who were looking to strike it rich.

He returned in 1861, with the sobering realization that money is better made by hard work and using your brain. In Shelbyville he made his mark and fortune in the dry goods business along with other investments he made from his profits . . . the usual success story of those willing to take advantage of the opportunities in America.

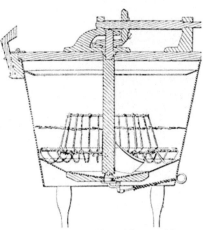
111-Cochrane's dishwashing machine

Because of her husband's success as a businessman, she had servants to do dishes, but the amount of chipping manual washing caused led her to seek a mechanical solution. Making a machine to wash dishes was her first goal and not really to make a new startling discovery from which to reap millions in profit.

196

Her friends were very impressed with her new machine and had her make dish washing machines for them, calling them "Cochrane Dishwashers". This is what she began to call it, and later led to the naming of her new company, Garis-Cochrane Manufacturing Company.

Josephine designed the first model of her dishwasher in the shed behind her house located in Shelbyville, Illinois. George Butters[162], the mechanic that assisted her in the construction of the first dishwasher, became her first employee at the dishwasher factory.

She designed the wire racks to hold the dishes and a hand crank to splash soapy water on them, and worked on her invention until it was perfected. She then filed for her patent, which she received in December of 1886, and immediately installed the machine in her kitchen for all to see.

Her husband passed away before she completed her invention, but Josephine continued on by herself, opening the factory and mass producing dishwashers for high end restaurants and hotels, and of course her friends. When Josephine died in 1913 of a stroke believed to be caused by exhaustion, her company was purchased by the Hobart Manufacturing Company.

In 1949 Hobart introduced *home* dishwashers under the *Kitchen Aid* brand, which is now owned by Whirlpool. By the 1950's, dishwashers became a standard feature in all newly constructed homes in America

Stephanie Louise Kwolek - There isn't a law enforcement officer or a soldier alive today, that isn't eternally grateful for the life of Stephanie Kwolek. She was an American chemist who toiled for DuPont Company for over forty years. She is best known for inventing the first of a family of synthetic fibers of exceptional strength and stiffness: poly-paraphenylene terephthalamide—better known as Kevlar®[163].

There is a link to immigration for Kwolek in bringing civilization forward. She was born to Polish immigrant parents in the Pittsburgh suburb of New Kensington, Pennsylvania, in 1923.

113-Stephanie Kwolek inventor of Kevlar®

Her father, John Kwolek , originally *Jan Chwałek*, died when she was ten years old. He was a naturalist and Kwolek spent hours with him exploring the woods and fields near her home filling scrapbooks with nature's treasures. She credits her mother for her interest in fashion and science.

She graduated from the women's college (Margaret Morrison Carnegie College) of Carnegie-Mellon University in 1946 with a BS in Chemistry, and applied for a position as a chemist with the DuPont Company. She interviewed with DuPont's research director, W. Hale Charch.

The interview process went well, but Charch, not being one to make an instant decision, told her he'd get back to her in a couple of weeks. Kwolek's response was that she'd like to know soon as she was already waiting for a reply from another company, and was more interested in an up or down answer at the end of her interview. Her forcefulness got a positive reply.

She never revealed to DuPont that her job would only be temporary because she wanted to go to medical school. She needed the job at Dupont's textile fabrics laboratory in Buffalo, New York, because she did not have the funds to attend medical school. When Dupont's Pioneering Research Laboratory opened in 1950 she was already losing interest in becoming a doctor and so, excepted a move down to Delaware.

At DuPont she worked on many polymer projects which she found most interesting and challenging. She decided she needed to look no further than DuPont for greater challenges, and decided to make it her career. She dropped any pretense of wanting to attend medical school, and dove head-first into researcher in polymer chemistry.

Kevlar opened the door for Kwolek and for DuPont as well. It was an exciting discovery which no one realized at the time, there would be hundreds of applications and vast numbers of products and industries that would be effected. Kwolek's Kevlar became one of the most famous synthetic fibers ever made. It had exceptional strength, stiffness, and durability.

Most people today have heard of Kevlar, from its use in bullet-proof vests, but that's only because the film industry had the "good guys" wearing the Kevlar vest in every action scene. Not often does Hollywood get it right, but with Kevlar, there are thousands upon thousands of law enforcement officers, and military personnel who will be glad to testify as to the validity of those movie scenes.

A USA Today article[164] documented two satisfied customers who are still alive today and not statistics in the files of the Defense Department thanks to Kevlar. An Army private showed a congressional budget official representative (see photo) a flak vest that stopped two bullets from an AK-47 in Afghanistan, during a daylong firefight last year against the Taliban in a snow-covered Afghan valley.

In another instance, N.Y. Navy corpsman Thomas Smith survived an Iraqi ambush on the outskirts of Baghdad this after a bullet ricocheted off his Kevlar vest, leaving a large hole.

113-Army Pfc. Jason Ashline of the 10th Mountain Division, Fort Drum, N.Y. discusses how Kevlar saved his life when he was hit by an AK-47 bullet.

We are confident that going through police files, we would see thousands more satisfied customers of this remarkable product. While Kevlar is best known for its use in bullet-proof and, fragmentation-resistant protective gear used by bomb diffusion device teams, there are more than 200 other applications for this product in boats, airplanes, ropes, cables, tires, tennis racquets, skis, helmets and so forth, with more uses coming all the time.

Like most who invent a new product while working for a company, Kwolek never reaped any financial benefit from DuPont from the sale of Kevlar or the other 28 patents she obtained in their name. That probably doesn't sit well with those who sit on the sidelines and throw rocks at publically held companies, but to many dedicated American workers, there is far more to life than money.

In the business world Kwolek was widely recognized as one of the top women in polymer chemistry and was awarded the DuPont Lavoisier Medal for outstanding technical achievement. As of 2015, she was the only female employee to have received that honor. You will find her name alongside three other women in the National Inventors Hall of Fame, and find that she won many top awards[165] including the National Medal of Technology, the IRI Achievement Award and the Perkin Medal.

James Ritty - Hopefully it is obvious to all that inventing something new does not always lead to wealth and prosperity. Sometimes people just take years and years to see the value of what one person recognizes, and some never see any value at all.

Developing a new product or idea takes sales and marketing skills in order to bring it to market and even more savvy to make it a financial success. Just inventing something and living in America is no slam-dunk that one will get rich off his idea.

114-James Ritty

James Ritty was one such individual that had an idea to stop employee theft in his business. His business? Owning a saloon. To those unfamiliar with the old term *saloon,* people today would call it a *bar* - notorious for shrinkage (employee theft). With a reputation of having a high rate of thievery, one would think Mr. Ritty's new invention would be a sure-fire hit.

James Ritty was born on October 29, 1836, in Dayton, Ohio, where he briefly attended college to study medicine. When the American Civil War broke out, Ritty left school and enlisted in the Fourth Ohio Volunteer Cavalry as a first lieutenant. He served honorably for the duration of the war. He left the Union Army in 1864, having attained the rank of captain.

Ritty opened his first saloon in Dayton, Ohio in 1871, billing his establishment as a business "Dealing in Pure Whiskies, Fine Wines, and Cigars". The time-honored tradition in saloons and honkytonks with employee theft is still a big problem today.

In 1878, while on a ship bound for Europe, Ritty observed a machine that the crew used to count the revolutions of the ship's propellers, and his mind went to work. He inquired how the counter worked and using the same sort of technology, he became convinced that he could solve the theft problem at the saloon.

When he returned to the United States, he commandeered his brother to assist him in applying what he had learned aboard

115-James Ritty's 1879 Cash Register

ship. His brother was a mechanic and had skills he didn't possess himself. Together they built *Ritty's Incorruptible Cashier*. It didn't have a cash drawer, but simply recorded the number of sales and also the number and amount of each sale. The machine allowed Ritty to look at a day's take and balance it with the day's receipts. If they didn't jive, someone was stealing. Ritty had invented the early version of the cash register.

In 1879, Ritty applied for and was granted a patent. It looked like he was the only saloon keeper excited by it. None-the-less he decided to go into business to manufacture and sell cash registers after his patent was approved. Ritty established his company in Dayton, Ohio. Unfortunately, Ritty's invention did not draw much enthusiasm from other business owners, and Ritty's new company quickly closed.

Eventually Ritty sold his patent to a group of Ohio investors. Among them was Jacob H. Eckert, who re-named the company National Manufacturing Company.

As popularity grew so did the need for cash to expand to meet the demand, and in 1884, Echert sold the company to John

Patterson, a businessman who wanted the machine for his retail coal business in Dayton. Patterson got a "deal of a lifetime" for just $6500. Patterson renamed the National Manufacturing Co. to the National Cash Register Company and put the registers into large scale production with a promotional budget to match.

Eighty-four other companies jumped on the bandwagon and entered the business with variations of their own cash registers, between 1888 and 1895, but only three actually survived the competition. Ritty returned to running his saloon until he retired in 1897, and finally passed away from heart failure on March 29, 1918. National Cash Register, continued to improve on Ritty's concept, adding a cash draw to keep the money secure.

116– The cash register became an import accounting tool to help merchants keep records of sales and hold employees accountable

In 1902 The NCR cash register began offering shopkeepers cumulative totals automatically and to provide audit trails of transactions, helping users collect market-research data. In 1906, and engineer in the NCR factory designs the first register to run on an electric motor. Improvements on the original register design continued through the years as NCR grew into a sizeable company.

Ritty's simple idea to help him keep his saloon in business by stopping the internal theft by employees, matured throughout the 20th and 21st centuries, to become a huge conglomerate, which included mergers and acquisitions enabling the company to become publically traded on the New York Stock Exchange.

The new NCR[166] is more than just a cash register company these days with annual revenue nearing $7 billion, of which 44% comes from the sale of products, and 56% of the revenue from services, leaving a net income for shareholders of more than $350 million, while retaining a healthy $500+ million in cash reserves. NCR has grown to 32,000 employees and today its operation are global . . . rest in peace James Ritty!

King Camp Gillette- During the past decade, television and movies have featured actors, both on-the-screen in leading roles, and in key positions in the commercials *unshaved*. To many of us this all started with *Casual Fridays*, and escalated to casual business attire for every day of the week.

It seems Madison Avenue advertising agencies have simply thumbed their noses at proper business decorum as Americans in general, simply accept the unkempt look as normal today.

117-King Gillette

Europeans and the population of many other countries look at the way Americans dress as an insult to civilization, and in particular, those Americans who make a living in the high tech and financial worlds. Gone are the $1000 suits with their silk ties and freshly shined shoes, replaced by a pair of grubby blue jeans, tee shirts, tennis shoes without socks, and an unshaven face.

Along with the physical change in the way business people dress, out the window was thrown much of what was once considered proper business etiquette, honestly, hard work, and meaningful business relationships. It has been going downhill along with the quality of education our children receive in school.

Meet King Camp Gillette . . . Born on January 5, 1855, back when a closely shaved face, perfectly combed hair, and a clean suit with a stiffly starched shirt was the mark of a successful business man. Such a look demanded respect and it was most often extended regardless of whether the well heeled individual was worthy or not.

For thousands of years man has been fighting a battle with his facial hair and spent over 3000 hours during their lives trying to win the endless battle to stay clean-shaven; that is, until the last couple of decades when many men gave-up.

According to the *Modern Gent* website[167], Egyptians shaved their beards and heads which was a custom adopted by the Greeks and Romans about 330BC during the reign of Alexander the Great. Being clean shaven was meant as a defensive maneuver to keep the enemy from grabbing their hair in hand-to-hand combat.

Shaving spread through the world, because men of unshaven societies became known as "barbarians" meaning they were "unbarbered". To not shave one's face would be the equivalent of a women not shaving her legs and underarms, though that practice came somewhat later on the civilization calendar.

For early man to shave, they scraped the hair away with crude items made from stone, flint, clam shells and other material

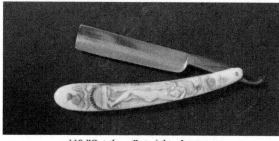

which they sharpened with stone. As man progressed up the civilization chart he reached a point that he began experimenting with bronze, copper and

118-"Cut-throat" straight edge razor

iron razors, honed on finer and finer stone and pumice[168].

Eventually man reached the sophistication of learning to shave with razors made of steel, the first of which were straight edge razors, sharpened and highly polished to a super fine edge. The need to sharpen these razors, which gained the reputation as "throat cutters" for obvious reasons, before each use and re-sharpened (honed) and re-polished using a leather strop, was to cause less irritation and nicks. These tools required sufficient skill, least one inadvertently cut his own throat, which is why the task was usually left up to local barbers in most cases.

A simple rule of thumb was that hair needed to be cut all the time and the longer the hair, the more likely one was to attract lice. The less hair one had the easier life was.

Shaving continued to evolve through the ages. Beginning in the1800's shaving and grooming for men became a self-indulgent pastime thanks in part to George Bryan (Beau) Brummell who was a *dandy* known for his impeccable manners and style of dress. It was said of Brummell that he shaved his face several times a day and pluck out any remaining hairs with tweezers. After inheriting a sizeable fortune, Brummell dedicated himself to becoming famous as gentleman of fashion.

By the late 1800's man entered the Victorian Age and had become extremely critical over his personal appearance. Men found that daily shaving was time consuming and skin irritation became a problem that could only be solved by the use of warm soapy water that would be used to soften the beard. Following a close shave men began using lotions prepared at home using cherry laurel water[169] - a derivative of hydrogen cyanide - being careful not to drink any while using it as an after-shave lotion.

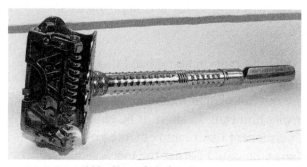
119– Kempft Safety Razor

In 1895, The Kampfe Brothers filed a patent for the first Safety Razor featuring a wire skin guard along one side of the blade's edge. Only one side of the blade was used for shaving which meant the guard had to be removed often for sharpening. The Kampfts followed their first safety razor with a later version a few years later that more closely resembles the razors that were to follow.

1901 - In the United States King Camp Gillette, a salesman for the Baltimore Seal Company came up with the idea for a new type of *disposable* safety razor blade that could be used in a handle-type razor like the Kempft razor, only it never needed to be sharpened. Once it became dull, the user simply threw the blade away. Over the next six years Gillette developed his safety razor kit, complete with handle and a *throw-a-way* package of blades.

King Camp Gillette was born in Fond du Lac, Wisconsin. While working as a salesman for the Crown Cork and Seal Company[170] (today it is known as Crown Holdings Incorporated), in the 1890s, Gillette saw bottle caps, with the cork seal his company made being thrown away after the bottle was opened. He was no dummy, and he recognize the value of a business with a product that was purchased, used once or twice, and discarded.

Being a man who shaved regularly, he was quick to see how such a concept could be applied to razors. Men shaved with straight razors that needed sharpening every day using a leather strop. The newly developed "safety razor concept" wherein a relatively inexpensive razor had recently been invented, but its blades too, dulled quickly and needed continuous sharpening, was not the right answer, but was close. *This was opportunity just knocking at his door.*

With such astute observation he realized that if he could make a *safety* razor that was cheap, could be used several times, and then thrown away instead of sharpening it, such a concept had real possibilities to make him rich. In short, if he could offer consumers a sturdy, permanent razor supplemented by cheap, easily replaceable blades, he could corner the men's facial grooming market *and* create a massive, repeat customer base.

To produce his yet to become world famous *disposable blade concept*, Gillette had many obstacles to overcome. Making them cheap and thin as possible, using inexpensive steel was difficult to work with and sharpen. Overcoming these obstacles was the reason for the delay between *concept* and *production*, but the ever tenacious Gillette stayed diligently on track until he solved the production problems.

The first prototype was produced using Gillette's drawings

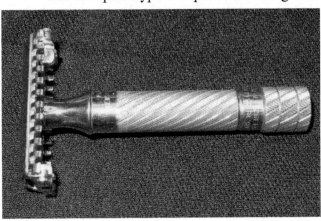

by Steven Porter, his machinist, and after seeing it, Gillette changed a few things and let another machinist and a partner of his, William Emery

120-Gillette safety razor with disposable blades

Nickerson, change the original model with an improved longer handle and sturdier frame so that it could better support the thin steel blade, and then went on to design the machinery to mass-produce it.

From the records of the Gillette Safety Razor Company[171] as it was named, *"Gillette sold 90,884 razors and 123,648 blades, thanks in part to Gillette's low prices, automated manufacturing techniques and good advertising. Sales and distribution were handled by a separate company, Townsend and Hunt, which was absorbed by the parent company for $300,000 in 1906. By 1908, the corporation had established manufacturing facilities in the United States, Canada, Britain, France and Germany.*

"In 1910 King Gillette decided to sell a substantial portion of his controlling share of the company to the company's major investor, John Joyce. Gillette had succeeded in fighting off challenges for control of the company from Joyce in the past, but this time he took approximately $900,000 and bowed out.

"Gillette retained the title of president and frequently visited foreign branches, but he no longer played an active role in company management. Joyce was made vice-president, a position he used to manage day-to-day operations. When Joyce died in 1916, his longtime friend, Edward Aldred, a New York investment banker, bought out the Gillette shares left to Joyce's estate and took control of the company. Aldred remained on Joyce's management team."

A lasting remembrance of the Gillette story was his legacy of the razor and blades business *model*[172], still taught in business schools today. The model is that one item is sold at a low price (or given away for free) in order to increase sales of a complementary good, such as supplies. We see this today being followed by many successful companies, but most notable that come to mind are the computer printer companies. They sell you a low price printer with low capacity ink cartridges, that are replaceable at relatively high prices . . . and we wait in lines to purchase them.

Joseph Gayetty- *Gayetty* Is a name no one recognizes today, yet his invention was considered "The greatest necessity of the ages! Gayetty's medicated paper[173] for the water-closet".

121-Joseph Gayetty

So little is known about Joseph Gayetty that documenting much of his story is one of the most difficult inventors we have the privilege of reviewing. The United States Census Records, shows a Joseph Gayetty lived in New York in 1860 with his family and lists his birthplace as Massachusetts.

From the Prezi website[174] we read: *"Gayetty first marketed toilet paper in 1857 which originally sold for US$0.50 in packs of 500 bearing a watermark of his name"*. . . What did they do before?

"Prior to Gayetty's invention, Americans would stock their restrooms with mail order catalogs so that their pages could be torn out and used as toilet paper". Was it successful? One can only guess as to how successful this was, but one can be sure the catalog companies were not too impressed with how their catalogs *tamed the west.*

The website goes on to further document Gayetty. . . *"Joseph C. Gayetty created the first commercially packaged toilet paper in 1857. His toilet papers were loose, flat, sheets of paper. Joseph founded The Gayetty Firm for toilet paper production in New Jersey and his first factory-made toilet paper was 'The Therapeutic Paper'. This first toilet paper in flat sheets was medicated with aloe. Gayetty named it Gayetty's Medicated Paper. Joseph Gayetty printed his name on every sheet. Unfortunately, this invention failed"*.

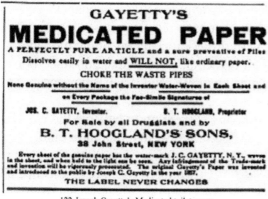

GAYETTY'S
MEDICATED PAPER
A PERFECTLY PURE ARTICLE and a sure preventive of Piles
Dissolves easily in water and <u>WILL NOT,</u> like ordinary paper.
CHOKE THE WASTE PIPES
None Genuine without the Name of the Inventor Water-Woven in Each Sheet and
on Every Package the Fac-Simile Signatures of
JOS. C. GAYETTY, Inventor.   **B. T. HOOGLAND, Proprietor**
For Sale by all Druggists and by
B. T. HOOGLAND'S SONS,
38 John Street, NEW YORK
Every sheet of the genuine paper has the water-mark J. C. GAYETTY, N. Y., woven in the sheet, and when held to the light can be seen. Any infringement of the Trade-mark and invention will be rigorously prosecuted. The original Gayetty's Paper was invented and introduced to the public by Joseph C. Gayetty in the year 1857.
THE LABEL NEVER CHANGES

122-Joseph Gayetty's Medicated toilet paper

Its Impact however, was widely recognized as a necessity of nature but his design didn't sell well, so catalogs pages continued to be the paper of choice for bathroom connoisseurs. His patent however, did open up the subject of the need for commercial toilet paper, a subject most people would not mention in public.

Could it have been a big business back then for Gayetty? Well, you can be the judge. Today toilet paper sales in the U.S. are about a $6 billion dollars industry.

And what does that dollar amount translate to in the average usage per individual per year? The average American uses about 50 pounds of toilet paper each year, totaling millions of rolls per year. We don't need to cry for Mr. Gayetty. Though his idea was not a commercial success for himself, he did lead the way for 3 brothers - Thomas Scott, Irvin Scott, Clarence Scott and their cousins Thomas Seymore and Zerah Hoyt. They established The

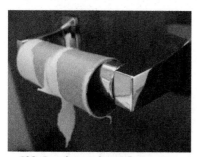

123-A sad experience for anyone

Scott Paper Company[175] in 1874 located in Philadelphia, PA. They began experimenting with bathroom tissue and in 1890 introduced *toilet paper on a roll.*

They quickly became the nation's leading producer of toilet paper, or as we politely call it today, TP. Scott bought large rolls of paper from paper manufacturers and then converted them to become toilet paper on a small roll. The TP was sold through intermediaries, private labelers and drug stores. Scott private labeled the wrappers and cut the paper according to the specification that each reseller wanted. Scott did not want to be associated with this Victorian era "unmentionable" product and didn't want their name appearing on the product, but soon they had some 2000 resellers in the toilet paper business.

The Scott Paper Company[176] went on to become the world's

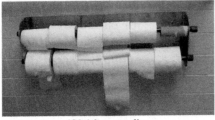

largest manufacturer and marketer of sanitary tissue products with operations in 22 countries. Its products were sold under a variety of well-known brand names, including *Scott Tissue, Cottonelle, Baby Fresh, Scottex* and *Viva*.

124-A happy ending

Consolidated sales of its consumer and commercial products totaled approximately $3.6 billion in 1994, and led to it being acquired by Kimberly-Clark Corp [177] for $9.4-billion . . . the Scott brothers families thank you Mr. Gayetty!

Marion Donovan - Image what life was like for generations before us. The purpose of this book is to acquaint the reader with American inventions that have led to the advancement of civilization. We contend there is no nation on earth that has contributed more to advancing mankind than America, and as the genius of Americans step to the plate to bring forth their ideas . . . and yes, even profit from them . . . imagine how life would be without their contributions. For items of convenience, none has had a greater impact that the *disposable diaper*!

125-Marion Donovan

For millions, if not billions of

mothers, disposable diapers, have given them freedom to travel, work, and enjoy the millions of other tasks, life has found for them to do in raising their families. This is not just confined to the United States. While our detractors of American genius always have something negative to say about American Exceptionalism, the *disposable diaper* is a convenience few in the world could live without today.

In the old days and that is just a half century ago, mom's toiled daily with house work, ironing, and everything needed to support *Joe Husband* who had to go to work every day. When children began to appear (must be magic) she had the added duties of childcare and raising kids. Little did she need to be burdened spending half a day to change, rise, and clean cloth diapers.

Marion Donovan became an inventor out of *necessity*. There were a myriad of problems she saw as needing to be addressed. The first was the diaper situation, which took so much of her time.

Not only did changing diapers eat away at the clock, of which there was no getting around, but the problems caused by a leaky diaper just meant more work for her . . . the urine from the leaky diaper ran onto the bed covers and baby's clothes, which added more "stuff" to be cleaned in the pile of laundry already in the hamper on the basement floor. But even before she could add a dirty diaper to the hamper, it had to be rinsed in the toilet to remove the stool.

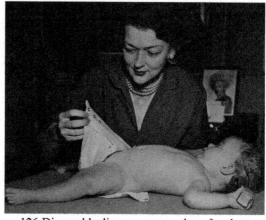

126-Disposable diapers gave mothers freedom

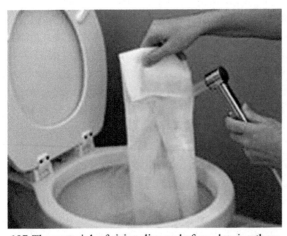

127-The nasty job of rising diapers before cleaning them

Her first invention was to stop the leaky diaper problem. It came about in 1946, when she came up with the idea of using a piece of her shower curtain from her bathroom to create a diaper cover - a plastic cover to be donned outside a diaper . . . neat idea.

In her quest her shower curtain caught her eye and a light went off in her head. Before you could say *waterproof*, the curtain was missing a panel and Mrs. Donovan was up in the attic at her sewing machine. Three years and many shower curtains later she came up with the Boater, a *re-usable diaper cover* made of surplus nylon *parachute cloth so it was breathable*.

Her first *Boater,* as it was called, was sold in 1949 at Saks Fifth Avenue's flagship store in New York City, and patents were later issued in 1951. So well did the Boater work, she was able to sell the idea of the waterproof diaper for $1 million to Keko Corporation. In those days everyone used safety pins to hold diapers in place. Her idea incorporated the use snaps to close the diaper cover, meaning that mothers could do away with safety pins, killing two birds with one stone.

Donovan's next goal was to get rid of so much laundry. She wanted to create a completely *disposable diaper*, and she set out to find a different type of paper that would be absorbent but also pull the moisture away from the baby's skin to prevent diaper rash, which any mother will tell you is a constant problem with wet diapers.

214

She came up with a prototype of a paper diaper and began visiting paper manufacturers. However, no one was interested. The men all responded with the fact that the disposable diaper was *not necessary*, because nobody had ever asked about it. Men are sometimes not to bright. Though she continued to discuss the idea, she was never able to find the right company to manufacture her idea.

128-The time and labor of cleaning and drying diapers

Her list of inventions that allowed women more freedom and better ways to provide for their children had helped spearhead an industrial and domestic revolution by inventing the forerunner of the disposable diaper, for which is she given the credit.

The first totally disposable diaper in the U.S. was introduced by Proctor & Gamble in 1961. The company had purchased the Charmin' Paper Company in 1957, and they assigned one of their chemical engineers, Victor Mills[178], to look into creating new paper products. No one knows for sure whether Victor Mills ever met Donovan, but there was much discussion about paper disposable diapers in the air.

Mills was a grandfather and had probably changed a few diapers in his time; and one can be sure, out of necessity, even had to rinse, launder, and dry them as well. Procter and Gamble credits Mills with suggesting disposable diapers to them, but the early designs still required pins. A short while later P&G changed over to tape closures and completed the simplification process that Marion Donovan began with her boater.

Today, 95 percent of American babies wear disposable diapers. The global baby diaper market[179] is expected to reach $64.62 billion by 2022, according to a new report by Grand View Research, Inc. Increasing disposable income levels coupled with increasing birth rates particularly in emerging markets is expected to remain a key driving factor for global baby diapers market. Can we get a round of applause for another great American invention.

Marion Donovan earned a place in the national Inventors Hall of Fame for her many patented contributions to making life more convenient. She was inducted in May of 2015.

131-The Grim Reaper

Cyrus Hall McCormick - Many of us are familiar with the term *Grim Reaper*. Throughout history he has been known as The Destroyer, The Hooded One, The Angel of Death, & The "God" of Death, and probably many other names. His image wearing a hood was first seen in the 15th century in England and perhaps most recognize him in that image.

In some mythologies, the Grim Reaper actually causes the victim's death by coming to collect them. In turn, people in some stories try to hold on to life by avoiding Death's visit, or by fending off Death with bribery or tricks . . . not to worry. *McCormick's reaper* had nothing to do with death, but has actually been a *life saver* to millions of farmers all over the world.

Reaping is synonymous

130-Cyrus McCormick

with harvesting and has been the hardest task done by farmers for close to 5000 years. Hand reaping is done by various means, including plucking the grains directly by hand, cutting the grain stalks with a *sickle* (a sharp blade swung by hand), or cutting the grain with a *scythe* (a sharp curved blade with a long handle that can be used with the field-hand standing in an upright position.

Reaping is usually distinguished from *mowing*, which uses similar implements, but is the traditional term for cutting grass for hay, rather than reaping or harvesting grain from crops.

Cyrus Hall McCormick was born on February 15, 1809, in the Blue Ridge Mountains of Virginia. he was the son of Robert McCormick, a long time grain farmer. Like father like son, as Cyrus too, wanted to follow in his father's footsteps and take over the farm when his father stepped down. He wasn't scared off by the hard work of farming and was convinced, after working for his father from his early youth, he could probably put some of his ideas to work to harvest grain faster than other farmers in the region.

As with all tasks done by hand on a farm, reaping is *back-breaking* work if done by hand and limits a farmer 's crop yield by the amount of stamina he has and the number of field workers he can hire. The *mechanical reaper* was an important step in the mechanization of agriculture during the nineteenth century.

132-The Patrick Bell Scottish Reaper

Before, reaping by hand, the amount of grain that could be cut during the short harvest seasons limited food supply, farm sizes, and revenue produced from the sale of grain the farmer didn't need to feed his family.

There were a number of mechanical reapers in various stages of development when Cyrus's father, Robert, first started working on a mechanical reaper, but no one had patented a machine yet.

Patrick Bell[180] of Scotland designed a reaper that worked quite well in his native Scotland, but being an ordained minister he desired no profit and felt it should be used to benefit all farmers, and never worried about a patent.

They were other kinds of reapers around the U.S. in the 1800's, but all had some problems that needed to be solved before becoming commercially viable.

McCormick started with his father's design and saw that he needed several key changes to build a reaper that would do the job of reaping and do it far faster than by hand thereby increasing a farmer's productivity and yielding greater harvests. Since mechanical harvesting was not a new concept, and since many attempts to build a mechanical reaper had failed, McCormick had to build a machine that overcame the inadequacies of other machines and produce the goals he was looking for.

133-The McCormick Mechanical Reaper

By 1828 the McCormick machine was fully functional. Cyrus and his father were using it with success on the family farm. Cyrus felt he needed to give his machine the hardest workout he could and so he went to other farms in his community and helped them with their harvests. His father had worked for two decades to invent a machine and when the task to complete the machine was given to Cyrus to carry on . . . carry-on he did.

By 1831, McCormick was convinced his machine was commercially viable. His patent was granted in 1834, and so he set up building units from the Virginia plantation where he was born.

One could not call his business "booming", but he wasn't dissuaded. For the next twelve years he continued to farm and build reapers, but by 1846, less than 100 had been sold.

A meeting with Illinois senator Stephen Douglas and a trip to the vast grain fields of the Midwest convinced McCormick to relocate his operation to Chicago in 1847. His first investor was William Ogden[181], a Chicago financier and president of Union Pacific railroad. The financial support enabled Cyrus to found McCormick Harvesting Machine Company, and most of the family relocated to Chicago as his plant began to turn out mechanical reapers.

McCormick was a visionary in bringing grain farming into the modern world, and his reaper enabled America to become the world leader in grain production. But don't confuse Cyrus with being a simple farmer or inventor; he was also the consummate *pitch man*. He so strongly believed in his reaper his tag-line became . . . "One Price to All and Satisfaction Guaranteed".

He guaranteed the performance of the McCormick "harvester" to deliver *15 acres a day or your money back*; revolutionized farm equipment purchase by enabling farmers to *buy on credit and pay over time*; he educated his customer base with demonstrations; and advertised with satisfied customer testimonials.

He set a fixed price of $120 per harvester and gave his customers a policy of *take it or leave it.* He removed the hassle of dickering over more money that has always been customary in equipment purchases. It would seem car salesmen of today could use a lesson in selling from Cyrus McCormick.

He was the first farm equipment manufacturer to develop interchangeable replacement parts and had them readily available to keep the farmer farming. Another first was his concept of traveling salesmen. He trained men on the mechanics of his machine and on his business and then sent them out as the first traveling salesmen. As was stated above, McCormick's motto was

"One Price to All and Satisfaction Guaranteed", and every salesman he had lived up to that motto.

In 1851, McCormick's machine won him the Gold Medal at London's World's Fair in the Crystal Palace. A tour of the European continent ended with his election to the French Academy of Sciences for "having done more for agriculture than any other living man."

By 1860, he was selling over 4000 reapers a year. McCormick's success in Chicago raised the fortunes of the Midwestern farmer and made Chicago the greatest grain center in the world. In 1902 McCormick Harvester Company became part of International Harvester Company[182], which today is a worldwide conglomerate and part of Navistar International Corp[183] headquartered in Warrenville, Illinois

By the end of the 1990s, Navistar, had become the nation's leading manufacturer of large trucks and employed about 2,500 people in the Chicago area, one-tenth of the number who once worked in and around the city for International Harvester. Its total revenues in 2002 stood at almost $7 billion.

Garrett Morgan - Imagine if you would, some 256 million vehicles[184], traveling at a variety of different speeds down 4.09 million miles of streets, highways, and recognized public roadways (basically roads with center-lines that create 8.61 million *lane*-miles), with no way to insure who has the right-of-way. One can only imagine the carnage and death that would occur from the many accidents that would take place.

134-Garrett Morgan

Thanks to a little known, African-American, born in Paris, Kentucky, on March 4, 1877. . . problem solved with his patented invention . . . the *traffic signal* which we will discuss in a minute.

Garrett Morgan[185] was the seventh of 11 children. His mother, Elizabeth (Reed) Morgan, was of Indian and African descent, and the daughter of a Baptist minister. It is uncertain whether Morgan's father was Confederate Colonel John Hunt Morgan or Sydney Morgan, a former slave freed in 1863, however, Morgan's mixed race heritage would play a part in his business dealings as an adult.

With only an elementary school education, he was in his mid-teens when he moved to Cincinnati, Ohio, to look for work, and found it as a handyman to a wealthy landowner. His lack of formal education didn't stop his enthusiasm to make the most of every opportunity, but he did recognize that his lack of education would limit those opportunities unless he could become more learned. He was able to pay for school lessons from a private tutor which increased his knowledge in almost every subject that would benefit his life.

Fortunately, like many great inventors, Morgan had an brilliant mechanical mind that enabled him to solve problems, but unlike many other inventors, he also was a born entrepreneur. Morgan began his career as a sewing-machine mechanic. He developed a keen sense for sewing machines and held jobs at several sewing-machine factories, which would capture his imagination and determine his future.

135-Garrett Morgan Improved Sewing Machine

He quickly learned the inner workings of the machines and how to fix them, and was always looking for ways to improve their performance. After receiving his first patent regarding an improved sewing machine, he decided he needed to opened his own repair business.

Morgan's business grew and by all accounts it was a success. With some degree of stability in his life he married a Bavarian woman named Mary Anne Hassek, and they moved to Cleveland, Ohio, and began selling his newly patented sewing machine. It might sound like he and his wife were off to a rather simple life to most people, but Garrett was one to seize any opportunity that might present itself.

Morgan decided he needed to open a tailor shop with his wife who had experience as a seamstress, and they built their business around his patented sewing machine, but even greater opportunities landed on their doorstep. He and his wife encountered woolen fabric that had been scorched by a sewing-machine needle which was a common problem at the time since sewing-machine needles ran at such high speeds.

222

To alleviate the problem, Morgan experimented with a chemical solution to reduce friction created by the needle and lower the heat generated. It worked but he noticed something else . . . the hairs of the cloth became straighter. He tried his solution on a neighboring dog's fur, and low and behold it worked. He then tested it on himself.

When that worked, he rightly figured he had a marketable product and opened G.A. Morgan Hair Refining Company to sell the cream to the African-American community. The company was incredibly successful, bringing his family financial security and allowed him to pursue other interests.

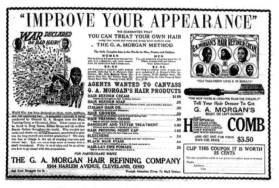

136-G.A. Morgan's Hair Straighten System

Life would have been good for the Morgan family had he stopped looking around for new things to tinker with, but that's just not his nature. In 1914, Morgan designed and patented a device, that piqued the interest of many, especially the fire departments.

His new product was a full head cover that would protect the wearer from smoke and fumes. Some might have thought him crazy, but he actually went around and demonstrated the mask's reliability to fire departments by wearing it himself in real fires.

Initially there was some resistance to Morgan's device among certain buyers, particularly in the South where racial prejudice was still a problem during and after the era of Jim Crow - Blacks were however, making advancements in civil rights in the North.

To deal with the resistance to his products, Morgan hired a white actor to pose as "the inventor". During presentations of the breathing device, while he would play the role of the inventor's sidekick disguised as a Native American man named "Big Chief Mason"[186], they became an unbeatable team. His genius paid big dividends and the sales of the device were brisk to firefighters and rescue workers.

Later in 1914, Morgan secured a patent for his device, which essentially *was a canvas hood*[187] *with two tubes. Part of the*

device held on the back filtered smoke outward, while cooling the air inside. Morgan's safety hood won accolades and wide adoption in the North, where over 500 cities added it to their list of essential gear for the protection of their firefighters.

137-Morgan's Life-Saving Gas Masks

He also sold the hoods to the U.S. Navy, and the Army, which used them in World War I. Obtaining big military contracts required a bit of skill and a whole lot of luck. It is obvious from the way he sold his masks to the fire departments that he had the skill pretty much under control, what he needed was the luck.

Between 1898 and 1916, Cleveland was undergoing construction of water intake tunnels for city's water system. The tunnels into Lake Erie were needed because by 1876 the increased sewage flow from the rapidly growing city had transformed its water supply into a health hazard. During this period the city experience a total of six disasters known as *The Cleveland Waterworks Tunnel Disasters,* which killed 58 men during the project.

The last disaster happened on July 24, 1916, when workmen digging in a 10' wide portion of the tunnel hit a pocket of natural gas. A spark triggered an explosion, killing 11 men and 10 would-be rescuers who were overcome by gas when they entered the pressurized tunnel.

Morgan along with his brother Frank and 2 others entered the gas-filled tunnel at the request of the Cleveland police to effect a rescue of those still trapped inside. Sustained by the Morgan's patented breathing apparatus, they rescued 2 men and recovered 4 bodies.

This was the luck that was needed to get the military to grant the gas mask contract. As Paul Harvey would say, *"Now you know the rest of the story"*, but that isn't the case, quite yet . . . Cleveland's newspapers[188] and city officials, according to a story PBS did on the Cleveland Tunnel Disasters, wrote Morgan and his brother out of the story even though they were the real heroes of the rescue, choosing instead to laud other men and ignoring Morgan's heroism. This was because Cleveland couldn't recognize heroes who were Black rescuing white people.

The military received the correct information however, and

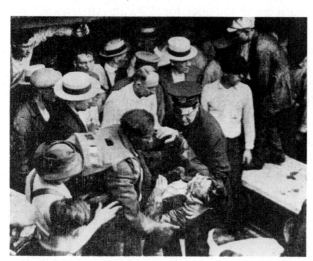

Morgan received his contact, but it would take years for the city to recognize the contributions of Garrett Morgan. Morgan died in 1963, vindicated as a hero of the Lake Erie rescue and restored to his place in history.

138-Garrett Morgan Life-Saving feat at Cleveland Tunnel

Getting back to the other contributions Garrett Morgan made in the march of civilization . . . In the same PBS story which set the record straight on the tunnel disaster, they talk about how Morgan made

225

money it seemed, on everything he invented, accidently or on purpose. Yet few historians ever knew he was the first black man in Cleveland to own a car.

When he branched out into cosmetic business with his hair straightening products he joined a new organization called the NAACP[189], (National Association for the Advancement of Colored People) and soon was donating money to Negro colleges. He was a sincere and true philanthropist with the money he earned.

139-Morgan's Traffic Signal

In 1920, he started a newspaper for African-Americans, *The Cleveland Call*, and opened an all-black country club. In 1923, he patented that mechanical traffic signal we told you about, which he sold to General Electric[191]. One has to believe an element of Black racism tainted this sale of the traffic light, but Morgan never said a word about it, perhaps because maybe his lack of education didn't equip him to be a *Donald Trump style negotiator*. Looking at the millions upon millions of lives traffic signals have saved over the decades, we can all agree it is worth far more than the paltry $40,000 General Electric gave him for his patent.

George Crum- There was a time, prior to fast food restaurants, when Americans traveled the roads across the country, went into a nice restaurant, ate, and continued on their journey or vacation. The meal was a time to relax.

Families almost always use to eat fairly wholesome foods at home and only went out on special occasions. All this changed half-way through the 20th century when we arrived at the Sixties, though an astute person could see things beginning to change in the mid-Fifties.

140-George Speck Crum

Going back even further in time, say the late 1800's, choices of where to eat were fairly slim. Meals were cooked at home and families sat around the dining room table, discussing important things like the news or family matters, and rested after hard day's work while the children talked about their school adventures. Rarely did families dine out, but the lonesome traveler or out-of-town salesmen had to dine where often there was not a real large choice of establishments from which to chose.

Restaurants in most towns and cities were not gourmet specialized *food-extravaganzas* one would find in almost any town or city large enough to sport a restaurant. The food was almost always the kind of food that was popular in the area . . . Southern fried chicken for the South, or ethnic style foods served in communities in the larger cities, particularly in the northern part of the country, for example. Life was very simple.

Restaurateurs making dramatic new discoveries, would not be something one would expect if we were revisiting those days, but occasionally they did happen. That brings us around to George Crum.

George Crum (born George Speck) an African-American of mixed ethnicity, some say he was Native-American[192], was born in 1828. Since George's invention or discovery was never patented, it is probably safe to assume much about George has been embellished by folklore to make him larger than life. We have no problem with that because his discovery has touched all of us.

Legend has it that George was a fur trapper and guide in the Adirondacks of New York. Considering that region of the country has numerous Indian tribes, there probably is good reason to believe that Native-American was part of his ethnicity.

As a trapper he was more than likely pretty handy with a skillet, and took to cooking much of what he trapped. He became renowned for his culinary skills when he became a cook and restaurant owner in Saratoga Springs, New York.

142-George Crum and Aunt Katie at Moon's Lake House Restaurant

By 1860 he owned *Crum's House*, which was a popular lakeside restaurant in nearby Malta, New York.

From Saratoga.com[193], the official popular voice for the local history of Saratoga Springs we get the full details of how George became the father of the most popular snack food in America, the one we love to hate, but can *never eat just one*.

As local legend goes, *"In 1853, when a gentlemen wore tight collars and too many layers of clothing, one wealthy patron - perhaps a little disgruntled from the summer weather - entered Moon's Lake*

House, a restaurant on the shores of Saratoga Lake in Saratoga Springs. George 'Speck' Crum worked at Moon's as a cook, where his sister Catherine Speck Wicks also worked.

"The grumpy patron ordered Moon's Fried Potatoes, their well-known house specialty. At that time, fried potatoes (or French fried potatoes) were commonly served in thick cut slices in the French tradition. The patron found the potatoes to be too thick and soggy. Dissatisfied, he sent them back to the kitchen and requested that they be cut thinner. He was duly served a second portion, and still not satisfied, he returned them yet again, insisting that they be cut thinner.

"Not particularly receptive to criticism of his cooking, the spirited Mr. Crum obliged by slicing them as paper-thin as he could manage and salted them heavily in an attempt to make them inedible. Deep fried, they became quite crispy and impossible to eat with a fork - Intending to teach the wealthy patron a lesson.

*"The reaction from the diner instead, was one of enthusiastic appreciation and a request a second serving of chips! Soon other diners requested Crum's chips, and **so began the illustrious history of 'Saratoga Chips'**, a Moon's Lake House specialty".*

141-Moon's Lake House Restaurant on the shores of Saratoga

But, like all legends, there will inevitably be variations, and probably a whole lot more than just one. The Saratoga website gives us this second one to ponder, just in case the first story doesn't ring true:

> Another version of the story claims "*That Catherine Speck Wicks accidentally dropped slices of potato into hot fat she was preparing for a batch of doughnuts, and when Crum fished it out, he tasted it and decided to put it on the menu as crispy Saratoga Chips*".

At any rate, the website goes on to complete their potato chip story about George Speck Crum, by following Crum in 1860, when he opened his own restaurant in Saratoga Springs, Crum's House.

> "*In 1860, Crum opened his own restaurant in Saratoga Springs on Malta Avenue near Saratoga Lake. Within a few years, he was catering to a large and wealthy clientele that included the Vanderbilts, Jay Gould, and Henry Hilton. A Saratoga historian claims in an article published in the Saratoga Springs newspaper, The Saratogian, that the reputation of Saratoga Chips*

stayed with Moon's and Crum focused on fish and game at his restaurant."

NOTE: The Snack Food Association claims Crum brought his invention to his newly opened restaurant where he placed them in baskets on all the tables, and marketed them in takeout boxes as Saratoga Chips, but never patented or protected his invention.

When Crum died in 1914, his obituary stated he was the originator of the Saratoga Chip. However, when his sister Catherine died in 1917, her obituary stated she was the inventor of the Saratoga Chip. This same obituary also claims she first came to Saratoga in 1861, a full eight years after the Chips were purportedly invented.

According to the Snack Food Association[194],

"Potato chips first became available in grocery stores in 1895. That was the year that William Tappenden began delivering potato chips to stores in his Cleveland, Ohio, neighborhood. He used a horse-drawn wagon to deliver the potato chip that he started making on his kitchen stove. As orders increased, Tappenden converted his barn into one of the first potato chip factories.

"The next milestone in potato chip distribution came in 1926. Up until this time, retailers dispensed potato chips in bulk from cracker barrels or glass display cases. The chips were then given to customers in paper sacks. Laura Scudder, working in her Monterey Park, Calif.- based family chip business, had a new idea.

"At night, women employees in the company took home sheets of waxed paper and hand-ironed them into bags. The next day, the workers hand-packed chips into the bags and sealed the tops with a warm iron. The bags of

chips were then delivered to retailers where they could be purchased by customers.

"The early 1900s gave birth to a number of companies that helped define the potato chip industry. In 1910, Daniel Mikesell and his wife started Mike-sell's in Dayton, Ohio.

"Wise Potato Chips was founded in 1921 when Earl Wise, Sr. decided to make potato chips out of the excess potatoes at his Berwick, Pa. delicatessen, and during that same year Bill and Salie Utz founded Utz Quality Foods in Hanover, Pa.

"The Magic City Food Company (which later became Golden Flake Snack Foods) opened in Birmingham, Ala., while in 1932, Herman Lay founded Lay's in Nashville, Tenn., which distributed potato chips from a factory in Atlanta, Ga. In 1938, Lay purchased the chip factory and Lay's Brand Potato Chips was born".

An industry was launched. Potato chips have become America's favorite snack. U.S. retail sales alone of potato chips are over $6 billion a year, and more than 65,000 people derive their income from jobs in the chip industry. Whatever bit of folklore you chose to believe about the discovery of this

143-Freshly made Potato Chips salted to taste

devilishly delicious and addictive snack, it is easy to remember that George is probably smiling down from heaven when people realize **his last name is all that's left in a bag of potato chips after it's passed around . . . CRUMS"**!

Leo Gerstenzang - Leo was born was born in Warsaw, the largest city and capital of Poland. He emigrated to Chicago, Illinois in 1912. From 1918–1919, he returned to Europe as a representative of the American Jewish Joint Distribution Committee[194], a humanitarian organization founded in 1914, to provide assistance to Jews living in Palestine under Turkish rule.

144-Leo Gerstenzang

In 1919 he returned to Chicago and became an American citizen before relocating to New York city. Gerstenzang did not send rockets to the moon, invent some highly technical product which revolutionized life in America, or radically change the way people did things. No, Gerstenzang was just an ordinary immigrant here in America looking for a way to make a life for his family.

He realized that having the fortune to be able to leave Poland and immigrate to America, came at some cost. Many who left Europe were not so fortunate. He heard a calling to help his Jewish brothers and sisters in Turkey who were suffering from a famine caused as a result of the First World War.

The war had forced many Jews to flee Europe for the Middle East and many ended up in Turkey. His position with the American Jewish Joint Distribution Committee was to provide relief aid in the form of food and money which had been solicited from wealthy Jewish business people in the United States. After four years traveling the cities of Turkey he completed his mission and returned to the U.S.

145-Q-Tips

Leo's American life really starts at the point he and his wife moved to New York city. One evening he observed his wife wrapping toothpicks with cotton to swab the inside of her ears. He immediately conceived the idea that his wife couldn't be the only one in New York that cleaned her ears in this manner, so there might just be a market for someone to make these cotton covered "swabs".

The story is a relatively short one with long range benefits for humanity. Leo Gerstenzang, then decided to manufacture a ready-to-use cotton swab and build his company around it as the *flagship* product when he opened Leo Gerstenzang Infant Novelty Co. to market baby care accessories.

146-Cotton swab applicators

Coming up with a name for the swab was probably the most difficult task he faced as there was an immediate interest by the people of New York as a personal hygiene product. The first name he conceived was Baby Gays, but in 1926 he changed the name to Q-Tips Baby Gays. The "Q" stood for *quality*. Shortly thereafter he dropped the name Baby Gays, and simply went with Q-Tips, registering the name with the U.S. Patent Office. The Leo Gerstenzang Infant Novelty Company became the Q-Tips® Company, which today is owned by publically-held Unilever Company.

Home sales of Q-tips are about $200 million annually, but with all the other cotton swabs that are made by other companies, along with the private brand production of swabs for Wal-Mart, K-Mart, and others, one can only guess as to how large the market really is. Additionally, the market for cotton swabs is far greater than Leo would have ever imagined with the medical industry, industrial trades, and arts and crafts aficionados purchasing *Cotton*

Swab Stick Applicators, which are swabs with only one end of an 8" stick wrapped in cotton.

Leo Gerstenzang, and immigrant from Warsaw, Poland, like millions of others, became a U.S. citizen. He assimilated into American culture, and made his mark in history. He is a classic case of not having to be brilliant to seek the American Dream, or to make a fortune from a single creative idea.

Dr. Percy LeBaron Spencer - You can smell popcorn popping in the microwave half-way across the office or in any room in the house, no matter where the microwave is located. Let's face it. the microwave has become the mainstay of American's culinary tastes for decades.

147-Microwave popcorn –a perfect snack in a matter of minutes.

The microwave craze really got its start in the 1940s, with the announcement by Jack Fisher[195] that his new company called FridgiDinners, was introducing a revolutionary concept in dining with a line of "just reheat" meals to bars and taverns. This was a mild prelude to the TV dinners that would follow in the Fifties.

When Albert and Meyer Bernstein[196] co-founded Frozen Dinners Inc. in 1949, the instant dinner, or as they were soon to be called, TV Dinner era had arrived. As the name implies, families on the go were headed into a time when both mom and dad would be off to work each day, and there would be little time for mom to spend standing over the stove cooking a big dinner for the family. World War II had unlocked the floodgates to an American economy that was ready to bust its seams producing goods and supplying services to rebuild Europe and put America on a path to blow the doors off the world's economies.

The opportunity for American families to improve their financial wellbeing as never before, was presented to the public with a boom in the housing business and the growth of related products, material, and services that support the housing industry. It seemed that everyone who wanted a paycheck could find a job. Nobody was going to have time to spend hours a day in the kitchen cooking food.

The Bernstein's realized the market was ripe for instant meals that could be prepared for a family of four or more in a matter of minutes, and their frozen dinners concept looked like a very viable business venture. According to Kathy Padden, editor of www.todayifoundout.com[196], *"The Bernsteins sold their aluminum dinner trays with three compartments in the Pittsburgh area, and by 1950 had manufactured an impressive 400,000 dinners.*

"As their product continued to grow in popularity, they reorganized into the Quaker State Food Corporation, and expanded their sales to the east coast. By 1954, their new company had sold over 2.5 million frozen dinners, presumably some of which were eaten while people watched TV, though at this point it certainly wasn't the focus."

The TV dinner crazy got into full swing when Swanson Food Company jumped into the fray and began calling the heat-and-eat tray dinners, "TV Dinners". Swanson put the product on the map, as they say, advertising that for just $.98 per dinner, customers could have a choice of wholesome meals which included Salisbury steak, meatloaf, fried chicken, or turkey, served with potatoes and bright green peas. That was just too good for *family-Americana* to pass up.

The TV dinners, no matter how convenient, began to see families no longer sitting together to have their dinner. Most families had fold-up TV trays that could be propped up in front of

236

the couch or dad's favorite chair and everyone could watch television with their TV meals right in front of them, or the kids could take them upstairs to eat while studying. With the *non-stop* American family we began to lose touch with each other as everyone simply began to eat whenever they were hungry.

148-Percy Spencer

As America rolled into the Sixties, things were about to move forward even faster in preparing the family meal, but before we get too far down that road we have to take a step back to 1946 when an engineer named *Percy Spencer* was experimenting with a magnetron tube (a tube which forms microwaves) at the Raytheon Corporation.

In the cool air conditioned laboratory Spencer noticed the candy bar in his pocket had melted after working with that magnetron tube! This incident piqued his curiosity so he decided to see if the process would repeat itself using popcorn. He put some popcorn kernels beside the magnetron tube and went to the far end of the room and hit the switch on the magnetron. Shortly thereafter the popcorn started popping. The next day they tried seeing what would happen to an egg and sure enough, in short order the magnetron cooked the egg so fast it exploded.

It wasn't long before Spencer began experimenting with all kinds of food and found out things cooked very quickly using the magnetron. One would have to think that such revelations were not just exciting but potentially there could be commercial appliances which were definitely not Raytheon's strong suit. Spencer and his associates thought perhaps that the magnetron could have a

148-First Raytheon Microwave

237

military purpose as well, for thawing large quantities of frozen food, like aboard ships, or on military bases. So initially that was the focus.

Raytheon was a company not well known to the average citizen in America. It was and still is a major defense contractor and industrial corporation with core manufacturing concentrating in weapons and military electronics. It would be three decades before Raytheon became known to most people because of the Patriot Missile Air Defense system[197] used during the First Gulf War, even though the company has tens of thousands of employees.

Never-the-less, Raytheon filed a patent on October 8, 1945 for a microwave cooking oven, which they called the *Radarange*. In 1947 the first commercially produced microwave oven was about 6 feet tall, weighed about 750 lbs, and cost between $2,000 and $3,000 in today's dollars . . . this again, was thought to be an application for military use. It wasn't until 1967, that the first relatively affordable ($495) and reasonably sized (counter-top) microwave oven became available for sale.

Just who was Percy Spencer? Spencer was an American physicist and inventor born in Howland, Maine, on the July 29, 1894. His father died when he was just 18 months old and his mother sent him to live with an aunt and uncle. He never completed grammar school, but that did not mean he was illiterate or dumb. In fact he was quite bright, but when his uncle died, he was just seven years old and he had to help support his aunt and himself by working from sunrise to sunset at a spool mill doing odd jobs. He was such a quick learner and so sharp, he took an interest in electricity and actually helped electrically wire the spool mill in which he worked.

At the age of 18, Spencer decided to join the U.S. Navy. He had increased his interest in electricity to include electronics and wireless communications after studying the wireless operators and the systems they had to work with aboard the Titanic when it sank.

While with the navy, he made himself an expert on radio technology.

From "Stories from History's Dust Bin - Volume 2"[198], we read about the furtherance of Percy's education, *"'I just got hold of a lot of textbooks and taught myself while I was standing watch at night'. He also subsequently taught himself trigonometry, calculus, chemistry, physics, and metallurgy, among other subjects"*.

Okay . . . so exactly what is a microwave and how does it cook food? Microwaves are essentially radiation. Microwave ovens cook so quickly and efficiently because they channel heat energy directly to the molecules (tiny particles) inside food. Microwaves heat food like the sun heats your face—by radiation. They can cook raw meat roughly six times faster than a conventional oven, and save energy, because you can cook immediately without waiting for the oven to heat up to a high temperature first. Interestingly they cook from the inside out, whereas regular ovens cook from the outside in.

"According to Explain that Stuff. com[199], *"A microwave is much like the electromagnetic waves that zap through the air from TV and radio transmitters. It's an invisible up-and-down pattern of electricity and magnetism that races through the air at the speed of light (300,000 km or 186,000 miles per second). While radio waves can be very long, microwaves have much shorter wavelengths and frequencies. The microwaves that cook food in your oven are just 12 cm (roughly 5 inches) long.*

"Despite their small size, microwaves carry a huge amount of energy. One drawback of microwaves is that they can damage living cells and tissue. This is why microwaves can be harmful to people—and why microwave ovens are surrounded by strong metal boxes that do not allow the waves to escape."

Microwave technology has come a long wave since those early days in the Forties. The magnetron has certainly paid big dividends to Raytheon yet Spencer received no compensation other than the traditional $2.00 "bonus", Raytheon presents to their employees for developing new patentable technology. Today the uses for such technology goes beyond most people's imagination: Here are some of the ways microwave technology had been put to use:

- Detecting speeding cars and motorcycles
- Sending telephone messages
- TV broadcasting
- Curing and drying plywood
- Treating muscle soreness
- Curing resins and rubber
- Raising bread and doughnuts
- Cooking potato chips.

Spencer became Senior Vice President and a Senior Member of the Board of Directors at Raytheon[200]. He received 300 patents during his career. Not too shabby for a grade-school drop-out. That could only happen in America.

Additionally a building at the Raytheon Missile Defense Center in Woburn,

150-Microwave transmission for use in radio, television, and communications

Massachusetts is named in his honor. Among honors too numerous to mention include the Distinguished Public Service Award by the U.S. Navy, membership in the Institute of Radio Engineers, Fellowship in the American Academy of Arts and Sciences, and an honorary Doctor of Science from the University of Massachusetts.

Percy Spencer passed away September 8, 1970, leaving the world far better off to handle today's fast pace. Suffice it to say, without the microwave oven and the other magnetron applications, perhaps we would not be able to keep up with life.

As to those early TV dinners . . . nearly any foods that you can purchase at the supermarket, you can also find in the frozen food aisle, packaged for cooking in a microwave oven. Every restaurant has one to quickly heat food that may have gotten cold waiting for the rest of an order, cook a baked potato in a minute or so, or simply boil water. Every company's break room has a microwave for the employees to eat a hot lunch on their half-hour break. Yes, the microwave was a product to match the speed Americans must maintain to lead a fast pace world.

151-Gourmet microwave dinners from pizza to bourbon steak . . .hmmm

Bibliography

1. "Some Thoughts on D-Day." *Restoring Honor Starts Here.* Twenty Ten Theme, 06 June 2011. Web. 26 Jan. 2016.

2. "Zero-Sum Game Definition | Investopedia." *Investopedia.* N.p., 18 Nov. 2003. Web. 15 Feb. 2016. <http://www. investopedia.com/terms/z/zero-sumgame.asp>.

2-1. Rothbard, Murray. "The End of Socialism and the Calculation Debate Revisited." *Mises Institute.* Mises.org, n.d. Web. 25 Feb. 2016. <https://mises.org/library/end-socialism-and-calculation-debate-revisited>.

3. "Professor Philip Hanson OBE." *Chatham House.* N.p., n.d. Web. 26 Jan. 2016.

4. "The End of Socialism and the Calculation Debate Revisited." *Mises Institute.* N.p., n.d. Web. 26 Jan. 2016.

5. "Top US Students Fare Poorly in International PISA Test Scores, Shanghai Tops the World, Finland Slips - Education By The Numbers." *Education By The Numbers Top US Students Fare Poorly in International PISA Test Scores Shanghai Tops the World Finland Slips Comments.* N.p., 03 Dec. 2013. Web. 26 Jan. 2016.

6. "Number of Countries" http://www.infoplease.com/ipa/A0932875.html

7. http://www.nytimes.com/2003/07/06/books/chapters/0713-1st-hedges.html?pagewanted=all

8. "American War Deaths Through History." *American War Deaths Through History.* N.p., n.d. Web. 26 Jan. 2016.

9. http://www.boston-tea-party.org/parties-summary.html "Boston Tea Party." Boston Tea Party Historical Society, n.d. Web.

10. "Crispin Attucks." *Infoplease.* Infoplease, n.d. Web. 26 Jan. 2016.

11. "Battles of Lexington and Concord." *History.com.* A&E Television Networks, n.d. Web. 26 Jan. 2016.

12. "FAQ about the American Revolutionary War." *FAQ about the American Revolutionary War.* N.p., n.d. Web. 26 Jan. 2016.

13. "James K. Polk." *History.com.* A&E Television Networks, n.d. Web. 26 Jan. 2016.

14. "Charles Sumner." *History.com.* A&E Television Networks, n.d. Web. 26 Jan. 2016.

15. Jr., Henry Louis Gates. "100 Amazing Facts About the Negro: Henry Louis Gates Jr. Explains." N.p., n.d. Web. 26 Jan. 2016.

16. "Michael Medved - Six Inconvenient Truths about the U.S. and Slavery." *Townhall.com.* Town Hall, n.d. Web. 26 Jan. 2016.

17. "Powhatan | North American Indian Confederacy." *Encyclopedia Britannica Online.* Encyclopedia Britannica, n.d. Web. 26 Jan. 2016.

17-1. "Southeastern Virginia Historical Markers." *Southeastern Virginia Historical Markers.* Virginia Historical, n.d. Web. 12 Feb. 2016. <http://sevamarkers.umwblogs.org/2012/04/03/paspahegh-indians-v-50/>.

18. "New Mexico - History and Travel Destinations in the Land of Enchantment." *New Mexico - History and Travel Destinations in the Land of Enchantment.* N.p., n.d. Web. 26 Jan. 2016.

19. http://international.loc.gov/intldl/eshtml/es-1/es-1-3-5.html

20. http://www.slideshare.net/grieffel/spanish-explorers Slideshare "Spanish Explorers." *Spanish Explorers.* N.p., n.d. Web. 26 Jan. 2016.

21. http://www.nmgs.org/artcuar2.htm "New Mexico Genealogical Society." *New Mexico Genealogical Society.* N.p., n.d. Web. 26 Jan. 2016.

22. http://www.history.com/topics/native-american-history/american-indian-wars "American-Indian Wars." *History.com*. A&E Television Networks, n.d. Web. 26 Jan. 2016.

23. http://www.americaslibrary.gov/jb/recon/jb_recon_ custer_1.html "Custer's Last Stand." *Custer's Last Stand*. N.p., n.d. Web. 26 Jan. 2016.

24. "The Wounded Knee Massacre - The Ghost dance. *Ushistory.org*. Independence Hall Association, n.d. Web. 26 Jan. 2016.

25. "The Wounded Knee Massacre." *Ushistory.org*. Independence Hall Association, n.d. Web. 26 Jan. 2016.

26. http://www.history.com/this-day-in-history/the-maine-explodes "The Maine Explodes." *History.com*. A&E Television Networks, n.d. Web. 26 Jan. 2016.

27. http://www.history.com/this-day-in-history/the-battle-of-san-juan-hill "The Battle of San Juan Hill." *History.com*. A&E Television Networks, n.d. Web. 26 Jan. 2016.

28. Henry Gunther - https://en.wikipedia.org/wiki/ Henry_Gunther

29. Flying Tigers - http://www.flyingtigersavg.com/ *Flying Tigers Home Page*. Flying Tigers AVG Forum, n.d. Web.

30. "A Few Americans in the Battle of Britain." *History Net Where History Comes Alive World US History Online*. N.p., n.d. Web. 26 Jan. 2016. http://www.historynet.com/a-few-americans-in-the-battle-of-britain.htm

31. War in the Pacific - http://pwencycl.kgbudge.com/C/a/ Casualties.htm. "Casualties." *The Pacific War Online Encyclopedia:* N.p., n.d. Web. 26 Jan. 2016.

32. The Bomb - " Hiroshima: Was it Necessary?" http://www.doug-long.com/hirosh2.htm

33. John Clare - http://www.johndclare.net/cold_war5.htm. "Hiroshima and the Cold War"

34. http://www.japanfocus.org/-Herbert-P--Bix/1787/article.pdf. The Asia-Pacific Journal, Vol. 3, Issue 7, Jul 2005. "Japan's Surrender Decision and the Monarchy: Staying the Course in an Unwinnable War"

35. "The War." *PBS*. PBS, n.d. Web. 26 Jan. 2016. https://www.pbs.org/thewar/detail_5382.htm

36. http://web.stanford.edu/~jacksonm/war-overview.pdf, Matthew O. Jackson and Massimo Morelli, Revised: December 2009

37. http://www.brainyquote.com/quotes/quotes/j/josephstal

109571.html. "Joseph Stalin Quote." *BrainyQuote*. Xplore, n.d. Web. 27 Jan. 2016.

38. http://www.history.com/this-day-in-history/korean-war-begins. "Korean War Begins." *History.com*. A&E Television Networks, n.d. Web. 27 Jan. 2016.

39. https://history.state.gov/milestones/1945-1952/korean-war-2. U.S. Department of State, Office of Historian, n.d. Web.

40. http://www.ibiblio.org/hyperwar/OnlineLibrary/photos/

events/kowar/50-unof/inchon.htm. "Korea - The Inchon Landing." *DEPARTMENT OF THE NAVY -- NAVAL HISTORICAL CENTER*. N.p., n.d. Web.

41. http://www.fsmitha.com/h2/ch24kor4.htm. *Macrohistory and Worldwide Timeline*. N.p., n.d. Web.

42. http://www.kwva.org/graybeards/gb_99/gb_9910_final.pdf. Korean War Veterans Association file

43. https://en.wikipedia.org/wiki/Cuban_Revolution. *Wikipedia*. Wikimedia Foundation, n.d. Web. 27 Jan. 2016.

44. "26th of July Movement | Cuban History." *Encyclopedia Britannica Online*. Encyclopedia Britannica, n.d. Web. 27 Jan. 2016. <http://www.britannica.com/topic/26th-of-July-Movement>.

45. N.p., n.d. Web. <http://usforeignpolicy.about.com/od/alliesenemies/a/Fiftieth-Anniversary-Of-Cuban-Missile-Crisis.htm>.

46. "Monroe Doctrine." N.p., n.d. Web. <http://history1800s.about.com/od/1800sglossary/g/monroedocdef.htm>.

47. "What Was the Bay of Pigs Invasion?" *About.com Education*. About.com, n.d. Web. 27 Jan. 2016. <http://latinamericanhistory.about.com/od/historyofthecaribbean/a/09bayofpigs_2.htm>.

48. "Cause of the Vietnam War." N.p., n.d. Web. <http://www.english.illinois.edu/maps/ vietnam/causes.htm>.

49. "Tonkin Gulf Resolution (1964)." *Our Documents -*. Archives.gov, n.d. Web. 27 Jan. 2016. <http://www.ourdocuments.gov/doc.php?flash=true&doc=98>.

50. Agent Orange: The Congressional Record (August 11, 1969 pages s-9519 through **S-9524**) http://www.bluewaternavy.org/Congressional%20Record%20Aug%2011%201969%20CBW.pdf

51. Buckingham, Maj. Gen. William A., Jr. "Operation Ranch Hand: Herbicides In Southeast Asia." *Operation Ranch Hand: Herbicides In Southeast Asia*. N.p., n.d. Web. 27 Jan. 2016. <http://www.airpower.maxwell.af.mil/airchronicles/aureview/1983/Jul-Aug/buckingham.html>.

52. "What Happened During the Tet Offensive?" *About.com Education*. About.com, n.d. Web. 27 Jan. 2016. <http://history1900s.about.com/od/1960s/qt/tetoffensive.htm>.

53. "Vietnam: General Vo Nguyen Giap." *About.com Education*. N.p., n.d. Web. 27 Jan. 2016. <http://militaryhistory.about.com/od/army/p/giap.htm>.

54. Gomez, Salvador. "US Invasion Dominican Republic 1965." *US Invasion Dominican Republic 1965*. University of Pittsburgh, n.d. Web. 27 Jan. 2016. <http://sincronia.cucsh.udg.mx/dominican.html>.

55. Gunboat Diplomacy - "Big Stick Diplomacy." N.p., n.d. Web. https://en.wikipedia.org/wiki/ Gunboat_diplomacy>.

56. "History Is A Weapon." *History Is A Weapon*. Operation Limpieza.org, n.d. Web. 27 Jan. 2016. <http://hiaw.org/ defcon2/lam/powdomrep19651966.html>.

57. "Reagan Sends Aid, Troops to Lebanon." Congressional Quarterly, n.d. Web. <https://library.cqpress.com/cqalmanac/ document.php?id=cqal82-1163928>.

58. "Global Policy Forum." *The US Invasion of Grenada:*. N.p., n.d. Web. 27 Jan. 2016. <https://www.globalpolicy.org/ component/content/article/155/25966.html>.

59. *Wikipedia*. Wikimedia Foundation, n.d. Web. 27 Jan. 2016. <https://en.wikipedia.org/ wiki/Invasion_of_Grenada>.

60. "Security Council Resolutions - 1990." *UN News Center*. UN, n.d. Web. 28 Jan. 2016. <http://www.un.org/Docs/scres/1990/scres90.htm>.

61. "Persian Gulf Wars." *Infoplease*. Infoplease, n.d. Web. 27 Jan. 2016. <http://www.infoplease.com/encyclopedia/history/persian-gulf-wars.html>.

62. "Biography of Norman Schwarzkopf." *Bio.com*. A&E Networks Television, n.d. Web. 28 Jan. 2016. <http://www.biography.com/people/norman-schwarzkopf-9476401>.

63. "Gulf War Air Campaign." Wikipedia Foundation, n.d. Web. <https://en.wikipedia.org/wiki/Gulf_War_air_ campaign#cite_note-2>.

64. Chediac, Joyce. "The Massacre of Withdrawing Soldiers on "The Highway of Death"by Joyce Chediac." *The Massacre of Withdrawing Soldiers on "The Highway of Death"* N.p., n.d. Web. 28 Jan. 2016. <http://deoxy.org/wc/wc-death.htm>.

65. "Air Force Fact Sheet-Airpower in Operation Desert Storm." *Usmilitary.about.com*. U.S. Millitary. Com, n.d. Web. <http://usmilitary.about.com/library/milinfo/affacts/blairpowerinoperationdesertstorm.htm>.

66. Manuzak, Jeffrey. "Somalia 1992-1994." *Www.history.army.mil*. N.p., n.d. Web. <http://www.history.army.mil/brochures/somalia/somalia.htm>.

67. "Yugoslavia History." *Infoplease*. Infoplease, n.d. Web. 15 Feb. 2016. <http://www.infoplease.com/encyclopedia/world/yugoslavia-history.html>.

68. "Pan-Slavism." *Encyclopedia Britannica Online*. Encyclopedia Britannica, n.d. Web. 11 Feb. 2016. <http://www.britannica.com/event/Pan-Slavism>.

69. "Archduke Franz Ferdinand Assassinated." *History.com*. A&E Television Networks, n.d. Web. 11 Feb. 2016. <http://www.history.com/this-day-in-history/archduke-franz-ferdinand-assassinated>.

70. "Tito Is Made President for Life." *History.com*. A&E Television Networks, n.d. Web. 11 Feb. 2016. <http://www.history.com/this-day-in-history/tito-is-made-president-for-life>.

71. "Balkans." *Wikipedia*. Wikimedia Foundation, n.d. Web. 11 Feb. 2016. <https://en.wikipedia.org/wiki/NATO_intervention_in_Bosnia_and_Herzegovina>.

72. "Dayton Accords." *Wikipedia*. Wikimedia Foundation, n.d. Web. 11 Feb. 2016. <https://en.wikipedia.org/wiki/Dayton_Agreement>.

73. "Babrak Karmal | President of Afghanistan." *Encyclopedia Britannica Online*. Encyclopedia Britannica, n.d. Web. 11 Feb. 2016. <http://www.britannica.com/biography/Babrak-Karmal>

74. "Russia Sends Troops to Syria." *AllisChalmers Forum*. Allis Chalmers, n.d. Web. 11 Feb. 2016. <http://www.allischalmers.com/forum/forum_posts.asp?TID=111963&title=russia-sends-troops-to-syria>.

75. "Lengths of American War Participation." *Wikipedia*. Wikimedia Foundation, n.d. Web. 11 Feb. 2016. <https://en.wikipedia.org/wiki/List_of_the_lengths_of_American_participation_in_major_wars>

76. "Obama Has Touted Al Qaeda's Demise 32 Times since Benghazi Attack."*CNS News.* CNS News, 01 Nov. 2012. Web. 11 Feb. 2016. <http://cnsnews.com/news/article/obama-touts-al-qaeda-s-demise-32-times-benghazi-attack-0>.

77. "Thunder Pig." *Http://thunderpigblog.blogspot.com.* N.p., n.d. Web. <http://thunderpigblog.blogspot.com/2014/09/president-obama-addresses-nation.html>.

78. "Full Text of "Poor Richard's Almanack"" *Full Text of "Poor Richard's Almanack"* Benjamin Franklin, n.d. Web. 15 Feb. 2016. <https://archive.org/stream/poorrichardsalma00franrich/poorrichardsalma00franrich_djvu.txt>.

79. Crouch, Dennis. "Tracing the Quote: Everything That Can Be Invented Has Been Invented." *PatentlyO.* N.p., n.d. Web. 11 Feb. 2016. <http://patentlyo.com/patent/2011/01/tracing-the-quote-everything-that-can-be-invented-has-been-invented.html>.

80. "Mark Twain Quotes." *Brainy Quotes.* N.p., n.d. Web. <http://www.brainyquote.com/quotes/quotes/m/marktwain141773.html#LrBT1zoZf3qAtyR5.99>

81. "General Information Concerning Patents." *General Information Concerning Patents.* USPTO-Government, n.d. Web. 11 Feb. 2016. <http://www.uspto.gov/patents-getting-started/general-information-concerning-patents>.

82. "Samuel Hopkins." *Wikipedia.* Wikimedia Foundation, n.d. Web. 11 Feb. 2016. <https://en.wikipedia.org/wiki/Samuel_Hopkins_%28inventor%29>.

83. "Samuel Hopkins: Holder of the First U.S. Patent." *: Notable Pittsburgh Inventors: Reference Services: Carnegie Library of Pittsburgh.* Carnegie Press, n.d. Web. 11 Feb. 2016.

84. Williams, Matt. "How Many Patents Have Been Issued since the U.S. Patent and Trademark Office Was Created in 1836?" *How Many Patents Have Been Issued since the U.S. Patent and Trademark Office Was Created in 1836?* Government Tech, n.d. Web. 11 Feb. 2016. <http://www.govtech.com/question-of-the-day/Question-of-the-Day-for-081911.html>.

85. "Isambard Kingdom." *Wikipedia*. Wikimedia Foundation, n.d. Web. 11 Feb. 2016. <https://en.wikipedia.org/wiki/Isambard_Kingdom_Brunel>.

86. "Robert Grove." *Wikipedia*. Wikimedia Foundation, n.d. Web. 11 Feb. 2016. <https://en.wikipedia.org/wiki/William_Robert_Grove>.

87. "William Armstrong." *Wikipedia*. Wikimedia Foundation, n.d. Web. 11 Feb. 2016. <https://en.wikipedia.org/wiki/William_Armstrong,_1st_Baron_Armstrong>.

88. "Laissez-faire | Economics." *Encyclopedia Britannica Online*. Encyclopedia Britannica, n.d. Web. 11 Feb. 2016. <http://www.britannica.com/topic/laissez-faire>.

89. Ghosh, Pallab. "'First Human' Discovered in Ethiopia - BBC News." *BBC News*. N.p., n.d. Web. 11 Feb. 2016. <http://www.bbc.com/news/science-environment-31718336>.

89-1. Gibbons, Ann. "Fossil Pushes Back Human Origins 400,000 Years." *Fossil Pushes Back Human Origins 400,000 Years*. Science Magazine, 04 Mar. 2015. Web. 25 Feb. 2016. <http://www.sciencemag.org/news/2015/03/fossil-pushes-back-human-origins-400000-years>.

90. "Bipedal Humans." *ScienceDaily*. ScienceDaily, n.d. Web. 11 Feb. 2016. <http://www.sciencedaily.com/releases/2009/08/090810162005.htm>.

91. Bryner, Jeanna. "The World's Oldest Cave Art." *Livescience.com*. N.p., n.d. Web. <http://www.livescience.com/48199-worlds-oldest-cave-art-photos.html>.

92. "HISTORY OF LANGUAGE." *HISTORY OF LANGUAGE*. History World Net, n.d. Web. 11 Feb. 2016. <http://www.historyworld.net/wrldhis/PlainTextHistories.asp?historyid=ab13#ixzz3yVRiqrUT>.

93. "Roy J. Plunkett | Chemical Heritage Foundation." *Roy J. Plunkett | Chemical Heritage Foundation*. Chemical Heritage Foundation, n.d. Web. 11 Feb. 2016. <http://www.chemheritage.org/discover/online-resources/chemistry-in-history/themes/

petrochemistry-and-synthetic-polymers/synthetic-polymers/plunkett.aspx>.

94. "The Manhattan Project." *Ushistory.org*. Independence Hall Association, n.d. Web. 11 Feb. 2016. <http://www.ushistory.org/us/51f.asp>.

95. "Alexander Graham Bell." *Bio.com*. A&E Networks Television, n.d. Web. 11 Feb. 2016. <http://www.biography.com/people/alexander-graham-bell-9205497>.

96-97. "Bell, Alexander Graham." Leading American Businesses. 2003. "Bell, Alexander Graham." *Encyclopedia.com*. HighBeam Research, 01 Jan. 2003. Web. 15 Feb. 2016. <http://www.encyclopedia.com/topic/Alexander_Graham_Bell.aspx>.

98. "Full Text of "Poor Richard's Almanack"" *Full Text of "Poor Richard's Almanack"* N.p., n.d. Web. 11 Feb. 2016. <https://archive.org/stream/poorrichardsalma00franrich/poorrichardsalma00franrich_djvu.txt>.

99. "What Hath God Wrought?" *History.com*. A&E Television Networks, n.d. Web. 11 Feb. 2016. <http://www.history.com/this-day-in-history/what-hath-god-wrought>.

100. "Samuel F.B. Morse." *Bio.com*. A&E Networks Television, n.d. Web. 11 Feb. 2016. <http://www.biography.com/people/samuel-morse>.

101. "Thomas Edison." *History.com*. A&E Television Networks, n.d. Web. 11 Feb. 2016. <http://www.history.com/topics/inventions/thomas-edison>.

102. "The Legal Profession." American Eras. 1997, "Legal Profession." Dictionary of American History. 2003, "Legal Services." Encyclopedia of Small Business. 2007, TOM McARTHUR, "Legalese." West's Encyclopedia of American Law. 2005, "legalese." The Oxford Pocket Dictionary of Current English. 2009, and "legalese." Oxford Dictionary of Rhymes. 2007. "The Legal Profession." *Encyclopedia.com*. HighBeam Research, 01 Jan. 1997. Web. 11 Feb. 2016. <http://www.encyclopedia.com/topic/Legal_Profession.aspx>.

103. "Personal Life of Eli Whitney." *Bio.com.* A&E Networks Television, n.d. Web. 11 Feb. 2016. <http://www.biography.com/people/eli-whitney-9530201#personal-life>.

104. "Eli Whitney Museum." *Arms Production.* Bio.com, n.d. Web. 11 Feb. 2016. <https://www.eliwhitney.org/7/museum/eli-whitney/arms-production>.

105. "Levis Strauss - Won the West." *Nashville Scene.* Nashville Scene, n.d. Web. <http://www.nashvillescene.com/nashville/could-the-quest-for-the-perfect-pair-of-blue-jeans-end-in-a-former-12south-gas-station/Content?oid=1727532>.

105-1. Madison, Mandy. "Levi's Digital Fitting Experience." *Prezi.com.* Prezi.com, n.d. Web. 11 Apr. 2016. https://prezi.com/054bhq3qz9tr/levis-digital-fitting-experience/

105-2. Franchia, Charles. "FoundSF." *Levi Strauss -.* FoundSF Foundation, n.d. Web. 11 Apr. 2016. http://foundsf.org/index.php?title=Levi_Strauss

106. "Our Story - Levi Strauss." *Levi Strauss.* Levis Foundation, n.d. Web. 11 Feb. 2016. <http://www.levistrauss.com/our-story/>.

107. "Journal of Black Studies." *Journal of Black Studies.* Sage Publishing, n.d. Web. 11 Feb. 2016. <http://jbs.sagepub.com/>.

108. "History of Trains." *Train History.* Train History Museum, n.d. Web. 11 Feb. 2016. <http://www.trainhistory.net/>.

109. Klein, Maury. "Financing the Transcontinental Railroad." *Financing the Transcontinental Railroad.* Gilder Lehrman Foundation, n.d. Web. 11 Feb. 2016. <https://www.gilderlehrman.org/history-by-era/development-west/essays/financing-transcontinental-railroad>.

110. "The Big Four." *The Big Four.* CA. Railroad Museum, n.d. Web. 11 Feb. 2016. <http://www.csrmf.org/explore-and-learn/railroad-history/the-transcontinental-railroad/the-big-four>.

111. "BHRA: Granville Woods." *BHRA: Granville Woods.* Brooklyn Railroad Historical Society, n.d. Web. 11 Feb. 2016. <http://www.brooklynrail.net/Granville_Woods.html>.

112. "Elias Howe Jr." *Wikipedia*. Wikimedia Foundation, n.d. Web. 11 Feb. 2016. <https://en.wikipedia.org/wiki/Elias_Howe>.

113. "Lock Stitch Design." *Wikipedia*. Wikimedia Foundation, n.d. Web. 11 Feb. 2016. <https://en.wikipedia.org/wiki/Lockstitch>.

114. "Elias Howe." *Elias Howe*. Nation Inventors Hall of Fame, n.d. Web. 11 Feb. 2016. <http://www.nndb.com/people/371/000103062/>.

115. Karen, McCally. "University of Rochester." *Rochester Review* ∴. University of Rochester, n.d. Web. 11 Feb. 2016. <http://www.rochester.edu/pr/Review/V76N1/0403_carlson.html>.

116. "Bakelite | Chemical Compound." *Encyclopedia Britannica Online*. Encyclopedia Britannica, n.d. Web. 11 Feb. 2016. <http://www.britannica.com/science/Bakelite>.

117. Phenol | Chemical Compound." *Encyclopedia Britannica Online*. Encyclopedia Britannica, n.d. Web. 11 Feb. 2016. <http://www.britannica.com/science/phenol>.

118. "Facts About Formaldehyde." *EPA*. Environmental Protection Agency, n.d. Web. 11 Feb. 2016. <http://www.epa.gov/formaldehyde/facts-about-formaldehyde>.

119. "Leo Baekeland." *Leo Baekeland*. American Pink, n.d. Web. 11 Feb. 2016. <http://america.pink/leo-baekeland_2579931.html>.

120. Brager, Bill. "Top Stories." *100 Years Later, Bakelite Shines*. Plastic News, n.d. Web. 11 Feb. 2016. <http://www.plasticsnews.com/article/20070809/NEWS/30809999 9/100-years-later-bakelite-shines>.

121. "Spingarn Medal Winners: 1915 to Today." *Spingarn Medal Winners: 1915 to Today*. NAACP Organization, n.d. Web. 12 Feb. 2016. <http://www.naacp.org/pages/spingarn-medal-winners>.

122. "Chegg.com." *Definition of NAACP*. Chegg Educational Material, n.d. Web. 12 Feb. 2016. <http://www.chegg.com/homework-help/definitions/naacp-43>.

123. "Night Riders in Black History." *Www.uncpress.unc.edu*. UNC Press, n.d. Web. <http://www.uncpress.unc.edu/browse/book_detail?title_id=999>.

124. "George Washington Carver - Scientist, Educator, Inventor." *George Washington Carver - Scientist, Educator, Inventor*. Legends of America, n.d. Web. 12 Feb. 2016. <http://www.legendsofamerica.com/ah-georgewcarver.html>.

125. "George Washington Carver's Bachelor's Thesis: "Plants as Modified by Man"" *Scribd.com*. Scribd Incorporated, n.d. Web. 12 Feb. 2016. <http://www.scribd.com/doc/45471564/George-Washington-Carver-s-Bachelor-s-Thesis-Plants-as-Modified-by-Man#scribd>.

126. "About Us." *George W. Carver*. Tuskegee Institute, n.d. Web. 12 Feb. 2016. <http://www.tuskegee.edu/about_us/legacy_of_fame/george_w_carver.aspx>.

127. Turner, Robert. "Black History Month: George Washington Carver."*DCBigPappas Blog*. DC Big Poppa, 23 Feb. 2012. Web. 12 Feb. 2016. <https://dcbigpappa.wordpress.com/2012/02/23/black-history-month-george-washington-carver/>.

128. "Inventors and Inventions: B - EnchantedLearning.com." *Inventors and Inventions: B - EnchantedLearning.com*. Enchanted Learning, n.d. Web. 12 Feb. 2016. <http://www.enchantedlearning.com/inventors/indexb.shtml#bloodbank>.

129. "About Charles R. Drew." *CDREWU.edu*. University of Michigan, n.d. Web. <http://www.cdrewu.edu/about-cdu/DrCharlesRDrew>.

130. "Amherst College." *Student Awards*. Amherst College, n.d. Web. 12 Feb. 2016. <https://www.amherst.edu/news/specialevents/commencement/speeches_multimedia/2012/senior_assembly/student_awards>.

131. "Home | Howard University." *Home | Howard University*. Howard.edu, n.d. Web. 12 Feb. 2016. <https://www2.howard.edu/>.

132. "Freedmen's Hospital/Howard University Hospital (1862--) | The Black Past: Remembered and Reclaimed." *Freedmen's Hospital/Howard University Hospital (1862--) | The Black Past:*

Remembered and Reclaimed. On Line Encyclopedia, n.d. Web. 12 Feb. 2016. <http://www.blackpast.org/aah/freedmen-s-hospital-howard-university-hospital-1862>.

133. "About Charles R. Drew." *CDREWU.edu.* University of Michigan, n.d. Web. <http://www.cdrewu.edu/about-cdu/DrCharlesRDrew>.

134 . "America's Lost Colleges." *America's Lost Colleges.* Lost Colleges, n.d. Web. 12 Feb. 2016. <http://www.lostcolleges.com/#!eastman-business-college/c8q4>.

135. "Kodak: History of Kodak: Introduction." *Kodak: History of Kodak: Introduction.* Eastman Kodak, n.d. Web. 12 Feb. 2016. <http://www.kodak.com/US/en/corp/kodakHistory/>.

136. *Bio.com.* A&E Networks Television, n.d. Web. 12 Feb. 2016. <http://www.biography.com/people/george-eastman-9283428>.

137. "Eastman, George." *Eastman, George.* Learning to Give, Inc, n.d. Web. 12 Feb. 2016. <http://www.learningtogive.org/resources/eastman-george>.

138. "Letters of Note: My Work Is Done. Why Wait?" *Letters of Note: My Work Is Done. Why Wait?* Letter of Note, n.d. Web. 12 Feb. 2016. <http://www.lettersofnote.com/2011/08/my-work-is-done-why-wait.html>.

139. "Inventor Otto Rohwedder Biography." *Inventor Otto Rohwedder Biography.* Ideafinder, n.d. Web. 12 Feb. 2016. <http://www.ideafinder.com/history/inventors/r

140. "History." *Illinois College of Optometry.* ICO.edu, n.d. Web. 12 Feb. 2016. <http://www.ico.edu/about-ico/ico-timeline/>.

141. "Lt. Gen. John C. Premberton." *Council on Foreign Relations.* Council on Foreign Relations, n.d. Web. 12 Feb. 2016. <http://www.civilwar.org/education/history/biographies/john-pemberton.html>.

142. "Battle Of Vicksburg | History Net: Where History Comes Alive - World & US History Online." *History Net Where History Comes Alive World US History Online.* History.Net, n.d. Web. 12 Feb. 2016.

143. "John Stith Pemberton." *American Civil War Stories*. A Civil War Story, n.d. Web. 12 Feb. 2016. <http://www.americancivilwarstory.com/john-stith-pemberton.html>.

144. "Cephalanthus Occidentalis Page." *Cephalanthus Occidentalis Page*. Missouri Plants, n.d. Web. 12 Feb. 2016. <http://www.missouriplants.com/Whiteopp/Cephalanthus_occidentalis_page.html>.

144-1. McDonald, Jennifer. "Prickly and Bitter." *: A Northern Coffee Relative*. N.p., n.d. Web. 11 Apr. 2016. http://botanicalmusings.blogspot.com/2012/12/a-northern-coffee-relative.html

145. "John Stith Pemberton." *American Civil War Stories*. A Civil War Story, n.d. Web. 12 Feb. 2016. <http://www.americancivilwarstory.com/john-stith-pemberton.html>.

146. "May 8th, 1886 – Confederate Chemist Creates "Intellectual Beverage"." *The Pandora Society*. Pandora Society, 08 May 2015. Web. 12 Feb. 2016. <http://thepandorasociety.com/may-8th-1886-may-8th-2015/>.

147. "Neurasthenia." *Merriam-Webster*. Merriam-Webster, n.d. Web. 12 Feb. 2016. <http://www.merriam-webster.com/dictionary/neurasthenia>.

148. "What Are Some Famous Companies with Mindblowing History?" - *Quora*. Ouora.com, n.d. Web. 12 Feb. 2016. <https://www.quora.com/What-are-some-famous-companies-with-mindblowing-history>.

149. "Asa Candler (1851-1929)." *New Georgia Encyclopedia*. N.p., n.d. Web. 12 Feb. 2016. <http://www.georgiaencyclopedia.org/articles/history-archaeology/asa-candler-1851-1929>.

150. "Flight Mythology." *Science Learning Hub RSS*. N.p., n.d. Web. 12 Feb. 2016. <http://sciencelearn.org.nz/Contexts/Flight/Looking-Closer/Flight-mythology>.

151. "Myth Man's Icarus and Daedalus Two." *Myth Man's Icarus and Daedalus Two*. N.p., n.d. Web. 12 Feb. 2016. <http://thanasis.com/icarus02.html>.

152.. "FLYING MACHINES - Alphonse Penaud." *FLYING MACHINES - Alphonse Penaud*. N.p., n.d. Web. 12 Feb. 2016. <http://www.flyingmachines.org/pend.html>.

153. "Wright Brothers' Wing Warping." *Wright Brothers' Wing Warping*. N.p., n.d. Web. 12 Feb. 2016. <http://wright.nasa.gov/airplane/warp.html>.

154. "Aircraft Roll." *Aircraft Roll*. NASA, n.d. Web. 12 Feb. 2016. <http://wright.nasa.gov/airplane/roll.html>.

154-1. "Amusements of America - Our Midway and Attractions Carnival Rides, Games, Food." *Amusements of America - Our Midway and Attractions Carnival Rides, Games, Food*. American Amusements, n.d. Web. 11 Apr. 2016. http://www.amusementsofamerica.com /aoa/midway/midway.asp

155. "Wilbur Wright." *Bio.com*. A&E Networks Television, n.d. Web. 12 Feb. 2016. <http://www.biography.com/people/wilbur-wright-20672839#synopsis>.

156. "Orville Wright." *Bio.com*. A&E Networks Television, n.d. Web. 12 Feb. 2016. <http://www.biography.com/people/orville-wright-20672999>.

157. "Salem Witch Trials." *History.com*. A&E Television Networks, n.d. Web. 12 Feb. 2016. <http://www.history.com/topics/salem-witch-trials>.

158. Cox, Stan. "In the Heat Wave, the Case against Air Conditioning."*Washington Post*. The Washington Post, 11 July 2010. Web. 12 Feb. 2016. <http://www.washingtonpost.com/wp-dyn/content/article/2010/07/09/AR2010070902341.html>.

159. "How Air Conditioning Improved Employee Productivity by 30%."*Noobpreneur.com*. Noobpreneur, 15 July 2014. Web. 13 Feb. 2016. <http://www.noobpreneur.com/2014/07/15/air-conditioning-improved-employee-productivity-30/>.

160. "Willis Carrier - Beyond the Factory - 1923-1929." *Willis Carrier - Beyond the Factory - 1923-1929.* Carrier Air Conditioning, n.d. Web. 12 Feb. 2016. <http://www.williscarrier.com/1923-1929.php>.

160-1. "God Bless Willis Carrier." *Adams Insurance Service.* Adams Insurance, n.d. Web. 16 Feb. 2016. <http://www.adamsinsurance.com/content/god-bless-willis-carrier>.

161. "John Fitch - Inventor." *PBS.* PBS, n.d. Web. 12 Feb. 2016. <http://www.pbs.org/wgbh/theymadeamerica/whomade/fitch_hi.ht ml>.

162. "JOSEPHINE COCHRANE (1839-1913) Invented the Dishwasher."*FORGOTTEN NEWSMAKERS.* N.p., 20 Apr. 2010. Web. 12 Feb. 2016. <http://forgottennewsmakers.com/2010/04/20/ josephine-cochrane-1839-1913-invented-the-dishwasher/>.

163. "Better, Stronger and Safer with Kevlar® Fiber." *Kevlar® Aramid Fiber.* N.p., n.d. Web. 12 Feb. 2016. <http://www.dupont.com/products-and-services/fabrics-fibers-nonwovens/fibers/brands/kevlar.html>.

164. "Kevlar Bullet-Proof Vests -http://usatoday30.usatoday.com/ money/world/iraq/2003-04-15-kevlar_x.htm

165. "Stephanie Kwolek." *Stephanie Kwolek.* Pennsylvania Books OnLine, n.d. Web. 12 Feb. 2016. <http://pabook2.libraries.psu.edu/palitmap/bios/Kwolek__Stephani e.html>.

166. Ribbeck, Joshua. "NCR Report: NYSE." *1This Research Presentation Report Expresses Our Research Opinions, Which We Have Based upon Interpretation of Certain Facts and Observations, All of Which Are Based upon Publicly Available Information, and All of Which Are Set out in This Research Presentation Report. Any Investment Involves* (n.d.): n. pag.*Valuewalk,com.* Spruce Point Capital Management. Web.

167. Rouah, Daniel. "History of Shaving." *Moderngent.com.* Modern Gent, n.d. Web. <http://www.moderngent.com/history_ of_shaving/history_of_shaving.php>.

168. "Everyday Chemistry - Why Do Pumice Stones Float in Water?" *Everyday Chemistry - Why Do Pumice Stones Float in Water?* Human Touch of Chemistry, n.d. Web. 12 Feb. 2016. <http://humantouchofchemistry.com/why-do-pumice-stones-float-in-water.htm>.

169. "The Handlebar Club Forum." • *View Topic.* Handlebar Club, n.d. Web. 12 Feb. 2016. <http://www.handlebarclubforum.org/diy-aftershave-recipe-wanted-t492.html>.

170. Brand-Building Packaging | Crown." *Brand-Building Packaging | Crown.* Crown Cork, n.d. Web. 12 Feb. 2016. <http://www.crowncork.com/>.

171. "The Gillette Company History." *History of The Gillette Company – FundingUniverse.* Funding Universe, n.d. Web. 12 Feb. 2016. <http://www.fundinguniverse.com/company-histories/the-gillette-company-history/>.

172. "What Is the Razor/Razorblade Model? | Investopedia." *Investopedia.* Investopia, 23 Sept. 2008. Web. 12 Feb. 2016. <http://www.investopedia.com/ask/answers/08/razor-blade-model.asp>.

173. "Gayetty Medicated Papers." *Http://www.lemen.com.* Lemen, n.d. Web. <http://www.lemen.com/dict/D_LOC Gayettyb001dr.jpg>.

174. "Joseph Gayetty." *Prezi.com.* Prezi, n.d. Web. 12 Feb. 2016. <https://prezi.com/wtpge6316zd7/joseph-gayetty/>.

175. "Toilet Paper History – Complete Historical Timeline." *Toilet Paper History & Timeline.* The Toilet Paper Encyclopedia, n.d. Web. 12 Feb. 2016. <http://encyclopedia.toiletpaperworld.com/toilet-paper-history/complete-historical-timeline>.

176. "Kimberly Clark Corp Report." *Www.sec.gov/archives.* U.S. Government, n.d. Web. 12 Feb. 2016. <http://www.sec.gov/Archives/edgar/data/55785/0000950134-95-002721.txt>.

177. 13, December. "Kimberly-Clark Completes $9.4-Billion Purchase of Scott : Paper: Firm Likely to Cut Jobs, Take Hefty

Charge and Sell Several Units." *Los Angeles Times*. Los Angeles Times, 13 Dec. 1995. Web. 12 Feb. 2016. <http://articles. latimes.com/1995-12-13/business/fi-13466_1_scott-paper>.

178. Mcg, Robert. "Marion Donovan, 81, Solver Of the Damp-Diaper Problem."*The New York Times*. The New York Times, 17 Nov. 1998. Web. 12 Feb. 2016. <http://www.nytimes.com/1998/ 11/18/business/marion-donovan-81-solver-of-the-damp-diaper-problem.html>.

179. "Baby Diapers Market Size To Reach $64.62 Billion By 2022." *Baby Diapers Market Size To Reach $64.62 Billion By 2022*. Granview, n.d. Web. 12 Feb. 2016. <http://www. grandviewresearch.com/press-release/global-baby-diapers-market>.

180. "Undiscovered Scotland." *Patrick Bell: Biography on*. N.p., n.d. Web. 12 Feb. 2016. <http://www.undiscoveredscotland.co. uk/usbiography/b/patrickbell.html>.

181. "People & Events:William Ogden." *PBS*. PBS, n.d. Web. 12 Feb. 2016. <http://www.pbs.org/wgbh/amex/chicago/peopleevents/p_ogden.ht ml>.

182. "Wisconsin Historical Society." *McCormick-International Harvester Collection*. Wisconsin Historical Society, n.d. Web. 12 Feb. 2016. <http://www.wisconsinhistory.org/Content. aspx?dsNav=N%3A1167>.

183. "International Harvester Co." *International Harvester Co*. Chicago Encyclopedia, n.d. Web. 12 Feb. 2016. <http://www.encyclopedia.chicagohistory.org/pages/2723.html>.

184. "Number of Cars in United States 2013 | Statistic." *Statista*. The Statistics Portal, n.d. Web. 12 Feb. 2016. <http://www.statista.com/statistics/183505/number-of-vehicles-in-the-united-states-since-1990/>.

185. "Garrett Morgan." *Prezi.com*. Prezi, n.d. Web. 12 Feb. 2016. <https://prezi.com/rg8fxznckkw1/garrett-morgan/>.

186. "Garrett Morgan -Big Chief Mason." *PBS*. PBS, n.d. Web. 12 Feb. 2016. <http://www.pbs.org/wgbh/theymadeamerica/ whomade/morgan_hi.html>.

187. "1877." *Prezi.com*. PREZI, n.d. Web. 12 Feb. 2016. <https://prezi.com/dopmrqje_uu8/1877/>.

188, "Garrett Augustus Morgan." *PBS*. PBS, n.d. Web. 12 Feb. 2016. <http://www.pbs.org/wgbh/theymadeamerica/ whomade/morgan_hi.html>.

189. "People & Events - The NAACP." *PBS*. PBS, n.d. Web. 12 Feb. 2016. <http://www.pbs.org/wgbh/amex/scottsboro/ peopleevents/p_naacp.html>.

190. "Who Made America." *PBS*. PBS, n.d. Web. 12 Feb. 2016. <http://www.pbs.org/wgbh/theymadeamerica/whomade/edison_hi. html>.

191. "Potato Chip History - Invention of Potato Chips." *Potato Chip History - Invention of Potato Chips*. The Great Idea Finder, n.d. Web. 12 Feb. 2016. <http://www.ideafinder.com/history/ inventions/potatochips.htm>.

192. "Crispy Potato Chips Invented In Saratoga." *Saratoga Chips*. Everything Saratoga, n.d. Web. 12 Feb. 2016. <http://www.saratoga.com/news/saratoga-chips.cfm>.

193. "The Potato Chip Is 150 This Year!" *Snack Food Association*. Snack Food Association, n.d. Web. 12 Feb. 2016. <http://www.sfa.org/news/latest-headlines/story/the-potato-chip-is-150>.

194. "JDC Home." *Joint Distribution Committee*. American Jewish Distribution Committee, n.d. Web. 15 Feb. 2016. <http://www.jdc.org/>.

195. "The History of TV Dinners and Gerry Thomas." *About.com Inventors*. About.com, n.d. Web. 15 Feb. 2016. <http://inventors. about.com/od/inventionsalphabet/a/tv_dinner.htm>.

196. Padden, Kathy. "Peeling Back the Foil: The Origin of the TV Dinner." *Today I Found Out*. Today I Found Out, 19 Aug. 2013.

Web. 15 Feb. 2016. <http://www.todayifoundout.com/index. php/2013/08/peeling-back-the-foil-the-origin-of-the-tv-dinner/>.

197. Patriot Missiles - "Raytheon." : *Patriot Air and Missile Defense System*. Raytheon, n.d. Web. 16 Feb. 2016. <http://www.raytheon.com/capabilities/products/patriot/>.

198. Winterton, Wayne, PhD. "History's Dust Bin - Volume 2." Google Books, 2015. Web. <https://books.google.com/books ?id=ner7CgAAQBAJ&pg=PT255&dq=I+just+got+hold+of+a+lot +of+textbooks+and+taught+myself+while+I+was+standing+watch +at+night.%22&hl=en&sa=X&ved=0ahUKEwjM_5CgzvzKAhW D6SYKHTWqBtkQ6AEIHTAA#v=onepage&q=I%20just%20got %20hold%20of%20a%20lot%20of%20textbooks%20and%20taug ht%20myself%20while%20I%20was%20standing%20watch%20at %20night.%22&f=false>.

199. 199. Woodford, Chris. "Microwave Ovens." *Microwave Ovens*. Explain That Stuff, n.d. Web. 16 Feb. 2016. <http://www.explainthatstuff.com/microwaveovens.html>.

200. "Raytheon." : *Company: History*. Raytheon, n.d. Web. 16 Feb. 2016. <http://www.raytheon.com/ourcompany/history/>.

Photo references

1. "Free+public+images - Google Search." *Free+public+images - Google Search*. Colin Powell, n.d. Web. 26 Jan. 2016.

2. https://en.wikipedia.org/wiki/Crispus_Attucks Free public Domain

3. The Battle of New Orleans, with Andrew Jackson. Print of a painting by E. Percy Moran, 1910. Public domain.

4. Commander Lt. Col. William Barret Travis is from a 1953 painting of by Ruth Conerly that currently is displayed in the Alamo's Long Barrack. Free Public Domain image

5. William Travis gathered the Alamo garrison and drew the famous "line in the sand". www.pinterest.com/pin/445786063088912033/ Public Domain

6. James Polk - http://a3.files.biography.com/image/upload/ c_fit,cs_srgb,dpr_1.0, h_1200,q_80,w_1200/MTE1ODA0OT cxNzU2ODQ4NjUz.jpg. Public Domain

7. Charles Sumner - Free public image. https://en.wikipedia.org /wiki/Charles_Sumner

8. Abe Lincoln - Public Domain. https://www.zotero.org/ mattson0711/ items/VRJ5SS22/file/view

9. Chief Sitting Bull - https://commons.wikimedia.org/wiki/ File:En-chief-sitting-bull.jpg. Public Domain

10. Chief Crazy Horse - http://ducotedechezjoe.com/blog/cinq-grands-chefs-indiens. Public Domain

11. Gen. George Custer - http://www.wetcanvas.com/forums /showthread.php?t=848422. Public Domain access

12. Teddy Roosevelt and The Rough Riders - By W.G. Reed. Public Domain. http://www.bagemiya.ru/catalog/katalog_ kartin/shedevri.html?start=255

13.Henry Nicholas John Gunther - Public Domain. http://www.baomoi.com/Linh-My-cuoi-cung-chet-trong-The-chien-I/c/18047145.epi

14. Flying Tigers - First American Volunteer Group. https://en.wikipedia.org/wiki/Curtiss_P-40_Warhawk. Public Domain.

15. Eagle Squadron - File:American pilots of No. 71 (Eagle) Squadron RAF gathered in ... https://commons.wikimedia.org. Public Domain

16. Iwo Jima - https://en.wikipedia.org/wiki/Raising_ the_Flag_on_Iwo_Jima. Public domain use.

17. First Atom Bomb blast - https://commons.wikimedia.org/ wiki/File:Atomic_cloud_over_Hiroshima_%28from_ Matsuyama %29.jpg Public Domain

18. Outpost Harry - Photo of Outpost Harry courtesy of James Jarboe, June 15, 1953. http://www.ophsa.org/. Public Domain

19. Fidel and Raul Castro - http://www.theguardian.com/ commentisfree/2011/apr/20/cuba-reform-theatre-absurd. Public Domain

20. Vietnam - http://www.vintag.es/2011/02/35-years-after-fall-vietnam-war-in.html. Public Domain

21. Vietnam - http://tempsreel.nouvelobs.com/monde/ 20090227.OBS6565/les-photos-des-cercueils-de-militaires-americains-pourront-etre-publiees.html. Public Domain

22. Dominican Republic -http://nsarchive.gwu.edu/NSAEBB/ NSAEBB513/ Public Domain

23. Lebanon - http://www.nytimes.com/2012/10/23/ world/middleeast/clashes-break-out-overnight-in-lebanon.html? _r=0 Public domain

24. Marine Barracks Lebanon. http://historynewsnetwork.org/ article/151200 Public Domain

25. Granada - https://commons.wikimedia.org/wiki/ File:US_C141_Grenada.JPG Public Domain

26. Ronald Reagan - http://www.dodmedia.osd.mil/DVIC_ View/Still_Details.cfm?SDAN= DASC9003096&JPGPath=/ Assets/Still/1990/Army/DA-SC-90-03096.JPG Public domain

27. Panama - http://zeroanthropology.net/2015/01/02/ encircling-empire-report-25-remembering-panama/ Public Domain

28. Gulf War I USS Wisconsin fires Tomahawk Missle. Military photo Public Domain https://www.triposo.com/poi/ T__54e9b270b3b3

29. Norman Schwarzkopf - http://www.biography.com/ people/groups/famous-alumni-of-university-of-southern-california. Public Domain photo

30. Highway of Death - Public Domain use. http://o.canada.com/news/world/fisher-evil-on-the-horizon-casts-shadow-across-highway-of-death

31. Somalia Warlords - http://www.theepochtimes.com/n 3/542947-weak-somali-government-struggles-to-oust-al-shabab/ Public Domain

32. Somalia Blackhawk Down - http://becuo.com/black-hawk-down-1993 Public Domain

33. Yugoslavia Break-up - http://sambrook.weebly.com/how-did-yugoslavia-start-to-fall.html map of new Yugoslavia Public Domain

34. Yugoslavia - http://www.ouramazingworld.org/life/category/refugees Public Domain

35. Albanians fleeing Kosovo - http://what-happened.org /2015/09/in-kosovo/ ethnic albanians flee Public Domain

36. Twin Towers - http://www.patriotdude.com/september-11/september-11-2001-remembering-911 Public Domain

37. Soviets in Afghanistan - https://www.pinterest.com/pin/ 494692340292545961/ Public Image

38. Fall of Baghdad- ttps://commons.wikimedia.org/wiki/ File:UStanks_baghdad_2003.JPEG Public Domain

39. ISIS - http://www.commondreams.org/views/ 2014/09/02/how-america-made-isis Public Domain

40. ISIS Map - http://www.foreignpolicyjournal.com /2014/08/29/the-islamic-state-approaches-a-turning-point/ Public Domain

41. US Patent Office - https://commons.wikimedia.org/wiki/ File:United_States_ Patent_Office_c1880.jpg Public Domain

42. Early Man-http://www.rawstory.com/2015/05/early-men-and-women-were-equal-say-scientists/ Public domain

43.Cave drawings - https://www.pinterest.com/ahmedalley /cave-paintings/ Public Domain

44. Meteors - Meteor shower https://www.youtube.com/ watch?v=aEP_noo_ucs Public Domain image

45. Roy Plunkett - https://spravy.cohladas.sk/Roy_Plunkett Public Domain

46. Enrico Fermi - https://en.wikipedia.org/wiki/Enrico_Fermi Public Domain image

47. The Bomb - http://nationalinterest.org/feature/no-other-choice-why-truman-dropped-the-atomic-bomb-japan-13504 Public Domain

48. Alexander Bell - https://bksduaisyiyah.wordpress.com/2015/02/ Public Domain

49. Thomas Watson - https://commons.wikimedia.org/wiki/File:Thomas_Watson_b1792b.jpg Public Domain

50. Ben Franklin - http://upload.wikimedia.org/wikipedia/commons/2/24/Joseph_Duplessis_-_Portrait_of_Benjamin_Franklin_-_WGA06871.jpg Public Domain

51. Samuel Morse - https://commons.wikimedia.org/wiki/File:Mathew_B._Brady_-_Photo_of_Samuel_F.B._Morse_%28c.1850%29.jpg Public Domain

52. Dying Hercules - http://www.smithsonianmag.com/arts-culture/samuel-morses-other-masterpiece-52822904/ Public Domain

53. Thomas Edison - https://commons.wikimedia.org/wiki/File:Thomas_Edison2-crop.jpg Public Domain

54. Edison Bulb - http://www.history.com/topics/inventions/thomas-edison Public Domain

55. Henry Ford - http://www.thefamouspeople.com/ profiles/henry-ford-122.php Public Domain

56. Ford - https://en.wikipedia.org/wiki/Henry_Ford Public Domain

57. Ford 2- http://myautoworld.com/ford/history/ford-t/ford-t-2/ford-t-3/ford-t-3.html Public Domain

58. Whitney - http://kids.britannica.com/comptons/art-52123/Eli-Whitney Public Domain

59. Gin - http://www.pddnet.com/blog/2015/10/today-engineering-history-eli-whitney-applies-cotton-gin-patent

60. Musket - http://firearmshistory.blogspot.com /2013_04_01_archive.html Public Domain

61. Levis Strauss - http://www.germany.info/Vertretung/ usa/en/__pr/GIC/2013/22-Levi-Strauss.html Public Domain

62. Levis factory - http://www.levistrauss.com/our-story/ Public Domain Image

63. Levis miners - http://www.levistrauss.com/unzipped-blog/2011/10/levis-connoisseur/ Public Domain

64. Granville T. Woods - https://commons.wikimedia.org/wiki/ File:Granville_T_Woods_1903.png Public Domain

65. Union Pacific - https://www.gilderlehrman.org/history-by-era/development-west/essays/financing-transcontinental-railroad*Advertisement for shares in the Union Pacific Railroad, Harper's Weekly, August 10, 1867. (Gilder Lehrman Collection)* Public Domain

66. The last spike - https://en.wikipedia.org/wiki/Central_P acific_Railroad Public Domain

67. Train robbers - http://sptddog.com/sotp/pictorial.html Public Domain

68. Trolley patent - http://www.brooklynrail.net/Granville_ Woods.html Public Domain

69. Elias Howe- https://commons.wikimedia.org/wiki/ File:Elias_Howe_1867.jpg Public Domain

70. Sewing machine- http://www.marysrosaries.com/ collaboration/index.php?title=File:The_first_Howe_sewing_machi ne_001.jpg Public Domain

71. Lock stitch design - https://en.wikipedia.org/wiki/ Lockstitch Public Domain

72. Stamp - http://www.stampboards.com/viewtopic.php? f=17&t=538&start=50&view=print Public Domain

73. Chester Carlson - https://ms.wikipedia.org/wiki/ Chester_Carlson Public Domain

74. First image - First_xerographic_copy_-_10-22-38_ASTORIA_.jpg Public Domain with credit given to Astoria

75.Copy machine - http://fineartamerica.com/featured/chester-carlson-1906-1968-everett.html public Domain

76. Beakeland - https://commons.wikimedia.org/wiki/File:Leo_Baekeland_ca_1906.jpg Public Domain

77. Bakelite - Bakelite - http://blog.fxdurkin.com/page/8/ Public Domain

78. Carver - https://commons.wikimedia.org/wiki/File:George_Washington_Carver_ c1910.jpg Public Domain image

79. Carver in Lab- http://www.livescience.com/41780-george-washington-carver.html Public Image

80.Drew-https://commons.wikimedia.org/wiki/File:Charles_R._Drew_-_NARA_-_559199.jpg Public Domain

81.Blood Bank-https://commons.wikimedia.org/wiki/File:Blood_Donation_12-07-06_1.JPG Public Image

81. Dr. Drew Commemorative Stamp - http://usstampgallery.com/view.php?id=1db74d1e 7956e5f896cc6754bb2bda796eecf09c Public Domain

82. George Eastman - http://archive.org/details/menwhoaremakinga00forb Public Domain

83. Patent - "DigiCamHistory." *DigiCamHistory*. DigiCam, n.d. Web. 15 Feb. 2016. <http://www.digicamhistory.com/>. Public Domain

84. Kodak Bownie - https://commons.wikimedia.org/wiki/File:Kodak_six_20_brownie_e 003.jpg Public Domain

85.Otto Rohwedder - http://www.saveur.com/article/Kitchen/history-of-sliced-bread Public Domain

86. Rohwedder Bread Slicer - http://americanhistory.si.edu/collections/search/object/nmah _1317263 Public Domain Image

87. John Stith Pemberton - http://vanishingsouthgeorgia. com/2015/09/06/dr-john-s-pemberton-house-1840-columbus/ Public domain

88. Coca Cola and Temperance - https://origins.osu.edu article/43/images   Public Domain

89 Coca cola and ad sign - https://commons.wikimedia. org/wiki/File:1922_bottled_Coca-Cola_ad.png   Public Domain

90. Flight - https://inkbluesky.wordpress.com/2013/03/page/4/ Public Domain

90. Wright Brothers - http://www.vintag.es/2015/04/pictures-of-wright-brothers-first.html Public Domain

91. Daedalus - https://commons.wikimedia.org/wiki/ File:The_Fall_of_Icarus_LACMA_

65.37.158.jpg Public domain images from the Los Angeles County Museum of Art

90. Flight - http://www.ancient-origins.net/news-general/speakers-science-congress-says-ancient-india-mastered-advanced-space-flight-020155   Public Domain

90. Wright bicycle - https://en.wikipedia.org/wiki/Wright_ brothers Public Domain

94-Otto-lilienthal portrait - https://en.wikipedia.org/wiki /Otto_Lilienthal Public Domain

95-German Otto Liliethal - http://www.newstatesman.com /lifestyle/2014/03/will-self-fearless-flying-act-collective-delusion Public Domain

90. Wright first in flight - http://www.vintag.es/2015 /04/pictures-of-wright-brothers-first.html Public Domain

96. Wright - http://www.vintag.es/2015/04/pictures-of-wright-brothers-first.html Public Domain

97. Wright - http://www.vintag.es/2015/04/pictures-of-wright-brothers-first.html Public Domain

94. https://www.pinterest.com/dylangrif/artwork-i-enjoy/ Public Domain

106. Young Willis Carrier - http://www.williscarrier. com/ 1876-1902.php Public Domain

107. Engineers Hand-Book - https://commons.wikimedia.org/ wiki/File:Willis_Carrier_Engineers_Handbook.jpg Public Domain

108. First A/C system - http://www.williscarrier.com/1876-1902.php Public Domain

109 - First multi story A/C - http://www.williscarrier.com/ 1923-1929.php Public Domain

110. Josephine Cochrane - http://www.thesnug.com/3-things-you-might-not-know-were-invented-by-women-1052666994.html Public Domain

111. Cochrane dishwasher - http://www.thesnug.com/3-things-you-might-not-know-were-invented-by-women-1052666994.html Public Domain

112. StephanieKwolek - https://en.wikipedia.org/wiki/ Stephanie_Kwolek

113. Kevlar vest - http://archive.defense.gov/news/newsarticle. aspx?id=43627 Public Domain

114. James Ritty - http://steampunker.ru/blog/history /11339.html Public Domain

115. Ritt's Register - http://www.delraycc.com/ interestingmoney/24-amazing-pictures-of-money/ Public Domain

116. Registers help merchants - http://www.ncr.com/wp-content/uploads/1920x430-history-timeline.jpg

117. Gillette - https://commons.wikimedia.org/ wiki/File:King_Camp_Gillette.jpg Public Domain

118. Straight edge - http://www.atlasobscura.com/articles/how-green-bay-wisconsin-became-the-toilet-paper-capital-of-the-world Public Domain

119. Kempft Brothers safety razor - http://theoriginalsafetytoo. com/thread/503/kampfe-bros-star Public Image

120. Gillette safety razor - http://www.razorarchive.com/ gillette-toggle-adjustable Public Domain image

121. Joseph Gayetty - http://www.atlasobscura.com/articles/how-green-bay-wisconsin-became-the-toilet-paper-capital-of-the-world Public Domain

122. Gayetty Medicated toilet paper - https://ephemeralnewyork.wordpress.com/2014/08/04/a-19th-century-new-yorker-invents-toilet-paper/ Public Domain

123. Toilet paper - http://thestir.cafemom.com/being_a_mom/176698/dad_toilet_paper_roll_video Public Domain

124. Multiple toilet paper - http://mainetoday.com/page/132/?id=6784&cat&tag&srt&total=42&next=40 Public Domain

125. Marion Donovan - http://www.ranker.com/list/renaissance-woman-list/mike-rothschild Public Domain

126. Disposable Diaper - http://invention.si.edu/papers-illustrate-woman-inventors-life-and-work Public Image

127. Cloth diaper - http://www.wikihow.com/Category:Diaper-Changing Public Domain

128. Washing out diapers - http://mamamuzzle.com/?cat=1 Public Domain

129. Hanging diagers - http://fatherandchild.org.nz/magazine/issue-32/in-praise-of-cloth-nappies/ Public Domain

130. McCormick - http://www.thefamouspeople.com/profiles/cyrus-mccormick-6675.php Public Image

131. Reaper- http://pixgood.com/the-reaper-cyrus-mccormick.html   Public Domain

132. Bell's Reaper - http://fineartamerica.com/featured/bells-improved-reaping-machine-sheila-terry.html Public Domain

133. McCormick's Reaper -http://history1800s.about.com/od/1800sglossary/ Public Domain

134. Garrett Morgan - http://www.kevinwilliams.net/famous-black-scientists-garrett-morgan/ Public Domain

135. http://pzrservices.typepad.com/vintageadvertising/vintage_trading_cards/ Public Domain

136. http://www.mirandaalyse.com/?paged=2&page_id=234 Public Domain

137. http://www.theatlantic.com/technology/archive/2014/10/the-peril-of-being-a-black-inventor-in-the-old-south/381323/ Public Domain

138. http://www.robinsonlibrary.com/technology/mechanical/biography/morgan.htm Public Image

139. Traffic Light - http://intisari-online.com/read/sejarah-lampu-lalu-lintas- Public Image

140. George Crum - http://www.famousinventors.org/george-crum Public Domain

141. http://chipscrumsandspecksofsaratogacountyhistory.com/tag/loomis-lake-house/ Public Domain

142. http://www.timesunion.com/sports/article/Historical-photos-Saratoga-Springs-through-the-1469618.php#photo-1121931 Public Domain

143. http://www.julescatering.com/blog/tag/homemade-potato-chips/ Public Domain

144. Leo Gerstenzang - https://www.pinterest.com/pin/326722147939263897/ Public Domain

145. Q-Tips - http://www.popsugar.com/beauty/photo-gallery/34888319/image/34888356/Mistake-5-Using-Q-tips-clean-up-your-mistakes Public Domain

146. Swap Applicators - https://www.zoro swab-non-sterile-3in-pk25- Public Domain.com/swift-cotton-tip-

147. Percy Spencer - http://sqeets.com/articles/top-10-accidental-inventions/ Public Domain

148. Popcorn - http://recorderstandard.com/2015/12/act-ii-butter-delight-popcorn-50-g/ Public Domain

149. First microwave - http://motivasi.win/post/percy-spencer-microwave-oven Public Domain

150. Microwave in communication - http://shorttermmemory loss.com/nor/tag/microwaves/ Public Domain